The Role of Federal Agencies in Technology Transfer

The Role of Federal Agencies in Technology Transfer

Samuel I. Doctors

The M.I.T. Press
Cambridge, Massachusetts, and London, England

Set in Linotype Baskerville and printed by
Indiantown Printing Co. Bound in the
United States of America by The Maple Press Co.

Library of Congress catalog card number: 69–14403

To Susan

Foreword

During the period since the end of World War II, federally sponsored research and development has become one of the most dynamic and rapidly growing sectors of the American economy. In fiscal year 1968, 57 percent of the $14.6 billions spent by the federal government for research and development went to industry, and federal funds made up exactly half of all research and development expenditures by industry. The impact on the economy as a whole may in fact be considerably greater than suggested by the relatively small percentage of the gross national product represented by such expenditures. Many of the fastest growing sectors in the economy are those which derive from science-based technological innovations, and because the government finances so high a proportion of the organized activity directed at such innovation, its policies and decisions must have considerable influence on the directions of economic growth and capital investment. The technological activities of the federal government occupy a very high proportion of the nation's technical manpower, and probably an even higher proportion of the most technically sophisticated segment of this manpower.

Federally funded R & D by itself, however, does not generate innovations that contribute to growth in the civilian economy. The results of this R & D must be translated into products and services which can be sold on the commercial market. Since much of the research and development sponsored by the federal government is not directly related to commercial products, there must be a complicated technology transfer process that intervenes between the R & D expenditure and the final generation of economic growth. This transfer can occur in the form of direct adaptation of products or processes originally developed for government end use: for example, nuclear power plants, passenger jet aircraft, and communications satellites. Transfer can also occur when government demand accelerates the transition of an industry-originated innovation into full-scale application. The government demand helps development and production through the early and expensive phases of the learning curve and also assists in the early probing of the market. Examples of this form of transfer occur in the production of computers, integrated circuits, analytical instruments, and air navigation radar. More indirect or horizontal transfer can occur, requiring considerable adaptive research before a technology developed for one purpose can be applied to a wholly different purpose. Examples here are the application of many new research technologies such as neutron activation analysis, radioactive and stable isotope tracer techniques, and ultra high vacuum to commercial processes and controls.

Because federal expenditures for R & D preempt so large a part of our technical resources of manpower and facilities, it is important for the health of the economy that these expenditures be as effective as possible in generating additional economic growth without detriment to the original public objective for which they were made. This suggests that if the federal government is to ensure that the maximum benefit accrues to the national economy, it should devote considerable attention to the technology transfer process itself and tailor its policies in all areas of technological activity to make this transfer as effective and as rapid as possible.

About 84 percent of federal R & D expenditures in fiscal year 1968 were made by three agencies, the Department of Defense, the Atomic Energy Commission, and the National Aeronautics and Space Administration. The technologies of atomic energy and space were originally developed under military auspices but subsequently placed under the direction of civilian agencies, largely to ensure that these new technologies would be used as broadly as possible for the benefit of the nation and mankind and not exclusively for military purposes. Thus, in a sense, technology transfer became an integral part of the primary missions of both the Atomic Energy Commission and the new Space Agency, and both agencies were expected to devote some effort to the transfer process. For the most part, they interpreted their technology transfer mission to require broad public dissemination of scientific information, and they accordingly took steps to place as large a part of their research and development results in the public domain as seemed wise to them, consistent with national security and with their relationships with proprietary organizations. The leaders of both agencies approached their main task with an enthusiastic conviction that there were civilian benefits to be derived from their programs, and they used these claimed benefits as a major selling point to obtain continuing appropriations from the Congress. Thus technology transfer became not only an explicit purpose of each of the major nonmilitary agencies but also an instrumentality for selling its program to the public.

In view of the importance of the process of technology transfer, both to the national economy and to the continued political approbation of the agencies, it is, perhaps, surprising how little scholarly effort has been devoted to the understanding of the technology transfer process or to finding out what has actually happened during the history of these major technological agencies. A number of obstacles have tended to inhibit scholarly research in this area. In the first place, the process of technology transfer is exceedingly complex and elusive. Much of the most significant communication is informal, and technologists are usually much hazier than pure scientists as to the origins of their ideas. The innovators responsible for turning knowledge into products, processes, and services are oriented toward internal communications within their own organizations rather than toward their external professional communities; their communication processes, because they are not documented, are not easily available for study by outside scholars.

In the second place, the importance of technology transfer as a selling argument for agency appropriations has tended to discourage objective examination of the process, especially under agency sponsorship. There was always a gnawing fear that the civilian benefits of agency expenditures might turn out to be less extensive than believed and hoped and that if this were well documented, the results would reflect adversely on appropriations and public support. It was thought better to let sleeping dogs lie in this field or to have studies performed only under careful agency supervision.

In the third place, federal agencies have tended to interpret their technology transfer mission in terms of documentation and formal information dissemination. They regarded it as important to help the scientific community with its information problems but assumed that information which was primarily applications-oriented would be handled more or less automatically through commercial channels once the scientific information was properly documented and disseminated. The AEC, for example, published *Nuclear Science Abstracts* and financed the publication of several editions of a reactor handbook and of specialized bulletins on various aspects of reactor technology, such as safety, materials, and nuclear cross sections. In addition, it established a declassified report series and created a system of depository libraries for its reports. NASA also took steps to secure a wide dissemination of its reports and contracted with a professional association, the American Institute of Aeronautics and Astronautics, to produce an abstract journal in the field of space science and technology. NASA went somewhat further than AEC in creating a special program aimed at technology transfer, the Technology Utilization Program. This aimed explicitly at fostering transfer of space technology to civilian business, through consulting and information centers (Regional Dissemination Centers) scattered around the United States. The creation of these centers recognized more explicitly than did the other information programs that scientific information often requires reorganization, reinterpretation, and repackaging before it can be made useful to the technologist. In theory the NASA program was especially aimed at being helpful to small business, but in practice this aim appears to have been defeated by bureaucratic habit and by the less well-organized information handling capacities of small firms.

Despite all these efforts, however, most of the government's efforts to foster technology transfer have been based on conventional wisdom and intuitive judgment as to how the process *ought* to occur rather than on empirical knowledge or research on how it actually occurs. Much of what has been written on the subject consists of sparsely documented assertions and opinions by people with some experience in the process of technology transfer. *The Role of Federal Agencies in Technology Transfer* by Samuel I. Doctors is one of the first attempts at a thorough empirical study of a specific technology transfer program, the Technology Utilization Program of NASA, measured against its own announced objectives. It has important implications, both for future government policy and for the posture of business firms in relation to government R & D. It may also have a bearing on the degree to which firms that specialize in space and defense work can hope to diversify successfully into civilian business, making use of the experience and technology developed largely by government funding. Doctors' conclusions with respect to the transfer of space and defense technology from large firms are not very encouraging, although he shows that transfer has sometimes been successful in a few small, specialized high-technology firms with sufficiently small organizations so that the government and nongovernment parts of the company do not tend to become isolated from each other.

The study has broader implications for public policy if relaxation of political tensions in the world should encourage or permit a reallocation of research and development resources towards nonmilitary, social purposes. How easily can the massive and sophisticated defense industry diversify into new areas? How can the federal government best assist and encourage this process of diversification? How effective is direct government subsidy of industrial R & D in achieving technology transfer which results in salable products?

Doctors' book concentrates largely on the technology transfer efforts of NASA. This is a reasonable choice as a case history, since NASA has devoted more explicit thought and attention to the area than has any other technology-oriented federal agency and has used technology utilization as one of its chief selling points. It would be of great interest to extend this type of research to other federal agencies. One of the oldest technology transfer programs in the federal government is the Agricultural Extension Service; a substantially larger part of Agriculture Department resources is devoted to extension in comparison with its research expenditures than is the case for the technology transfer activities of any other federal agency. However, Agricultural Extension dates from before the days when technology transfer became an object of scholarly study. It is widely held to have been very successful and to have been an important factor in the superior economic performance of American agriculture, complementing a broad and extensive research program. As measured by growth in man-hour productivity, agriculture is one of the greatest success stories in the utilization of science for economic benefits. There have been several scholarly studies of the economic payoff of agricultural research, especially the studies by Theodore Schultz and his students at the University of Chicago. A few studies have examined elements of the transfer process in agriculture and the role of the extension program, but attempts to provide an overall model of transfer including government, farm support industry, and the farmer have been quite rare. It is important also to note that in agriculture there has developed a large nongovernmental research and development program in agricultural machinery, in fertilizers, and in pesticides. The funds expended by industry in research related to food production and processing actually exceed those expended by the states and federal government on agricultural research and extension. Very little has been written on how this remarkable research establishment has grown up, how it operates, and in particular, how the various parts couple and what kinds of information flows occur between them. One would like to know to what extent the agricultural model, believed to be such a success, is a valid model for technology transfer in other areas.

Similar studies might be rewarding in the fields of atomic energy and health, in which government research has played a seminal role. In each case the technology has matured to the point where a large nongovernmental industry has developed. It would be interesting to study the relationships between the government programs and the associated industries using the same concepts and insights as in the technology transfer program of NASA. To what extent are these insights and concepts applicable to these other programs? Are there lessons that could be learned from the experiences in agriculture, atomic energy, and health which could be applied to obtaining more successful technology transfer from the space program? How successful have these other programs been? It is my hope that Doctors' study will provide a model for further work in the area and lay the groundwork for the development of a new subject of research, fully worthy of the attention of serious scholars and at the same time having important implications for public policy.

Harvey Brooks

Cambridge, Massachusetts

Preface

At no time has the United States spent so large a portion of its national income on reasearch and development as it has since World War II. Government sponsorship of a large portion of this R & D has had a profound impact on education, industry, and the general economy. Measuring the effects of this vast public investment is difficult, if not impossible, at our present level of knowledge, and only a little has been done to expand our knowledge or our ability to measure them. While tens of billions of dollars have been spent on R & D, only a few million have been spent in analyzing the effects of this R & D investment.

Some effects—the intercontinental missiles, the space ships, the atomic reactors—can be easily discerned. But not so easily perceived are effects on the overall economy, such as patterns of innovation, patterns of education, and influences on foreign trade. We are all familiar with the growing use of computers, jet transports, microelectronics, and other new technology initially supported by federal R & D funding. The mechanisms which made possible the transfer of these new areas of technology from the space/defense market to the commercial market are, however, only poorly understood. Nor is it known today whether this important transfer is increasing or decreasing or even whether it is possible to increase the transfer rate by direct or indirect intervention.

The federal government has initiated a number of programs to facilitate technology transfer. These programs range all the way from the very extensive, venerable Agricultural Extension Service to the very limited industrial extension service (The State Technical Service Program) initiated in 1965. The advent of a large-scale space program generated great interest in the prospect of large-scale technology transfer from the public investment in space R & D. Unfortunately, very little measurable transfer was discernible early in the space program and public enthusiasm became public disaffection and disillusionment. To offset criticism and to facilitate transfer, NASA established an Office of Technology Utilization. A large part of this study, Chapters 6 through 10, is a case study of this unique and significant agency program.

No single work of this size could possibly encompass as much detail about federal agency technology transfer programs as an interested reader might wish. This book does, however, attempt to provide a concise survey of developments that are otherwise described only in a large number of government and secondary sources, many of them unavailable to the general reader. Moreover, it offers the first detailed analysis of the NASA Technology Utilization Program and its relevance for understanding the present role of federal transfer programs.

My interest in technology transfer was the result of a number of years' work as a systems engineer in the aerospace industry and work during the past two years with the NASA Technology Utilization (TU) Program. I have had the opportunity to work with the program both at the input side, as a staff engineer for a NASA contractor during the summer of 1966, and at the output side, as a staff member of the new Regional Dissemination Center (RDC) at the University of Connecticut. Both opportunities provided valuable insights into the mechanisms of the program and some of the more general problems of technology transfer in a federal agency setting.

I owe a debt of gratitude for assistance in this book to several score people in private industry, at NASA, at various Regional Dissemination Centers, at Harvard, and at MIT. I am particularly indebted to Professor Harvey Brooks for his extensive comments on several drafts and his continuing encouragement. By consenting to write a foreword, he has done me an undeserved kindness and has helped to place the problems of technology transfer in proper perspective. Professor Edward Roberts of MIT made valuable suggestions for changes in several of the chapters dealing with the transfer process. Comments and guidance from Professors Richard Rosenbloom, Raymond Bauer, Paul Cherington, and Derek Bok of Harvard were very helpful.

The Science and Public Policy Program of the Harvard School of Public Administration contributed greatly to the creation of this book through its library and through the opportunities it provided for discussions with eminent scientists and administrators.

Gayle Parker of the NASA Headquarters legal staff and John Manning of the Cambridge Electronic Research Center legal staff have been most helpful in providing data on various aspects of government patent/license policies and other legal matters.

The New England Research Applications Center supported part of the research and for that assistance I am most grateful. S. William Yost, Director of the Center, read several early versions of the manuscript and made numerous helpful suggestions.

Robert M. Jolkovski of Arthur D. Little was most generous of his time and offered me much insight into the transfer process.

Some of the information presented here is the result of confidential interviews. Of necessity, some footnote citations as to persons, times, and places of interviews are intentionally vague, for the NASA Technology Utilization Program has been sensitive to criticism and to political influences. I have tried to make those sections dealing with the Program as objective and factual as possible. Of course, reasonable men may differ over the interpretation of facts and data I gathered, but I believe that this case study of technology transfer in the federal agency setting is one reasoned interpretation.

Two Harvard Law students provided most important assistance. Michael Moore, LL.B. '67, assisted in the preparation of Chapter 10. Edward Hines, Jr., LL.B. '69, provided substantial help in the preparation of Appendix A and assisted in rewriting Chapter 9.

A number of very kind and patient women have assisted in the preparation of this book, among them Ann Kelly, Nancy Matthews, Lenore Abraham, and Jane Lew must be cited for especially valuable assistance, Ann Kelly and Nancy Matthews for their persistence and patience in typing a number of drafts of this manuscript. Lenore Abraham helped relieve the book of a large amount of graceless prose.

I am grateful to the Minnesota Law Review Foundation for permission to reprint portions of the article, "Transfer of Space Technology to the American Consumer: The Effect of NASA's Patent Policy," which appeared in the March 1968 issue of *The Minnesota Law Review*. I am grateful also to the American Society of Tool and Manufacturing Engineers for permission to reprint portions of the paper, "The Role of Federal Agency Patent Policy in Technology Transfer," presented at the 1968 National Engineering Conference.

SAMUEL I. DOCTORS

Cambridge, Massachusetts
November 1968

Acknowledgment

Nations rise and fall through their response to change in their environments. At the heart of such change is technology: creating new machines, of war, of transportation, of consumer-goods production. These developments give the adaptive nation a competitive advantage, leaving the unchanging nation at the military or economic mercy of the innovator. Given the fact that creation and application of new technology are vital to survival, where does the new technology come from—how is it applied effectively?

In the United States most research and development (R & D)—the breeding ground of technology—is supported by federal expenditure. Most of this effort is directed toward specific missions, yet technology cannot be bound to specifics; it is knowledge. How can this technical knowledge be generalized, extrapolated to other needs in our society? This is the crux of the situation vital to our existence. A critical question, then, is: What is the impact of federal policy on technology transfer from government to private and other public sectors?

NASA's recognition of this problem and its experimentation to eliminate barriers that might exist led to their support of the New England Research Application Center, which is an action program devoted to transferring technology on a person-to-person, firm-to-firm basis. Our belief that the very survival of our society hinges on the effective creation and utilization of knowledge, coupled with the fact of federal domination of R & D spending, makes very timely this intensive study of policies that have grown "like Topsy."

While we do not necessarily agree with each and every conclusion and recommendation, we believe that this volume represents a highly competent and unique analysis of federal policies and their impact on technology transfer and, accordingly, we have wholeheartedly sponsored its completion and publication.

S. William Yost
Director, New England
Research Application Center

Contents

Tables and Charts

PART I
Technology Transfer and the Federal Agency

Chapter 1
Introduction

Definitions and Concepts

The concept of *technology transfer* is not a simple one to define, for the meaning of the phrase seems to depend upon the audience considering it and the point in time. For the purposes of this book, technology transfer will denote the process whereby technical information originating in one institutional setting is adapted for use in another institutional setting. The transfer typically requires active participation by both the transferor and the transferee and implies more than the mere dissemination of technical information; it implies the adaptation of new technology through a creative transformation and application to a different end use. The end use may be similar to that for which the technology was originated, in which case the adaptation will be by way of analogous application; or the end use may be quite different, in which case, creative adaptation and application will be equally important elements of the transfer process. In either case, the availability of *relevant* new technology is a first step in the transfer process and itself requires careful planning and structure in the transferor institution.

Technological spin-off and *spill-over* are terms often used to delimit a certain portion of technology transfer. However, these terms are sometimes used more generally, as when spin-off is used to refer to the process whereby a new company is spun off from a parent organization, either nonprofit or commercial. Often this type of spin-off also involves the transfer of technology to a new field, as in the case of the many new electronics and instrumentation firms along Boston's Route 128; where this occurs, it will also be considered a form of technology transfer. In order to clarify the usage of terms, it seems appropriate to consider some general notions about technology, its transfer, and various methods of transfer.

As Brooks has noted, our image of *technology* is a nineteenth century notion, and "we tend to view it primarily in terms of machines and physical tools, that is, hardware."[1] Increasingly, however, such "software" as systems concepts, management control techniques, and computer programs may all be viewed as being as much a part of the common store of technology as a rocket vehicle or a linear accelerator. Schon has defined technology as "any tool or technique, any product or process, any physical equipment or method of doing or making by which human capability is extended."[2] It is this broad definition of technology that underlies all subsequent discussion.

Different strategies of transfer may be appropriate for different types of technology, for the spectrum of technology extends from very specific, visible inventions, to the collocation of such simples to form a broad area of new hardware technology such as the digital computer, to a new area of software such as a mangement control system. A discussion that omitted any portion of this spectrum would be deficient.

As discussed in Chapter 2, the transfer process appears to be a function of several interrelated variables, including an input or acquisition variable and an output or dissemination variable. In shaping policies affecting either variable, some recognition must be given to the fact that the various portions of the technology spectrum require different strategies for effective acquisition or dissemination. Part of the problem of a dissemination program lies in motivating the technologist to adopt externally generated information for his own use. It appears that motivating a technologist to adopt a new widget is a different problem from motivating him to adopt a digital computer to control manufacturing processes in place of the current method of control, and still a different problem from motivating him to install a Pert control system either to manage the production of new widgets or to optimize computer usage.[3] Of course, there is

[1] Harvey Brooks, "National Science Policy and Technology Transfer," in Harvey Brooks, *The Government of Science* (Cambridge: The M.I.T. Press, 1968), pp. 254–278.

[2] Donald Schon, *Technology and Change* (New York: Delacorte Press, 1967), p. 11.

[3] It has been suggested by some researchers at Arthur D. Little, Inc., in a report prepared for the United Kingdom that the transfer of broad areas of aerospace or weapons-systems technology is easier to effect than that of a discrete item. Arthur D. Little, Inc., *Transfer of Aerospace Technology in the United States—A Critical Review*. Report to the Subcommittee of Enquiry into the Aircraft Industry, United Kingdom (known as the Plowden Committee) (Cambridge,

not always a sharp division between these types of technology, but as one moves further from specific hardware items, it appears that transfer may be less dependent on entrepreneurial activities and the control of legal rights to a specific item, and more dependent on the selective dissemination of technical information.[4]

Innovation will be taken to mean the application of a new technique (hardware or software) which increases performance at existing or lower costs. The innovation, of course, may not only increase performance in existing products or processes, but also may make it possible to do things which could not be done before. As Rodgers notes, an innovation need not be objectively new:

> An innovation is an idea perceived as new by the individual. It really matters little, as far as human behavior is concerned, whether or not an idea is objectively new as measured by the amount of time elapsed since its first use or discovery. It is the newness of the idea to the individual that determines his reaction to it. . . .[5]

Invention will be used in the narrower sense of the patent definition, "any *new* and useful process, machine, manufacture or composition of matter."[6]

Technology transfer differs from the usual dissemination of scientific knowledge in that it is more concerned with the usage of end items or processes than with the incorporation of new conceptual schemes into the general framework of the technologist's work. Thus, the mechanisms developed for transferring technology, as distinct

---

Mass.: Arthur D. Little, Inc., July 1966), p. 10. This suggestion seems unwarranted in view of the negligible amount of data that has been gathered and the short time during which people have been concerned with measuring the so-called spin-off of specific innovations in the federal agency context.

4 See Arthur D. Little, Inc., *Technology Transfer and the Technology Utilization Program,* Report to the NASA Office of Technology Utilization (OTU) (Washington, D.C.: NASA Headquarters, January 1965), pp. 1–17 and Arthur D. Little, Inc., *Technology Transfer and Technology Utilization Program, 1965,* Report to the NASA OTU (Washington, D.C.: NASA OTU, April 1966), pp. 7–17, for a discussion of different transfer techniques for different levels of transfer.

5 Everett Rodgers, *Diffusion of Innovations* (New York: The Free Press of Glencoe, 1962), p. 13.

6 35 U.S.C. Sec. 101 (1954).

from technical data dissemination, should be oriented more toward suggesting methods and areas of application and motivation than toward supplying generalized theoretical results or general scientific data.

This book will be primarily concerned with what Brooks has called *"horizontal transfer,"*[7] as distinct from *vertical transfer* of scientific knowledge. In vertical transfer a general principle is applied to produce a new product, device, or process within a given scientific or technical discipline, and, generally, within an organizational entity such as a single corporation or government agency. In horizontal transfer, on the other hand, one technology is adapted to a different area of application, generally across institutional lines. An example of this distinction might be seen in the incorporation of a new rocket fuel into a booster system as contrasted with the use of a new metal alloy developed for a rocket engine in a boiler for a steel mill.[8]

Issues and Themes

This monograph will discuss the present federal role in technology transfer within the federal agencies and relate this role to current agency policies on the preparation, evaluation, and dissemination of technical data for parties outside the ambit of the federal agencies and their contractors. The focus will be on current programs and the problems associated with them.

---

[7] Brooks, *op. cit.,* pp. 256–59. Harvey Brooks observes that both federal agencies and private companies are better organized for vertical transfer, but horizontal transfer is an important economic and motivational stimulus, since many innovations are produced outside the confines of a given institutional setting. See, for example, David Hamberg, *R & D Essays on the Economics of Research and Development* (New York: Random House, 1966), pp. 69–112; Mueller, "The Origins of the Basic Inventions Underlying DuPont's Major Product and Process Innovations, 1920 to 1950," in National Bureau of Economic Research, *The Rate and Direction of Inventive Activity: Economic and Social Factors* (Princeton: Princeton University Press, 1962), pp. 323–46; Donald Schon, "Innovation by Invasion," *International Science and Technology,* No. 27 (March 1964), pp. 52–60.

[8] See U.S. Congress, House of Representatives, Committee on Science and Astronautics, Subcommittee on Advanced Research and Technology, *1967 NASA Authorization, Hearings,* 90th Congress, first session, H. Reports 4450 and 6470 (Washington, D.C.: U.S. Government Printing Office, 1967), part 4, pp. 681–92, for a NASA list of horizontal transfer items from the TU Program.

As the sponsor of most research and development (R & D) performed in this country, the federal government controls much of the technical information and data resulting from it. Thus its policies toward the dissemination and exploitation, private or public, of these R & D results is of prime importance in any meaningful technology transfer program. I believe that the federal government should play a more active role in such transfer than it does at present.

It is most important that technology transfer be viewed as a political, social, and economic problem that we know very little about, otherwise, as with present agency transfer programs, the main thrust will be to *do* something that yields tangible, quantitative results, but is not necessarily designed to promote optimal transfer in the long run. Although numerous papers have been written and some field studies have been conducted, real field experiments have been rare, and it has been difficult to obtain measurable feedback on the process of transfer. Such feedback is essential in formulating transfer policy, both in the inital stages and on a continuing basis, to provide for program modification and adaptation to a changing environment. In short, there is a need for comprehensive experiments by social scientists which would investigate the acquisition, evaluation, and dissemination of technical information and the measurement of its use after dissemination. Since such projects are unlikely to be supported by business until a market can be established for such activities, the federal government should become the sponsor of social science R & D projects designed to study the transfer process.

An experimental program of this kind would not necessarily increase technology transfer or increase productivity or social well-being. The results may not lead to any increases in transfer over what is now occurring with little or no federal assistance or studies in the area. But only by conducting a careful, non-politically-motivated study of technology transfer can a reasonable judgment be made as to what, if any, programs the federal government should support in order to promote technology transfer.[9] At present, the

---

[9] The ultimate aim of federal programs in the area of technology transfer should be to accelerate transfer beyond what would occur "naturally" and to channel this natural transfer more effectively, particularly to satisfy broader economic

federal government is supporting a number of transfer programs in several agencies and departments, but they do not appear to be very effective and it is very difficult to measure their results.

To illuminate some of the problems that an experimental program would encounter, this book will discuss portions of the problem of technology transfer not limited to spin-off or spill-over. The discussions will, however, be limited to technology transfer from government-sponsored R & D, both intra- and extramural, primarily as a result of funding by the three largest procurement agencies, the Department of Defense (DOD), the Atomic Energy Commission (AEC), and the National Aeronautics and Space Administration (NASA), denoted as space/defense-generated technology. Some attention will be given to vertical transfer because the AEC, as well as NASA, is already committed to large programs of this type, but primary emphasis will be placed on horizontal transfer, transfer across mission lines to areas outside the ambit of these three agencies and their industrial base.[10]

There are many barriers to this type of transfer. They are found in the mission orientation of most agency technical personnel, in the vertically integrated nature of the agencies, in the conflicting policies concerning the legal rights to patentable inventions and

---

and social needs as in assisting in balance-of-payment problems or in ameliorating unmet human needs. The possibility of such channeling of transfer should be examined as part of the proposed experimental program.

The basic problem in accelerating the process of transfer may be that of finding methods of enhancing the "natural" process of technical transfer rather than effecting new processes. However, this enhancement may require finding some novel institutional arrangements such as rewarding federal R & D contractors for reporting innovations by granting them a "royalty" payment when the innovations are used for governmental purposes, or by providing an industrial extension service.

[10] See Brooks, *op. cit.,* for a discussion of some of the institutional barriers to transfer in the federal agencies, in universities, and in private industry. See Richard Lesher and George Howick, *Assessing Technology Transfer,* NASA SP-5067 (Washington, D.C.: U.S. Government Printing Office, 1966), pp. 34–43, for a more general listing of barriers to transfer of the results of federal R & D to commercial industry.

See President's Science Advisory Committee (PSAC), *Science, Government, and Information* (Washington, D.C.: U.S. Government Printing Office, January 1963), generally known as the Weinberg Report, for a discussion and summary of the problems associated with the collection and evaluation of technical information from federal agency R & D.

other proprietary data among the agencies, in the institutional barriers to information flow in the aerospace/weapons-systems industry, in the low rate of technologist mobility from the aerospace/weapons-systems industry to the commercial sector, in the low value placed on the transfer function by the scientific and technical personnel engaged in federally sponsored R & D, in the political nature of institutions for transfer, in overzealous security restrictions, in poor and antiquated methods of information retrieval and evaluation, in poor understanding of the transfer process, and in the very power structure of the agencies themselves.

Not all the problems will be dealt with comprehensively, but all of them will be discussed, particularly as they relate to the activities of the NASA technology transfer program, the Technology Utilization Program (TUP).

This book is divided into three parts: the first will discuss the framework of federal R & D spending, the value of technology produced under federal sponsorship for use by other sectors of the economy, the results of some recent research in the transfer of technology and their relevance to understanding the process of transfer in this federal setting, and finally a general analysis of present agency programs. The second part will be devoted to the analysis of the NASA TU Program as the first example of an attempt by a federal agency to provide an integrated acquisition, evaluation, and dissemination program designed to serve commercial-industrial needs. Part III offers a series of conclusions concerning this NASA Program and its relevance for a truly experimental program in technology transfer designed to yield data for more meaningful federally sponsored technology transfer programs.

Chapter 2

The Framework of the Transfer Problem

Patterns of Federal R & D Spending

> Peacetime utilization of military technology is an old story. The canning of food was first developed to preserve supplies for Napoleon's army. The electronic computer, now ubiquitous in industry, was invented and improved in a World War II project.[1]

As Rosenbloom notes, the process of technology transfer is not new. What is new is the increasingly large part the federal government is playing in the production of new technology. As measured by increased R & D expenditures of the federal government, this involvement has grown from $74 million in 1940 to $15.9 billion in fiscal 1966, not including amounts spent on R & D plant totaling $1.1 billion and $0.6 billion for technical data activities. In 1940, 0.8 percent of the total federal budget was spent on science and technology; in fiscal 1966, it is estimated that 15 percent was spent on science and technology.[2] Not only has federal R & D spending increased absolutely, but it has become an increasingly larger part of federal budget expenditures from 1940 to 1964. Also important is that quantitative estimates of R & D spending by NSF and the federal agencies do not reveal the full magnitude of the federal contribution to total R & D spending in this country, for a significant portion of this federal contribution is buried in overhead funding

[1] Richard Rosenbloom, *Technology Transfer—Process and Policy* (Washington, D.C.: National Planning Association Special Report No. 62, July 1965), p. 1.

[2] The 1940–1966 comparison probably overstates the acceleration of federal involvement in R & D since a fraction of what is now classified as development and all of what is now classified as test and evaluation was considered part of production and procurement prior to 1950. See Harvey Brooks, "Future Needs for the Support of Basic Research," in *Knowledge and Power: Essays on Science and Government,* Sanford Lakoff, ed. (New York: The Free Press of Glencoe, 1966), pp. 432, 435.

of agency contractors.[3] Federal R & D spending is divided between basic research (12 percent), applied research (22 percent), and de-

---

[3] National Science Foundation, *Federal Funds for Research, Development and Other Scientific Activities: Fiscal Years 1965, 1966, 1967,* XV, NSF 66–24 (Washington, D.C.: U.S. Government Printing Office, July 1966) (hereafter cited as *1966 NSF Report on R & D Funding*).

If R & D plant and technical data activities are included, the NSF data yield a total of $17.6 billion spent in R & D related activities. FY 1966 figures represent best estimates by NSF. In FY 1965 actual expenditures were $14.6 billion for R & D *per se,* $1.1 billion for plant and $0.568 billion for technical data activities.

Even the $17.6 billion figure probably understates federal spending for extramural R & D. The major procurement agencies fund some R & D through reimbursement of corporate spending for "independent research and development" (IR & D), "product improvement" (PI), and bid-proposal (BP) costs. The amount may be as high as five percent of contractor sales to the federal government. The percentage is not based on R & D contract worth; it is a percentage of total procurement sales to the federal government including R & D and production. U.S. Congress, Senate Committee on the Judiciary, Subcommittee on Patents, Trademarks, and Copyrights, *Government Patent Policy, Hearings,* 89th Congress, first session. S. 789, S. 1809, and S. 1899 (Washington, D.C.: U.S. Government Printing Office, June 1965), part 2, pp. 399–401. The funding is negotiated with the particular agency or service that is the largest customer and is added to allowable overhead rates. See ASPR, section 15-205 (November 1963, revision 3) and NASA PR, section 15 205-35 (November 1965, revision 6). See also Brooks, *op. cit.,* p. 439.

Most AEC R & D is performed in AEC facilities and there is apparently little of this type of funding in AEC procurement contracts. In any case DOD procurement figures dwarf combined AEC and NASA R & D, with $30.7 billion estimated for FY 1967 for procurement plus $7.2 billion for research, development, test and evaluation (RDT & E), as against total estimated budgets of NASA and AEC of $7.2 billion. (Figures from *Aviation Week,* January 30, 1967, pp. 22–29.)

It is very difficult to obtain reliable, accurate data as to the amounts actually paid to contractors for this in-house, indirectly funded R & D, since the total amount of IR & D, PI, and BP expended by any given company is considered highly proprietary. Government participation may run to 80 or 90 percent of the total cost, the balance is funded from corporate profits. Even the percentage allowed any given company is considered highly proprietary since both amount and percentage are thought to reflect the ability to compete in the rapidly changing areas of space/defense technology. See Merton Peck and Frederick Scherer, *The Weapons Acquisition Process: An Economic Analysis* (Boston: Division of Research, Graduate School of Business Administration, Harvard University, 1962), pp. 581–93, for a discussion of contractor market insecurity due to "rapidly changing requirments of military technology."

However, some estimate of DOD funding may be obtained from a statement made by H. H. Rubin (Associate Director of Defense Accounting and Auditing Division, GAO), and some extrapolation from 1962–63 DOD funding rates.

"The extent of the independent research programs (apparently including IR & D, PI, and BP costs) is rather significant in many cases. We have received an estimate made within the Department of Defense that indicates that the amount of the total of such programs, I think about a year or two ago, was in the neighborhood of $900 million annually. This is a rather significant figure." Senate Subcommittee on Patents, Trademarks, and Copyrights, *op. cit.,* p. 400.

This estimate of $900 million is about 4.5 percent of total DOD procurement and RDT & E expenditures in FY 1962 or FY 1963. Frederick Scherer, *The Weapons Acquisition Process* (Boston: Division of Research, Graduate School of Business Administration, Harvard University, 1964), p. 57. Assuming that the percentage has remained relatively constant, DOD would be spending about $1.6 billion in FY 1967 (not including the NASA program). A conservative estimate of total federal funding of this type would probably be about $2 billion. This money is all allocable to in-house company R & D. The fruits of this R & D are considered the property of the private corporation; the government obtains no rights to any data, know-how, innovations of patentable items resulting from such work, unless the contractor wishes to sell it (again) to the government. See Senate Subcommittee on Patents, Trademarks, and Copyrights, *op. cit.,* pp. 399–401.

This 1962 figure was confirmed by Secretary McNamara, U.S. Congress, House of Representatives, Subcommittee of the Committee on Appropriations, *1967 Department of Defense Appropriations, Hearings,* 89th Congress, second session (Washington, D.C.: U.S. Government Printing Office, 1966), part 2, p. 251. However, director of Defense Research and Engineering Foster in 1967 indicated that there had been little growth in the absolute value of this overhead R & D funding since 1962, although the testimony is not entirely clear in this area. U.S. Congress, House of Representatives, Subcommittee of the Committee on Appropriations, *1968 Department of Defense Appropriations, Hearings,* 90th Congress, first session (Washington, D.C.: U.S. Government Printing Office, 1967), part 3, pp. 28, 64.

This type of funding may amount to as much as 10 percent of total federal spending on all R & D funding and to almost 20 percent of all industrial R & D funding. This $2 billion is in addition to the NSF figure of $15.9 billion. But see *1966 NSF Report on R & D Funding,* p. 61, n. 3, for ambiguous wording about covering some overhead charges within $15.9 billion figure. Apparently this overhead reference covers costs attributable to administrative overhead on R & D programs *per se,* not overhead R & D programs. A more serious problem than this probable inaccuracy in NSF figures for the extent of federal private-industrial R & D spending is the distortion created when comparing federal with private R & D funding if this $2 billion plus figure is included in private-industrial spending figures. See Brooks, *op. cit.,* p. 439. Private R & D expenditures are used in partial justification for a number of DOD policies: the proprietary data policy; the patent/license policy; and the general concern for protecting the commercial competitive positions of private firms allegedly established by the use of corporate profits to support R & D projects. See for example Letter DOD to GAO. Explaining DOD Policy as to Rights in Technical Data Resulting from Independent Research and Development Defense Procurement Circular #22 (Washington, D.C.: DOD or GAO, January 29, 1965.) This letter is a recent statement of DOD policy in this area.

velopment (66 percent), as defined by NSF.[4] Table I shows federal R & D spending, excluding plant and overhead reimbursement, for

[4] *1966 NSF Report on R & D Funding*, pp. 9, 14, 19. *Basic research* is defined as the "pursuit of knowledge for its own sake. Like basic research, *applied research* is systematic, intensive study directed toward fuller knowledge of a given subject. However, it differs from basic research in that it seeks to show or indicate the means by which a recognized need may be met. In *development* the findings are directed toward the production of useful materials, devices, systems or methods: this work includes design and improvement of prototypes and processes."

Another problem with the NSF figures (besides that discussed in footnote 3) is that the various agencies apparently disagree about what is or is not R & D or RDT & E. Arthur D. Little, Inc., *Transfer of Aerospace Technology in the United States—A Critical Review* (Cambridge, Mass.: Arthur D. Little, Inc., July 1966), pp. 4, 9. This report suggests that DOD and NASA definitions of R & D do not agree.

> In considering the size of the space program, however, it is important to bear in mind that it consists of a continuing program of basic research and unmanned scientific exploration or near-earth space, . . . upon which is superimposed a massive engineering project (Apollo). . . . It would not be completely accurate to characterize Apollo as "research." . . . It should be considered in the same category as a Department of Defense production program.

Arthur D. Little, Inc., *op. cit.*, p. 4.

Apollo accounts for over 70 percent of the NASA budget for R & D for the last several years, about $3.5 billion for FY 1966, or about 22 percent of the total federal R & D estimate for FY 1966. See *1966 NSF Report on R & D Funding*, p. 3.

Such conceptual differences in definition over categorization can clearly have a significant impact on the relevance of the NSF figures for assessing the amount of transferable technology as well as in assessing total R & D expenditures. This problem can also cause difficulty in determining the types of technology spin-off since production engineering data and techniques are likely to have quite different audiences from applied research or laboratory development.

The same problem of categorization of R & D spending exists in private industry, and it has some effect on the total attributed to private risk capital and, therefore, to arguments for preserving contractor rights to know-how and/or patents developed under federal R & D.

> There is good reason to believe that the public's stake in total R & D is greater than 70 percent. The reason for this is that industry in many cases is merely reclassifying traditional outlays in terms of the now fashionable "research and development" effort.

Statement by Mr. Benjamin Gordon (Staff Economist to Senator Russell Long), Senate Subcommittee on Patents, Trademarks and Copyrights, *op. cit.*, part 1, p. 372.

Table 1

Federal Obligations and Expenditures, R & D, Fiscal Years 1940-67 (millions of dollars)

		Research, Development, and R & D Plant		
Fiscal Years	Total Federal Budget Expenditures	Obligations	Expenditures	Expenditures as Percentage of Budget
1940	$ 9,055	b	$ 74	0.8
1941	13,255	b	198	1.5
1942	34,037	b	280	0.8
1943	79,368	b	602	0.8
1944	94,986	b	1,377	1.4
1945	98,303	b	1,591	1.6
1946	60,326	b	918	1.5
1947	38,923	$ 691	900	2.3
1948	32,955	868	855	2.6
1949	39,474	1,105	1,082	2.7
1950	39,544	1,175	1,083	2.7
1951	43,970	1,812	1,301	3.0
1952	65,303	2,914	1,816	2.8
1953[a]	74,120	3,361	3,101	4.2
1954	67,537	3,039	3,148	4.7
1955	64,389	2,745	3,308	5.1
1956	66,224	3,267	3,446	5.2
1957	68,966	4,389	4,462	6.5
1958	71,369	4,905	4,990	7.0
1959	80,342	7,116	5,803	7.2
1960	76,539	8,074	7,738	10.1
1961	81,515	9,601	9,278	11.4
1962	87,787	11,060	10,373	11.8
1963	92,642	13,650	11,988	12.9
1964	97,684	15,310	14,694	15.0
1965	96,507	15,731	14,875	15.4
1966[c]	106,428	17,069	15,963	15.0
1967[c]	112,847	16,650	16,152	14.3

[a] Beginning in fiscal 1953, amounts include pay and allowance of military personnel in research and development for both obligations and expenditures.

[b] Not available.

[c] The figures for 1966 are estimates based on amounts shown in "The Budget, 1967," subject to subsequent administrative action; estimated figures for 1967 do not reflect Congressional action.

NOTE: Data for FY 1952 and subsequent years are based on surveys of the National Science Foundation. Data for 1940 through 1951 were prepared by the Bureau of the Budget. Since the NSF surveys began, agencies have, when necessary, submitted revised data to maintain historical comparability of reporting.

the period 1940-67. Private industry performs about 63 percent of the total R & D but about 81 percent of the development portion; the balance of the total R & D funding is divided primarily between intramural work (20 percent) and educational and other nonprofit institutions (16 percent).

The 1966 National Science Foundation (NSF) Report on federal R & D funding observes that this funding is largely concentrated in three space/defense agencies: DOD, AEC, and NASA. These three agencies accounted for about 85 percent of federal R & D funding during fiscal 1965, 1966, and 1967.

> NASA, of course, differs from the other two in that it is committed to the objective that "activities in space should be devoted to peaceful purposes for the benefit of all mankind." Also the AEC, despite its original orientation toward defense and security now devotes more than one-half of its R & D dollars to "civilian" ends. At the same time, AEC's scientific work and that of NASA include cooperation with DOD on mutual programs and often in the use of the same industrial firms.[5]

Further, it appears that this concentration in these three defense/space mission-oriented agencies is likely to continue for the forseeable future though there has been some increase in R & D funding by some agencies (the Department of Health, Education and Welfare and Housing and Urban Development, for example) and a large percentage increase has been forecast by some economists. The magnitude of the actual increase is, however, only a fraction of the R & D expenditures of NASA alone.[6]

These three agencies appear to spend most of their industrial R & D funds in five industries: Aircraft, Electrical Equipment, Motor Vehicles, Machinery, and Chemicals with the first two receiving over 80 percent. Most of the money spent in these five industries is contracted to the eight largest companies in each industry: Aircraft (74 percent), Electrical Equipment (82 percent), Motor Vehicles (96 percent), Machinery (86 percent), and Chemicals (88 percent).[7]

---

[5] *1966 NSF Report on R & D Funding,* p. 3.

[6] Gerhard Colm and Peter Wagner, *Federal Budgets Projections* (Washington, D.C.: The Brookings Institution, 1966), Chapters VII, VIII, and IX.

[7] National Science Foundation, *Basic Research, Applied Research, and Development in Industry, 1964,* NSF 66-28 (Washington D.C.: U.S. Government Print-

Company-funded R & D in these five industries accounted for about 75 percent of total industrial spending in R & D in 1965.[8] Some of the money counted as company-funded R & D in these industries is probably attributable to federal overhead reimbursement expenditures in the form of overhead funding for independent research and development (IR & D) work, product improvement (PI) work, and bid proposal (BP) costs.[9] The stimulus given to industrial R & D by government expenditures in expensive capital equipment,[10] risk-taking, and indirectly by stimulating R & D through demands for higher quality products,[11] may be a significant, though indirect,

---

ing Office, June 1966) (hereafter cited as *NSF Industrial R & D Funding—1964*).

One problem with these NSF data, pp. 24–25, is that it is not entirely clear how much of the contract money is actually spent in the industrial categories given because: 1. NSF classifies a firm in one category if its primary business was in that field, even if only 51 percent; and 2. the degree and diffusion of subcontracting does not appear to be included. Thus General Electric would be included in the Electrical Equipment category, but in fact it supplies the government with R & D in almost every technical field. Also, in large R & D projects substantial amounts of the work are subcontracted, sometimes more than 50 percent, but some may, in fact, be subcontracted back to the original prime contractor.

8 National Science Foundation, *Basic Research, Applied Research, and Development in Industry, 1965*, NSF 67-12 (Washington, D.C.: U.S. Government Printing Office, June 1967) (hereafter cited as *NSF Industrial R & D Funding—1965*).

9 See footnotes 3 and 4 for a more detailed discussion of federal agency practices and expenditures in the area of IR & D, PI, and/or BP funding. According to the analysis and data presented there, the aircraft and electrical equipment industries may have received as much as $1 billion for this overhead R & D funding in 1965. Thus, about 70 percent of the R & D expenditures attributed to private-industrial spending in these two industries in 1965 by the NSF may have been paid for by federal overhead R & D funding.

Method of computation—

Assume—(a) $1.3 billion total for federal overhead R & D funding in 1964

Given—(b) 80 percent of (a) allocated to electrical equipment and aircraft industries in 1964

Given—(c) $1.5 billion attributed by NSF to these two industries

NSF Industrial R & D Funding—1964, p 27.

The ultimate issue is, In what sense should this overhead R & D funding be considered private risk capital? DOD argues that these funds should be viewed in the same category as those available to corporations from higher profits (relative to sales) in the commercial market and therefore "private."

10 Harvey Brooks, "National Science Policy and Technology Transfer" in *The Government of Science* (Cambridge: The M.I.T. Press, 1968), pp. 254–78.

11 *Ibid.*, pp. 267–68.

contribution to private R & D spending. Thus, the $15.9 billion or even the $17.6 billion figure may be far too low as an indication of the magnitude of federal spending and is clearly too low with respect to indirect benefits contributed through federal capital expenditures and overhead R & D funding.

NSF reports:

> In January 1965, industrial firms employed a full time equivalent of 346,300 R & D scientists and engineers, 2 percent above the number employed a year earlier and 51 percent above the January 1957 total . . . as in the case of both total and Federal R & D funds, the two industries most heavily involved in federally financed defense and aerospace R & D programs also accounted for the majority of industrial R & D scientists and engineers. The aircraft and missiles and the electrical equipment and communications industries employed respectively totals of 101,200 and 74,800 as of January 1965. . . .[12]

The 200 companies accounting for 92 percent of the federally funded R & D also employed 85 percent of all industrial R & D scientists and engineers.[13] (These totals do not include scientists and engineers employed under federally sponsored R & D done intramurally nor those employed at nonprofit institutions.) There appears to be little mobility of technical personnel from federally sponsored R & D to the commercial-industrial sector or back to universities.[14] This is especially important since it appears that

---

[12] *NSF Industrial R & D Funding—1964,* pp. 11–12. In January, 1966 the full-time equivalent of scientists and engineers in industry had increased four percent over the January 1965 figure to 358,900. *NSF Industrial R & D Funding—1965,* p. 10.

[13] This concentration of federal R & D spending among the largest firms in the given industry is not necessarily characteristic of private industrial R & D spending concentration. A recent article noted that, ". . . it appears that there are few instances where larger firms contribute a disproportionate share of industry resources for research and development." William Comanor, "Market Structure, Product Differentiation and Industrial Research," *The Quarterly Journal of Economics,* LXXXI (November 1967), p. 656. Thus, it may be that federal R & D spending patterns do not present the most efficient model from a competitive market standpoint. However, the scale of federal R & D projects may tend to encourage greater concentration in the space/defense industry.

[14] Although data are scarce in this area, a study by Richard Howell, *et al., The Structure and Dynamics of the Defense R & D Industry,* a Stanford Research Institute Report prepared for the Director of Defense Research and

mobility of technical personnel may be a key element in technology transfer and commercialization of federal R & D developed technology.[15]

Finally, over 60 percent of government R & D is concentrated in six states: California, New York, Maryland, Massachusetts, Texas, and Pennsylvania.[16]

Not only has the monetary expenditure increased greatly, but there is a growing awareness and interest in the effects of this public investment in new technology. Particularly since the large scale investment in the space program, there has been increasing concern with whether there has been enough transfer to the commercial sectors from this huge public investment in R & D.

The data presented in this chapter, although somewhat misleading in that they do not account for all indirect methods of federal funding of industrial R & D, indicate that federal R & D spending has increased dramatically since World War II; that these funds are primarily spent in industry, not intramurally as was true prior to 1941; that these funds are primarily spent by three powerful mission-oriented agencies; that they are spent in five industrial categories, and concentrated even more than privately funded R & D among the largest companies in each of these five industries; that a very large portion of the available R & D technical personnel, possibly the more talented,[17] is found in these industries and there

---

Engineering, Office of Director of Defense (Washington, D.C.: Clearinghouse for Federal Scientific and Technical Information, August 1966), p. 40, tends to confirm this statement.

[15] See Edward Roberts and Herbert Wainer, "Technology Transfer and Entrepreneurial Success," Miami Beach, Florida, paper presented to the Twentieth National Conference on the Administration of Research, Miami Beach, Florida, October 27, 1966.

[16] National Science Foundation, *Geographic Distribution of Federal Funds for Research and Development: Fiscal Year 1965,* NSF 67-8 (Washington, D.C.: U.S. Government Printing Office, April 1967), p. 48. This phenomenon and its apparent importance in the technology transfer process are discussed in conjunction with the mobility problem in Chapter 4. But, one problem with the data is that the NSF figures apparently refer to prime contract funds and it is not clear at the lower tier subcontractor level how the funding is, in fact, diffused geographically.

[17] They appear to be better paid and to have relatively more attractive work available, and there tends to be more glamor associated with aerospace R & D. This leads to a hypothesis that the more talented engineers and scientists tend to work on government projects and for that portion of private industry work-

is little movement by them to the commercial-industrial sector; and finally, this R & D is highly concentrated geographically.

This large federal investment establishes a *prima facie* case for some federal responsibility in assisting transfer of the technology thus acquired to other sectors of the economy. One issue that must be explored is the degree of responsibility. While the facilitation of transfer is a "good," it is no longer so simple as for the Napoleonic canners to identify, evaluate, and transfer new technology amid the increasingly large and complex government R & D programs, nor is it so simple to determine the value of this technology for commercial application.

Federal Responsibilities

> Since the federal government supports over two thirds of the scientific and technological activity in the nation, the way in which it does this may have a large influence on the process of technology transfer, whether it be in the vertical or the horizontal sense.[18]

The role played by the government could range from a mere nonselective library function, a sort of general clearing-house, to the carefully screened selection process advocated by the President's Science Advisory Committee (PSAC),[19] to the activist-librarian role suggested by Howick and Lesher,[20] to the entrepreneurial approach advocated by Arthur D. Little.[21] Presently, the vast majority of the work product of government R & D is not available, and what is available is often difficult and time-consuming to obtain and sift through.

---

ing on government projects. See generally, *NSF Industrial R & D Funding—1964,* pp. 8, 9, 49.

[18] Brooks, *The Government of Science,* p. 259.

[19] President's Science Advisory Committee, *Science, Government and Information* (Washington, D.C.: U.S. Government Printing Office, January 1963).

[20] Richard Lesher and George Howick, *Assessing Technology Transfer,* NASA SP-5067 (Washington, D.C.: U.S. Government Printing Office, 1966).

[21] See footnotes 35 through 45 of Chapter 8 for a discussion of the position advocated by Arthur D. Little, Inc. These three possible roles are neither exclusive nor exhaustive, nor do they necessarily represent a complete spectrum of possible roles from least to most government involvement, but merely indicate some suggested approaches for government involvement.

At present, the government has *sub silentio* instituted by inaction or half-hearted action severe restrictions on access to technical data. Some agencies (e.g., AEC) have tried and continue to try to surmount the problem of transfer. But often the institutional framework of federal R & D expenditures, particularly in the defense area, preserves a separation between public and private sectors so that even the aerospace divisions of many large companies communicate very little with their fellow commercial divisions.[22] The aerospace/defense industry appears, indeed, to follow a pattern of secrecy, and federal policies tend to foster this attitude. Thus not only does the government have some *prima facie* responsibility for disseminating so much of the work product as is consistent with national security, but also for altering its "data" policies so that this attitude can be modified. The secrecy that may have been a reasonable policy for a short crisis period is not applicable to a period of continuing use of large portions of the nation's R & D resources.

Although the federal government spends well in excess of the NSF figure of $278 million for the collection, evaluation, and dissemination of technical information from its yearly investment in R & D, most of the money is spent on routine library functions and within the ambit of the funding agency or its contractors. Little or no personalized transfer is funded except for the following four programs:[23]

a. AEC—Office of Industrial Cooperation and some other extramural activities
b. Department of Agriculture—Cooperative Extension Service

---

[22] Merton Peck and Frederick Scherer, *The Weapons Acquisition Process: An Economic Analysis* (Boston: Division of Research, Graduate School of Business Administration, Harvard University, 1962), pp. 128–30.

"In these companies [General Electric and Westinghouse] the defense business is largely carried on by specialized divisions. Judging from our limited observation of other 'mixed' companies, the defense business tends to be a corporate world in itself, with relatively little interchange of technical and managerial personnel between the defense and commercial division. At the operating level, we could discern little difference between these mixed and primarily defense firms." *Ibid.,* p. 129.

[23] See the beginning of Chapter 5 for a discussion of federal funding for the collection, evaluation, and dissemination of technical information.

c. Department of Commerce—State Technical Services Program
d. NASA—Technology Utilization Program

Aside from the agricultural area, the federal government spends less than $25 million yearly for systematic programs of collection, evaluation, and transfer.[24] No money at all is spent on a program which has a coordinated input-output operation backed by an integrated program for the control of proprietary data and patent/license regulations.

Precise measurement of the value to the economy of a given degree of federal participation is not yet possible. Yet the role of the federal government as the primary sponsor of R & D in the society argues for a larger role. The fact that this sponsorship has grown so dramatically—both absolutely and relative to the gross national product—during the fifties and early sixties provides an additional argument for an expanded role. Whether this sponsorship has in fact preempted valuable R & D resources from private use is less important than that it has directed them within a very narrow area. Thus even if the private sector has not been preempted, other public areas may be. In any case, if more value can be obtained from this resource within reasonable constraints of cost-effectiveness guidelines, then clearly an expanded program should be undertaken.

Technology Transfer Implied by the Charters of the Major Science Agencies

The role of the agencies in the transfer process has been under almost continuous debate in the Congress and the Executive branch since 1960 at least.[25] An early product of this debate, the so-called Weinberg Report, was published by PSAC in 1963. This report

[24] There are few or no accurate data available, except in the STS Program area which is limited by direct Congressional appropriations. STS had $5.5 million appropriated for FY 1967, the NASA TU Program spent about $7.5 million. Other federal programs are much smaller.

[25] U.S. Congress, Senate, Committee on Government Operations, Subcommittee on Reorganization and Internal Organizations, *Coordination of Information on Current Federal Research and Development Projects in the Field of Electronics,* 87th Congress, first session (Washington, D.C., U.S. Government Printing Office, 1961) (Committee Print).

called upon the agencies to become "information minded."[26] PSAC was primarily concerned with providing appropriate mechanisms for the collection of technical information, not with the problems of providing effective mechanisms for technology transfer. Since transfer is a function of both effective input and output, however, the reforms proposed are extremely important in establishing a transfer program. This report concluded that,

> Whether prompted by differences in Congressional directive or by differences in subject matter, the agencies vary most strikingly in the fraction of potentially useful material they cover . . . the DOD's technical information agency (ASTIA) collects not more than 40 percent of the reports that are byproducts of DOD's research and development program.[27]

Relevant also are Robert Solo's conclusions:

> Out of ten thousand prime contractors and the 300,000 sub-contractors, only 1,700 obtain any information from ASTIA. One important check on the use of ASTIA information, surely, is the peculiar "need-to-know" requirement as a prerequisite for the receipt of information from the DOD. The "need-to-know" requirement reflects (1) the extreme deference to the proprietary interest of individual contractors which characterizes DOD policy, and (2) the pervasive identification of scientific and technical information with military intelligence.[28]

This policy, Solo suggested, is pervasive throughout DOD. It also appears in NASA since Apollo Technical reports were not generally available (during 1965, 1966, and to a lesser degree during 1967) for some policy reason, evidently because of the so-called space race or possible military implications.[29]

Finally, the Report recommended that each government agency

---

[26] PSAC, *op. cit.*, p. 44.

[27] *Idem.*

[28] Robert Solo, *Studies in the Anatomy of Economic Progress,* Report prepared for the National Planning Association (Washington, D.C.: NPA, 1965), p. 258.

[29] Interviews with NASA personnel during Winter, 1966. Withholding of Apollo technical reports is important because Apollo spending represented about 70 percent of NASA's R & D budget for fiscal 1965, 1966, and 1967.

sponsoring R & D should recognize that the control and dissemination of information is an important part of its R & D function both intramurally and extramurally. The recommendations of the Weinberg Report called for each agency to establish ". . . a focal point of responsibility—for technical information," and to coordinate agency efforts through the Federal Council for Science and Technology (FCST). The FCST did establish a nominal coordinating body, Committee on Scientific and Technical Information (COSATI), in 1963, but its operation has been largely ineffectual, with each of the large procurement agencies continuing to follow policies consistent with what is believed to be its own political self-interest.[30] One relevant question that arises is: Why, after hearings, debates, executive recommendations, and numerous studies, has the power structure of the agencies been able to maintain the *status quo*?

In fairness to the nation's taxpayers, it would seem at the least that the results of public funding, after making due allowance for security requirements, should be made freely available to the economy, but they have not been.[31] In fact, it is probably true that only a small fraction of all R & D reports could ever be procured by an interested party not on the payroll of an agency or of an agency

---

[30] The similarity between the reaction of these agencies to these PSAC recommendations and their reaction to President Kennedy's Patent Policy message is striking. In both cases they have generally praised the two sets of recommendations and continued in the spirit of their former policies. This is indicative of the power (and inertia) of these large technology procurement agencies even as against the Executive branch.

See Robert Solo, *Patent Policy for Government Sponsored Research and Development*, Report (in three parts) prepared for the NASA Administrator's Office (Washington, D.C.: NASA, 1966), part 1, pp. 4–20 for a discussion of the divergent paths taken by federal agencies in response to the Kennedy Message. But see Federal Council for Science and Technology (FCST), *Annual Report on Government Patent Policy* (Washington, D.C.: U.S. Government Printing Office, June 1966) for a different interpretation of agency compliance with the Kennedy Patent Policy Statement.

[31] To promote private industrial development, it may, in some cases, be necessary to provide exclusive rights to specific inventions, since most of the cost (and therefore risk) in reducing an invention to marketable end product is incurred after the initial invention. See U.S. Department of Commerce, *Technological Innovation: Its Environment and Management* (Washington, D.C.: U.S. Government Printing Office, January 1967), p. 9 (estimating 5 to 10 percent of total innovation cost to develop the basic invention).

prime contractor.[32] Small contractors with narrowly defined contracts are often foreclosed from many areas of technical information whereas larger companies have much more rapid and comprehensive access to agency-sponsored or agency-generated R & D information.

Acquisition of technical information faces the additional barrier of agency policy regarding so-called company proprietary data of all types including patentable inventions. Appendix C presents a discussion of some of the difficulties of establishing effective means of promoting disclosure of so-called contractor proprietary information, including patentable inventions. All that need be said at this point is that if PSAC, with the backing of the Executive branch, was unable to promote even minimum standards for reporting, evaluating, and disseminating more project reports (that is, the specific work product of the contractors and grantees), the problems of promoting disclosure of company know-how must be even more intractable.

Although most of the literature in this field deals with federal patent policy,[33] the problem area extends to all types of company proprietary data, with patentable items only a small fraction of the information zealously guarded by the "system."

One of the realities that the Weinberg Report failed to come to grips with is that there is little incentive for the space/defense prime contractor and even less reason for his subcontractors to disclose or report any R & D results beyond those strictly required by the contract. The standard contract clauses combined with lack of interest in enforcement provide little incentive or coercive effect for disclosure, with the result that such disclosure is kept to a *pro forma* amount. The Report did note that agency technical personnel hold technical information reporting, evaluation, and dissemination in low regard.[34] However, a more serious problem may be that the

[32] There does not appear to be any study or agency report that would substantiate an exact figure; but if NASA, with its wide interest in transfer, withholds as much as 70 percent of its technical reports from general circulation, it appears likely that a far higher percentage of DOD's larger store of R & D results may be withheld or circumscribed with so much red tape as to be all but inaccessible.

[33] See bibliography in FCST, *op. cit.*, pp. 41–53. A thirteen-page bibliography of articles on federal patent policy, mainly post-1958.

[34] See PSAC, *op. cit.*, p. 19. But see Scherer, *op. cit.*

agencies, particularly DOD, have formed a close, continuing relationship with a group of large space/defense contractors and it is in the agencies' best interest not to insist too firmly on the reporting requirement.

Assuming that these agency institutional barriers to report do exist, what policy should the federal government adopt? To shed some light on this question, we will next consider some elements of the transfer process itself in terms of its constituent variables.

The Transfer Process and the Federal Agency

The transfer process appears to be a function of three primary interrelated variables, acquisition (the input variable), dissemination (the output variable), and agency policy with regard to proprietary data, including patent/license policy. Federal policy covering the control of contractor trade secrets and other company expertise including patentable inventions affects both the input and output variables. The granting or withholding of legal rights in patents to which the government has title appears particularly to affect the transfer of specific items.

The hypothesis that the input and output variables are interdependent rests on a general notion that if a Regional Dissemination Center (RDC) or other output mechanism is effective in transferring technology and can measure this transfer, then the output mechanism will provide some stimulus for the input function.[35] Similarly, if the input mechanism produced more quality reports and innovations, the output operation would have a wider choice of "wares," provided that the output "library" were not so poorly indexed as to be unmanageable. It appears that nothing would stimulate an aerospace contractor to report new innovations so much as the profitable sale in the commercial market of a license to a commercially successful innovation such as a new "Xerox" type

[35] An argument can be made that the effectiveness of any program for technology transfer depends on the quality and quantity of the input technical data and that it equally depends on the effectiveness of the output mechanisms. Further, the input will be influenced by the general space/defense industry strategy as to disclosure of company know-how, which is to some extent a function of the legal protection afforded for that know-how in the space/defense market.

process. The suggestion is, then, that the input and output function can be "forcing functions" on each other.

Not only are mechanisms for transfer established by an agency important in determining how successful a transfer program will be, but the attitude of an agency is also most important. In fact, the relative importance that an agency attaches to transfer will affect the institutional approach. Thus, the AEC, with its heavy commitment to nuclear research, appoints professional referees at each laboratory to screen technical reports for declassification, while the mission-oriented DOD leaves this task of review, where it is performed at all, to security officers. NASA, with its heavy commitment to commercial transfer, uses business-oriented engineers to screen technical reports for commercial content, while DOD does no commercial screening at all, merely passing on a portion of its unclassified, nonlimited reports to the Commerce Clearinghouse. The Department of Agriculture with its statutory responsibility for creating and diffusing agricultural technology has created an integrated transfer system from R & D to ultimate user, while other agencies do little in preparing and screening R & D results for the ultimate user.

Saying that technology transfer is a function of several variables does not, of course, remove the institutional barriers. Viewing the process of transfer in this way may, however, assist in analysis and methodology so that relatively more emphasis can be placed on an integrated functional approach as an alternative to the present ineffective, disjointed agency efforts. Failure to deal with the problem of transfer as a function of these interrelated variables is one of the primary reasons for lack of measurable success in existing programs and partially accounts for the fragmented approach taken by most agencies.

Chapter 3

The Value of Space/Defense Technology

The transfer and utilization of new technology offer immense opportunity to the Nation. There is widespread agreement among those who have studied the issue that the knowledge resulting from public investment in R & D constitutes a major, rapidly increasing, and insufficiently exploited national resource. Its effective use can increase the rate of economic growth, create new employment opportunities, help offset imbalances between regions and industries, aid the international competitive position of U.S. industry, enhance our national prestige, improve the quality of life, and assist significantly in filling unmet human and community needs.

Measurements exist to show that a considerable portion of the technology resulting from military/space/nuclear work is relevant to needs outside those mission areas. . . . (NASA TU Administrators Richard Lesher and George Howick)[1]

. . . A review of the potential for utilization of technical by-products of military and space research and development shows that: a) estimates of the magnitude of the potential are difficult to justify. . . . (Professor Richard Rosenbloom, Harvard Business School)[2]

The continuing visible technical accomplishments of the space program may be modifying attitudes toward technological innovation among those who previously have been hostile or neutral to innovation. To the extent that this is so, the very existence of the space program as a model of technological achievement may finally prove more important to the economy than either the multiplier effect of its investment or the "spill-over" of its technology. (Sumner Myers, National Planning Association researcher)[3]

---

[1] Richard Lesher and George Howick, *Assessing Technology Transfer,* NASA SP-5067 (Washington, D.C.: U.S. Government Printing Office, 1966), p. 5. Presently the authors are respectively Asst. Administrator for the TU Program and the Director of the TU Division. Studies to date indicate that transfer is not susceptible of quantitative measure. See the NASA-sponsored Denver Research Institute Report, *The Commercial Application of Missile/Space Technology* (Springfield, Va.: Clearinghouse for Federal Scientific and Technical Information, 1963). Other studies do indicate that there are some valuable by-products, but not such as are likely to eradicate major social, economic or foreign policy problems.

[2] Richard Rosenbloom, *Technology Transfer—Process and Policy* (Washington, D.C.: Special Report No. 62, NPA, July 1965), p. 11.

[3] Sumner Myers, "The Space Program: A Model for Technological Innovation," *Space Digest* (August, 1966), p. 82.

These quotations indicate the range of values assigned by commentators to the by-products of defense/space R & D and their measurability. There is widespread disagreement about the value of this investment for secondary application of technology,[4] but there is general agreement that it is not yet susceptible of measurement.

Soon after the initiation of the space program, there was enthusiastic expectation that the public sector would soon be receiving the benefits of this new endeavor.[5] The terms spin-off and spill-over themselves suggest an inevitable automatic process of tangible benefits. While these early estimates of specific benefits were in fact proven too sanguine, recent studies indicate that the pendulum has swung too far the other way toward assuming that specific, identifiable invention transfers are likely to be few and far between.[6]

There are some quantitative data on the amount of transfer that have resulted in patents,[7] but it is primarily obtained from larger aerospace or defense contractors, who have had a notably low patenting propensity under government-sponsored R & D.[8] These

---

[4] Compare Robert Solo, "Gearing Military R & D to Economic Growth," XL, No. 6 (November-December 1962), with Lesher and Howick, *op. cit.,* and both with Rosenbloom, *op. cit.,* for some range of opinions concerning the value of space/defense technology for secondary application. It is hard to find a subject about which there is less agreement.

[5] See, for example, General James Gavin's address before the International Bankers Association, December 1958; Leonard Silk, "The Impact on the American Economy," in *Outer Space: Prospects for Man and Society,* ed. Lincoln Bloomfield (Englewood Cliffs, New Jersey: Prentice-Hall, 1962), pp. 76–86.

[6] Arthur D. Little, Inc., *Transfer of Aerospace Technology in the United States —A Critical Review* (Cambridge, Mass.: Arthur D. Little, Inc., July 1965). (Report prepared for the Plowden Committee, United Kingdom.)

[7] Mary Holman, "Government Research and Development Inventions—A New Resource?" *Land Economics,* LXI (August 1965), pp. 231–38. Holman found that about 10 percent of the inventions assigned to the government had found some commercial use. Estimates of DOD contractor-owned patent commercialization range from 7 percent to 13 percent.

Compare U.S. Congress, Senate, Judiciary Committee, Subcommittee on Patents, Trademarks, and Copyrights, *Patent Practices of the Department of Defense, Report,* 87th Congress, first session (Washington, D.C.: U.S. Government Printing Office, 1961), pp. 23–29 and 86–129 (Committee Print), with Donald Watson, Harold Bright, and Arthur Burns, "Federal Patent Policies in Contracts for Research and Development," *The Patent, Trademark, and Copyright Journal of Research and Education,* IV, No. 4 (Winter 1960), pp. 321–23.

[8] See for example, Watson and Holman, *op. cit.,* pp. 1–60 and 189–203, or

space/defense contractors have also been least active in commercializing their specific inventions.

Measurement of Specific Invention Transfer

Some studies have indicated that specific invention spin-off, while easier to measure, is an inadequate measure of the amount of technology that is actually transferred.[9] There are, however, data that indicate that there is presently some measurable spin-off of specific inventions and that the amount of this spin-off is likely to increase in the next five to ten years. These data consist of the results of a study done at the National Planning Association (NPA), under Sumner Myers, to investigate the origins of 567 commercial innovations;[10] NSF data on the relative growth of federal R & D funding during the decade from 1954 to 1963 (see Table 1) versus the growth in privately funded R & D during this same period; and the diffusion rate of innovations from conception to end-item usage as determined by the studies of both Mansfield and Lynn (see Table 2).

No small number of case studies can be conclusive, but there is certainly evidence of a faster rate of technological development. The process, however, is still a fairly long one. Our studies suggest that major technological discoveries may wait as long as 14 years before they reach commercial application even on a small scale, and perhaps another five years before their impact on the economy becomes large. It seems safe to conclude that most major technological discoveries which will have a significant economic impact within the next decade are already at least in a readily identifiable stage of commercial development.

Christopher Freeman, "Research and Development in Electronic Capital Goods," *National Institute Economics Review,* No. 34 (November 1965), pp. 72–73.

[9] See for example, the Plowden Report, or Denver Research Institute, *The Commercial Application of Missile/Space Technology* (Springfield, Va.: Clearinghouse for Scientific and Technical Information, September 1963).

[10] National Planning Association, *Technology Tranfer and Industrial Innovation* (Washington, D.C.: NPA, Report to National Science Foundation, February 1967). Tables 3 and 4 are from this NPA report, pp. V-24 and V-29, respectively.

Table 2

Average Rate of Development of Selected Technological Innovations[1]

Factors Influencing the Rate of Technological Development	Mean Lapsed Time (years)		
	Incubation Period[2]	Commercial Development[3]	Total Development
Time Period			
Early 20th century (1885-1919)	30	7	37
Post-World War I (1920-44)	16	8	24
Post-World War II (1945-64)	9	5	14
Type of Market Application			
Consumer	13	7	20
Industrial	28	6	34
Source of Development Funds			
Private industry	24	7	31
Federal government	12	7	19

1 Based on study of 20 major innovations whose commercial development started in the period 1885–1950.

2 Begins with basic discovery and establishment of technical feasibility, and ends when commercial development begins.

3 Begins with recognition of commercial potential and the commitment of development funds to reach a reasonably well-defined commercial objective, and ends when the innovation is introduced as a commercial product or process.

The NPA study found that about 10 percent of the 567 innovations sampled had had their origins in information funded in whole or in part by the government (see Tables 3 and 4 for list of funding agencies and industry adopting the innovation). The study involved one relatively progressive industry, Computers, and two less progressive ones, Railroads and Housing Suppliers. The rate of diffusion of R & D from the defense or space R & D to a commercial end product varies enormously from innovation to innovation. Table 4 indicates the diffusion rate estimates of Lynn.[11] Mansfield's findings do indicate that the lag has decreased recently, but his estimate of average diffusion rate is almost the same as Lynn's, about 21 years between conception and practical application by one half

11 Frank Lynn, *An Investigation of the Rate of Development and Diffusion of Technology in Our Modern Industrial Society,* Report to the President of the National Commission on Technology, Automation, and Economic Progress (Washington, D.C.: U.S. Government Printing Office, 1966). Lynn concluded from a sample of 20 major innovations that the process from conception of an invention to actual application had accelerated somewhat over the last 70 years.

Table 3

Innovations Based on Information Partly or Wholly Government Funded, by Funding Agency and Industry

Government Agency which Provided Funds	Number of Innovations			
	Total	Railroads and Suppliers	Housing Suppliers	Computer Manufacturers and Suppliers
Military/Space Agencies				
AEC	4	3		1
DOD	34	11	3	20
NASA	3			3
Subtotal	41	14	3	24
Civilian Agencies				
DOA	10		10	
OTHER	5		3	2
Grand Total	56	14	16	26

Table 4

Percentage of Innovations Studied in Which Government-Funded Information Was Used as a Basis for Innovation, by Industry

Industry	Total No. of Innovations per Industry	No. of Innovations Based on Government Information	Percentage of Innovations Based on Government-Funded Information
Total	567	56	10%
Computer Manufacturers	90	19	21
Computer Suppliers	77	7	9
Housing Suppliers	196	16	8
Railroads	79	8	10
Railroad Suppliers	125	6	5

Table 4 and accompanying text are from the U.S. National Commission on Technology, Automation, and Economic Progress, *Technology and the American Economy* (Washington, D.C.: U.S. Government Printing Office, 1966), p. 4.

of an industry.[12] Based on extrapolation of Lynn's figures, an average rate of 17 years will be assumed for this diffusion process in 1967.

From 1954 to 1965 federal R & D expenditures grew from three-fourths of 1 percent of the GNP to 1.8 percent of the GNP, while the industrial share grew from three-fifths of 1 percent of GNP to 1 percent of the GNP; or the federal portion enjoyed a growth of 250 percent in the ten-year period compared with 66⅔ percent for private industry.[13] In addition, the private industrial portion may include sizable amounts attributable to federal agency overhead reimbursement procedures for independent research and development, product improvement, and bid proposal expenditures as well as indirectly through the building of costly development facilities and the permissive grant of commercial patent rights to DOD contractors.[14]

These data could be interpreted to support the contention that, in the years ahead, because of the greatly increased rate of federal R & D spending relative to GNP between 1954 and 1967,[15] com-

[12] Edwin Mansfield, "Diffusion of Technological Change," *Reviews of Data on Research and Development,* No. 31, NSF 61-52 (Washington, D.C.: U.S. Government Printing Office, October 1961). Mansfield surveyed 12 innovations in 4 industries, finding a lag of about 14 years, with another 1 to 15 years until one-half of the firms in the industry adopted the innovation.

[13] John Rubel, "The Impact of Government Research and Development on Industrial Growth: Trends and Challenges in Research and Development," paper presented to R & D symposium of the National Security Industry Association (March 13, 1963). Data gathered by Rubel from NSF, DOD, and other government sources. Also see, National Science Foundation, *Basic Research, Applied Research, and Development in Industry, 1964,* NSF 66-28 (Washington, D.C.: U.S. Government Printing Office, June 1966), pp. 1–11, 17–29, 37–41, 53–65, and 70–88.

See notes 3 and 4 in Chapter 2, for a discussion of why the NSF figures for R & D spending are potentially misleading as an indication of the growth of federal compared with private spending. The federal rates appear to be too low and the private too high, particularly in the electronics and aircraft industries. Errors of 20 percent or more are possible depending on how one defines R & D and what portion of federal agency overhead funding is considered private risk capital and what portion is considered public funding.

[14] All three terms refer to categories of allowable overhead charges in federal contracts. They are discussed in greater detail in footnotes 3 and 9 of Chapter 2.

[15] Mansfield found that there was a correlation between the rate of R & D expenditure and number of inventions capable of application in the commercial-industrial sector. However, efficiency does tend to diminish as the corporate R & D spending grows larger. Edwin Mansfield, "Industrial Research and Development Expenditures: Determinants, Prospects and Relation to Size

mercial industry will reap an increasingly larger number of specific innovation ideas from federally sponsored R & D expenditures even if little or nothing is done by way of an expanded or more inspired federal technology transfer program.

A number of arguments may be raised against this interpretation:

1. The sample used by the NPA study was quite small.

2. It is limited to three industries and the R & D spending rate increase is not directly related to those industries.

3. The relative commercial value of the 10 percent was not given although the innovations were considered recent "significant" innovations by the firms interviewed.

4. Many of the housing innovations resulted from Department of Agriculture (DOA) funding, not from DOD, NASA, or AEC funding.[16]

5. In view of Solo's argument that "Not only is space and military research growing further apart from industrial research in a technical way, but communication between the two sectors is becoming more unmanageable,"[17] projections of increasing transfer attributable to post-1954 R & D expenditures may be unrealistic.

6. The relative growth of government R & D may not be correlative to the number of innovations to be expected, nor has information been published by NPA on the relative rate of application for the 10 percent.

7. Increased spending on R & D appears to produce proportionately fewer innovations per R & D dollar after some efficiency limit is reached.

Even with all these limitations and possible changing patterns in defense/space R & D, the data still suggest that federally funded R & D may produce a larger number of measurable specific innovations, through horizontal transfer, in the future than in the past.

Measurement of General Area Transfer

Besides these specific examples of transfer there are earlier ex-

---

of Firm and Inventive Output," *Journal of Political Economy,* LXXII, No. 4 (August 1964), pp. 319–40.

[16] But 7 percent of the total excluding the innovations originating from the Department of Agriculture R & D, were based on space/defense funded R & D.

[17] Solo, *op. cit.*

amples of more general areas of technology that have been greatly facilitated by initial government funding, such as digital computers, the semiconductors, the commercial jet airliners, and others. If specific examples of transfer are difficult to identify, the amount attributable to federal R & D in more generalized transfer is even more difficult to identify and measure. However, as already noted, R & D spending in the aircraft and electronic industries is primarily funded by the federal government. Some diffusion of military/space-developed software has also occurred, but no measure of its overall diffusion or rate of diffusion appears to exist. In short, there appears to be transfer of federal R & D technology at many levels,[18] and it may be increasing, but the social benefits and costs are not yet susceptible of measurement. Nor does it appear likely that any significant amount of public investment in R & D can be justified by appealing to the value of transferable technology generated thereunder.

Thus, while there is some evidence of specific by-product spin-off from federal R & D, this alone would not justify a significant amount of public investment in a greatly expanded transfer program.

Economic Measure of Transfer

An argument for a greatly increased federal program for transfer would be a general economic one, that is, since productivity is mainly increased by new technology,[19] it follows that a program to transfer technology from federal R & D is bound to increase productivity and lead to all manner of benefits, from fulfilling unmet human needs to improving our balance-of-payments situation.[20]

---

18 See Denver Institute Research Report, *op. cit.*

19 See for example, Robert Solow, "Technical Change and the Aggregate Production Function," *Review of Economics and Statistics,* XXXIX, No. 3 (August 1957), pp. 312–20, estimating output per man-hour from 1909 to 1949, *seven-eighths* due to technological progress; Solomon Fabricant, "Resources and Output Trends in the United States since 1870," *American Economic Review,* XLVI (May 1956), estimating *90 percent* of the increase in output per man-hour in the 1871 to 1951 period due to technological progress; and, Edward Denison, *The Sources of Economic Growth in the United States* (New York: Committee for Economic Development, 1962), p. 270, estimated that about *36 percent* of the advance in GNP from 1929 to 1957 may be accounted for by "advances of knowledge," and projects a contribution of 46 percent in the 1960–80 period.

20 See Lesher and Howick, *op. cit.,* pp. 1, 10–16. "[I]t seems important first to ask if the benefits of employing new technology [from federal programs] war-

It is not clear that there is any measurable relationship between increased productivity as measured by increases in the rate of change of output per manhour and federal R & D spending. A recent study performed by the NPA for Lockheed Aircraft Corporation to determine the impact of the space program on the domestic economy reported that productivity statistics since 1948 do not indicate any spectacular increase in the private sector, which includes private enterprise filling government orders or working under government contracts. The average annual increase in total output (GNP) per manhour input are indicated in the accompanying figures.[21]

Annual Percentage Increase per Manhour Input

	1948–1955	1955–1960	1960–1964	1948–1964
Total private	4.3	2.3	3.2	3.4
Farm	5.4	4.9	5.4	5.2
Nonfarm	3.7	1.9	3.1	2.7
Manufacturing	3.2	1.4	3.6	2.7
Nonmanufacturing	2.9	2.2	2.9	2.7

Of course the rate of diffusion of new technology to marketable end items is a relatively slow process, and insufficient time has elapsed since large-scale federal R & D spending began, about 1954, to evaluate the impact on the commercial sectors of the economy. But, one point appears clear: economic productivity arguments for an increased program of federal technology transfer to the industrial sector are not justified by studies to date nor by any objective measures yet devised.[22] However, some investment in an

rants an investment in the means of making it available. *All* indications are that it will." P. 10 (italics added).

[21] National Planning Association, *The Impact of the U.S. Civilian Space Program on the U.S. Domestic Economy* (Washington, D.C.: NPA, July 1965), report prepared for the Lockheed Aircraft Corp., p. 6.

There is no strict data comparability between the nonfarm average, on the one hand, and manufacturing and nonmanufacturing on the other. Hence the peculiar relationships for 1948–55. *Ibid.,* footnote 1.

[22] There are at least four other possible measures of the effect of federal R & D spending on industrial productivity:

1. The federal R & D factor in international trade.
2. Specific industries' growth rates and the correlation of these growth rates to R & D spending.

experimental program does appear justified in order to determine the social costs and benefits of programs to stimulate the secondary application of federal R & D.

Conclusion

The rapid percentage and total increase of federal R & D spending between 1954 and 1965 compared with the lower percentage increase of private industrial funding during the same period, may indicate that more technology transfer, specific and end-item as well as generalized, can be expected. Or it may indicate that more effort is needed to produce a higher secondary yield from federal R & D spending as it occupies so much larger a share of the GNP than industrial R & D funding and is therefore partially preventing private industry from using these same technical resources. Or it may indicate that a rethinking of R & D goals is needed so that if the bulk of federally funded R & D is becoming more narrowly oriented and even further removed from secondary commercial application, then less spending on space, atomic energy, and nonessential defense R & D is required more fully to achieve the goals of our society. Or, it may be that all three possibilities are partially true and partially overstated. Thus, the lesson may be that more data are needed as to the actual amount and rate of transfer and that the public investment in a new area of technology cannot for many years be more than partially justified in terms of transferable new technology.

In considering any program of technology transfer, it is important to have in mind a working model of the transfer process. Such a model has not yet been advanced by leading researchers, but some concepts which should be constituent parts of such a model will be considered next since they are important as a guide in the evaluation of present federal programs.

---

3. Specific invention diffusion and the characteristics of this invention transfer.
4. Spin-off firms in such areas as Boston and Palo Alto and their significance in producing technological change.

These four measures are not exclusive, but are indicative of methods of supplementing classical economic approaches to measuring the effects of R & D spending on productivity. See footnotes 15 and 19 for references which discuss the classical economic measures of the effect of technology on productivity increases.

Chapter 4
The Transfer Process in the Space/Defense Context

There is a continuing dialogue about the relation of science and technology, particularly the difference between the relation in this century and in the nineteenth century. Brooks has observed that:

> Much of the technology in the 19th century owed little to contemporary science. On the other hand, an increasing component of today's technology is closely dependent on science—if not on contemporary science, then on science 10, 20 or 30 years old—but theoretical science nevertheless.[1]

Pattern of Transfer

Generally, scientific knowledge today appears to be diffused in a hierarchical manner from its origin in basic scientific research to its final application in the consumer market. Through the archival literature it is at first distributed to a limited audience; transferred to the still relatively sophisticated environment of the applied research laboratory, it reaches a slightly wider audience. It may then pass on to the still wider audience provided by the laboratory for the development of sophisticated space/defense hardware and eventually find its way into industrial processes, from there diffusing into the more cost-conscious consumer market. Not all new scientific knowledge spends equal time at each stage of the hierarchy, and in some cases, one or more steps in the transfer may be omitted. But this appears to be roughly the way scientific knowledge is translated into technology, which is in turn diffused in the form of innovations to form the basis of a new area of application.[2]

---

[1] Harvey Brooks, "Applied Research: Definitions, Concepts, Themes," in *The Government of Science* (Cambridge: The M.I.T. Press, 1968), p. 303. But see John Jewkes, David Sawers, and Richard Stillerman, *The Sources of Invention* (New York: St. Martin's Press, 1961), pp. 27–70 for a different explanation of this relation of science to technology.

[2] There is some question as to the appropriateness of such a hierarchical model for technology diffusion in other sectors of the economy. In other sectors per-

One of the primary reasons for such a hierarchical diffusion pattern from the space/defense sector to the commercial-industrial sector is that much of the technology developed in the space/defense sector is based on optimum performance almost without regard to cost, whereas in the commercial-industrial sector, cost plays a major role in the adoption of new products and processes. Thus, one may start with a device used purely for measurement in the research laboratory or used in a highly sophisticated space/defense system, and this may move down the line through routine industrial testing to process control and eventually into consumer industry. The transistor and integrated circuit form a classic illustration of this hierarchical transfer.

Apparently, little pure research is done in response to needs perceived by technologists in the commercial-industrial sector.[3] Commercial industry must therefore depend largely on a perception of a need coupled with knowledge of relevant technical data generated at a higher level. Methods of speeding this natural hierarchical diffusion process should therefore be explored.

Technology itself may create a need for investigation in a particular area of "pure" scientific research to help supply what Marquis and Allen call "gap-filling science."[4] Once developed, however, this gap-filling science is still likely to be diffused in much the same way that new scientific information originating in pure science is diffused except that its initial application is already partly predetermined. This makes the initial application simpler and more rapid but does not necessarily ease transfer to other levels.

By-product transfer in applied research, on the other hand, often appears to be the result of answering a specific need; that is, someone notes the correspondence between an existing requirement and

---

ceived consumer needs play a significant role and there may be much less reliance on science and the scientist for new products and processes. Indeed a number of different models and patterns of technology diffusion may be needed to explain diffusion patterns in various sectors of the economy. In the federal agency context, however, the suggested hierarchical diffusion pattern appears to provide an accurate description of the process.

[3] See the beginning of Chapter 2 for a detailed discussion of R & D funding characteristics.

[4] Donald Marquis and Thomas Allen, "Communication Patterns in Applied Technology," *American Psychologist,* XXI (November 1966), p. 1052.

some information that he has acquired.[5] Oversimplification as this is, it does indicate that a model for technology transfer in the context of specific by-product transfer should be need-oriented.

Another difficulty in the context of government originated technology today is that much of the technology created in space/defense research may be less applicable to present civilian needs than that created ten to twenty years ago. As environmental requirements become more rigorous, the commercial relevance of space/defense technology may be more difficult to perceive.

Transfer may require greater ingenuity and sophistication on the part of the transfer agent and a model for transfer must account for this different type of coupling agent. As Rosenbloom has noted, "To the extent that secondary innovation must come by analogy, rather than by imitation, we must contend with a new element—creative adaptation."[6]

Recent Research Findings

The results of recent research into aspects of the transfer process not only corroborate these observations but also point to ways of increasing the amount of transfer. Some of the most pertinent conclusions are as follows:

1. Interest in space/defense technology is highly correlated with the level of technical sophistication of corporate management.[7]

---

[5] Of course, there is often the situation where an enterprising individual will create a need. The Arthur D. Little, Inc., study for the NASA TU Program indicated that by combining a knowledge of general industrial needs with a fair measure of entrepreneurial skill, it was possible to sell NASA- developed innovations to industry where no specific need had been identified internally. Arthur D. Little, Inc., *Technology Transfer and the Technology Utilization Program,* Report to the NASA OTU (Washington, D.C.: NASA Headquarters, January 1965), pp. 1–17.

[6] Richard Rosenbloom, "The Transfer of Military Technology to Civilian Use," in Melvin Kranzberg and Carroll Pursell, Jr., eds., *Technology in Western Civilization,* Vol. II (New York: Oxford University Press, 1967), pp. 601–12. Secondary innovations may also occur by extension of existing primary innovations. This type of transfer is an important source of improvement innovations but does not typically produce major new innovations.

[7] A mail survey of 5100 firms was conducted during the spring of 1967 to determine the technology requirements of New England industry in terms of interests and types of services desired from an RDC in New England. Also,

2. Company size for science-based companies is not a significant factor in stimulating their interest in defense/space technology.[8]

3. Specific new aerospace developed inventions can be "sold" to technically entrepreneur-oriented firms where technical interest profiles have been developed *and* there is a champion for the innovation in the transferor organization.[9]

4. Government-funded information often influences the innovator to work in a wholly new area; also innovations originating in federal R & D require a larger amount of adaptation and are generally on a larger scale (see Tables 5 and 6).[10]

5. "Scientific entrepreneurship greatly accelerates the rate of in-

Table 5
Percentage of Innovations Actively Stimulated by Technical Information from Both Government- and Nongovernment-Funded Sources

	Innovator was working on a related problem	Innovator was not working on a related problem
Nongovernment-Funded Information	53%	47%
Government-Funded Information	12.5	87.5

over one hundred personal interviews were conducted to obtain much the same type of information as the mail survey, but in more detail and with opportunities for a good deal of give and take in the interview sessions. New England Research Applications Center, *NASA Technology Utilization Project-Feasibility Study for the Establishment of Regional Dissemination Center for New England* (Springfield, Va.: Clearinghouse for Scientific and Technical Information, April 1967).

8 A list of NASA RDC industrial clients reveals a high percentage of large firms, and Center personnel indicate that small firms in the Midwest, South, and Southwest are slow to invest in NASA RDC technical information services: 75%—ARAC; 60%—CAST; but 25%—KASC. The percentages refer to RDC client firms listed among the 500 largest corporations in the United States in 1966. However, the NERAC survey and client experience indicate that smaller firms (under 1,000 employees) in the Greater Boston area may be more likely to invest in services such as those offered by an RDC. As of July 1, 1968, over 60 percent of NERAC Massachusetts clients, 25 of 41, were smaller firms.

9 Arthur D. Little, Inc., *op. cit.*, pp. 1–17.

10 National Planning Association, *Technology Transfer and Industrial Innovation,* Unpublished Report prepared for the NSF by Sumner Myers, *et al.* (Washington, D.C.: NPA, February 1967), pp. V-22 and V-27.

Table 6
Innovations Based Partially or Fully on Government-Funded Technical Information as a Percentage of All Innovations Studied, by Type

	Total Number of Innovations Studied by Type	Number of Innovations Based on Government-Funded Information by Type	Percentage
Innovation Types	567	56	10.0%
More Innovative			
Larger Scale	140	21	15.0
Smaller Scale	198	21	10.6
Less Innovative			
Larger Scale	60	3	5.0
Smaller Scale	169	11	6.5

novation. . . . The importance of [technologist] mobility is generally greater as a technology is more complicated. . . ."[11]

6. The amount of entrepreneurial activity required to effect transfer may be greater with specific by-products than with the transfer of more general technology, especially where a need-oriented model is not used as a basis for transfer.[12]

7. Personal contact is significantly more important than mere dissemination of literature.[13]

---

[11] Daniel Shimshoni, "Aspects of Scientific Entrepreneurship" (unpublished Doctoral Dissertation, Kennedy School of Government, Harvard University), pp. 1–2.

[12] Arthur D. Little, Inc., *op. cit.,* p. 2.

[13] This has been the NASA TU experience since the inception of the transfer program. This information was obtained in numerous interviews with RDC and TU personnel during 1966–67 and from Arthur D. Little, Inc., *op. cit.,* pp. 3, 16–17. See also Edward Roberts, "Facts and Folklore in Research and Development Management," *Industrial Management Review,* VIII, No. 2 (Spring 1967), pp. 12–14.

Important Transfer Concepts for Policy Formulation

Analysis of these findings yields a number of conclusions about the transfer process and provides some guidance for formulating a policy for federal transfer programs.

1. Space/defense technology is more likely to be quality-oriented than cost-oriented, and higher up the hierarchical chain. Transfer should therefore concentrate on institutions, profit and nonprofit, where the participants can readily comprehend this sophisticated technology and where industry structure is more likely to allow introduction of this higher-cost technology. Otherwise more effort will be required in the transferor organization to adapt the innovation for use by the transferee lower in the hierarchical chain.[14]

2. Since innovations originating in government-funded information appear to require more adaptation for application,[15] transfer of this type is more likely to occur where the standards of performance are higher and seed money is available for initial development and exclusive rights to the invention are available to provide protection for the larger investment required.[16]

3. Since spin-off of organizations and mobility of technical personnel appear to be key elements, transfer may be fostered by assisting this dual mobility.

   a. Technical mobility is to be encouraged by assisting in the spin-off of new companies from parent organizations such as the MIT Instrumentation Laboratory, Lincoln Laboratory and

[14] Shimshoni, *op. cit.*, p. 2. "Thus heavy Federal support of R & D in all sectors has not only produced an outpouring of direct research results and of planned innovations, but it has also created a commercial demand for highly sophisticated instrumentation. . . ." Harvey Brooks, "National Science Policy and Technology Transfer," in *The Government of Science*, p. 267. As noted by both Brooks and Shimshoni, transfer to such industries as instrumentation has been facilitated by government standards for high quality devices. The influence extends to other industries using this instrumentation for process control, permitting better quality control, and generally creating a demand for higher quality products.

[15] National Planning Association, *The Impact of the U.S. Civilian Space Program on the U.S. Domestic Economy*, Report prepared for Lockheed Aircraft Corporation (Washington, D.C.: NPA, July 1965).

[16] See Edward Roberts and Herbert Wainer, "Technology Transfer and Entrepreneurial Success," Miami Beach, Florida, Paper presented to the Twentieth National Conference on the Administration of Research, October 26, 1966.

Stanford Research Institute. Seed money and need-oriented technology transfer centers would assist these new firms. Much of the technology used by these new companies originates externally to them in government-sponsored R & D.[17] Thus, by encouraging the formation of spin-off companies, space/defense technology may be commercialized at a more rapid rate than by attempting a direct transfer to commercial-industrial firms.

b. Mobility of individual technologists to these new spin-off firms should be encouraged since, as Daniel Shimshoni has demonstrated, "Technology is often transferred most effectively by the movement of a man into an existing company. . . . New technical companies have been particularly effective 'hosts' for such movement."[18]

4. Recent research findings indicate that smaller firms tend to be more innovative and more efficient in their R & D practices.[19]

---

[17] Shimshoni, *op. cit.,* pp. 1, 15–25.

[18] *Ibid.,* p. 2.

[19] See, for example, Daniel Hamberg, *R & D Essays on the Economics of Research and Development* (New York: Random House, 1963), parts 1 and 2; Edwin Mansfield, "Technical Change and the Rate of Imitation", *Econometrics,* XXIX (October 1961), pp. 741–66; Edwin Mansfield, "Size of Firm, Market Structure and Innovation," *Journal of Political Economy,* LXXI, No. 6 (December 1963), pp. 556–76; Mansfield found the diffusion of new technology higher in more competitive industries. Although the evidence is not entirely clear, Hamberg and Mansfield do agree that smaller firms tend to be more innovative and Hamberg concludes that ". . . the large industrial laboratories are likely to be minor sources of major, radically new and commercially or militarily important inventions; rather, they are likely to be major sources of essentially improvement inventions." P. 569.

See also Roberts and Wainer, *op. cit.,* "Technology Transfer and Entrepreneurial Success," and Shimshoni, *op. cit.* Arnold Cooper, "R & D Is More Efficient in Small Companies," *Harvard Business Review,* XLII, No. 3 (May-June 1964), pp. 75–83; National Science Foundation, *Basic Research, Applied Research and Development in Industry, 1964* (Washington, D.C.: U.S. Government Printing Office, June 1966), pp. 9–10, 56. The latter report shows clearly an increasing cost per technologist for larger firms. Smaller firms often spend as large a percentage or more for R & D than larger firms in any given industry. See William Comanor, "Market Structure, Product Differentiation and Industrial Research," *The Quarterly Journal of Economics,* LXXXI (November 1967), pp. 639–57.

Compare Roberts and Wainer, and Shimshoni, with U.S. Arms Control and Disarmament Agency, *Defense Industry Diversification,* prepared by John Gilmore and Dean Coddington of the Denver Research Institute (Washington,

The impressive success ratio for new companies spun-off from the various MIT laboratories suggests that companies such as these are a key element in technology transfer and in spurring competition. Their rapid rate of successful diversification into the commercial market as compared with the poorer results achieved by the larger aerospace firms in commercial diversification indicates the value of the small, technically based firm in the promotion of transfer.

5. The methods appropriate to the transfer of generalized areas of technology are not necessarily appropriate to the transfer of specific innovations and vice versa. The former can be accomplished by a variety of interpersonal contacts and probably require longer periods of time; the latter appear to be more dependent on entrepreneurial activities and careful need-oriented preparation by the transferor.

Some elements important in the transfer process have been suggested: the transferor must seek to match the level of technical sophistication of the information to that of the transferee organization; the higher investment required to develop government-originated innovations requires more effective legal protection for commercial application; mobility of technical personnel both by way of interfirm transfer and by way of the formation of spin-off firms provides an effective transfer mechanism, particularly where the technology is complex; the small, technology-based firm appears to be a good vehicle for spurring commercial development of space/defense technology; and the methods of transfer must be adapted to the type of technology being transferred.

Furthermore, if the transfer process is hierarchical and space/defense technology is high up the technology scale, then industrial transfer is most likely in areas where there is already a large tech-

---

D.C.: U.S. Government Printing Office, January 1966). The spin-off firms studied by Roberts and Shimshoni reported 40 percent of their sales were in the commercial market (end-item use is commercial), after 5 years, as compared with little or no commercialization of space/defense technology by larger space/weapons-systems contractors.

See U. S. Department of Commerce, *Technological Innovation: Its Environment and Measurement* (Washington, D. C.: Clearinghouse for Scientific and Technical Information, January 1967), pp. 19–23 and 46–47, for a discussion of the importance of the small firm in technological innovation and of the importance of federal assistance to the small science-based firm.

nology base (such as the Greater Boston or Palo Alto areas) and where the type of companies capable of accepting and using this technology, such as the prototype spin-off companies of Roberts' study, already exist. Transfer to universities and other research institutions may be more appropriate in other areas.

Thus the proposed experimental transfer program might well start in geographic areas where an impedance match already exists for space/defense technology or adapt its approach to various types of transferees depending upon the technology base in a given region.

The elements of the transfer process discussed are important in formulating federal transfer policies since they indicate some tangible methods of enhancing transfer as well as providing a framework for the proposed experimental program.

The federal government has initiated numerous programs aimed at making available to various segments of the economy the results of federally sponsored R & D. Some of these programs have been aimed at very narrow segments of the economy, such as the program of the Coal Research Office of the Department of the Interior; others, such as the Agricultural Extension Service, have been aimed at a broader area. Some programs include large-scale R & D efforts aimed at answering specific needs, others at merely disseminating information.

The importance of the transfer concepts discussed will be made clear in the discussion of the present federal role in technology transfer in the next chapter and, in particular, in the discussion of the NASA Technology Utilization Program in Part II.

Chapter 5
Present Federal Role in Technology Transfer

This chapter will briefly analyze some current federal programs aimed at technology transfer. Four agency programs, the NASA TU Program, the Department of Commerce State Technical Services (STS) Program, the AEC Industrial Cooperation Program, and the Department of Agriculture Cooperative Extension Service are of particular interest here since they are all especially concerned with technology transfer as well as document dissemination. The purpose of this brief analysis is to place the overall federal role in technology transfer in perspective and to relate that role to the new NASA technology transfer program.[1]

General Setting

In fiscal 1966 the federal government spent in excess of $603 million for the collection, documentation, publication, distribution, evaluation, and dissemination of information resulting from fed-

[1] Appendix A provides a more complete description of federal programs in the technical information area.

For a somewhat saccharine account of a few of these programs, see Richard Lesher and George Howick, *Background, Guidelines, and Recommendations for Use in Assessing Effective Means of Channeling New Technologies in Promising Directions,* Prepared for the U.S. National Commission on Technology, Automation and Economic Progress (Washington, D.C.: U.S. Government Printing Office, 1965), pp. 102–37; a survey of some federal programs besides those discussed in this chapter may be found at pp. A93–A101. *Background, Guidelines* is the complete version of Lesher and Howick's *Assessing Technology Transfer,* NASA SP-5067 (Washington, D.C.: U.S. Government Printing Office, 1966).

There are a large number of federal agencies offering different technical information or referral services. Many of the agencies offer several types of services for various reasons and for no apparent reason. Thirteen different agencies and parts of agencies offering several dozen different services are listed by Lesher and Howick, *Assessing Technology Transfer,* pp. 55–73, 107–14, and they do not even include detailed accounts of such agencies as NIH, the Patent Office, or NSF.

erally funded R & D and general purpose science information.[2] This chapter will be primarily concerned with information resulting from federally funded R & D. Of the total $603 million, $278 million was spent on R & D information, which is generally defined by NSF to include data collected and organized for R & D use.[3] These figures may be quite low since the three agencies with the largest extramural R & D programs (DOD, NASA, and AEC) all probably spent far more for scientific and technical information activities than is reported by the National Science Foundation Survey.[4]

Also, these figures probably do not include the NASA TU Program or the AEC Industrial Cooperation Program, to be described shortly, since they may be partially charged to agency administrative overhead or to the various laboratories' operating budgets or both. The NSF figures of $25 million for NASA and $5 million for the AEC seem too low to include both the cost of servicing internal Agency needs and their extensive extramural dissemination programs. The budget of the NASA TU Program for fiscal 1966 was in excess of $5 million, but this did not include salaries or that portion of STID activities which should be apportioned to the TU Program. The AEC estimated it would spend $28 million for fiscal 1966.[5]

---

[2] National Science Foundation, *Federal Funds for Research, Development, and Other Scientific Activities: Fiscal Years 1966, 1967 and 1968,* XVI (Washington, D.C.: U.S. Government Printing Office, August 1967), pp. 54–75 (hereafter cited as *1967 NSF Report on R&D Funding*). The sum of $684 million was projected for fiscal 1967 and $760 million for fiscal 1968. This total includes payment of charges to professional journals in connection with reporting of federally funded R & D as well as some professional society information activities (pp. 84–85).

[3] *Ibid.,* pp. 54, 66. A total of $315 million was projected for fiscal 1967 and $348 million for fiscal 1968.

[4] National Science Foundation, *Federal Funds for Research, Development and Other Scientific Activities: Fiscal Years 1965, 1966 and 1967,* NSF 66-24 (Washington, D.C.: U.S. Government Printing Office, July 1966), p. 46.

[5] *Assessing Technology Transfer,* p. 23. For an amusing account of how difficult these numbers are to pin down, see U.S. Congress, House of Representatives, Committee on Science and Astronautics, Subcommittee on Space Sciences and Applications, *1964 NASA Authorization, Hearings,* 88th Congress, first session, H.R. 5466 (Washington, D.C.: U.S. Government Printing Office, 1964), part 4, pp. 3430–60. Dr. Dr. Simpson, chief of the OTU at that time, struggles valiantly to explain to the Congressmen how much money was actually spent

Four agencies account for almost 80 percent of the total: DOD (43 percent), Commerce (15 percent), HEW (13 percent), and NASA (8 percent). DOD and HEW funding is almost entirely devoted to servicing their own R & D programs.[6]

Department of Defense

The Armed Services Technical Information Agency (ASTIA), established in 1951, was reconstituted as the Defense Documentation Center (DDC) on March 19, 1951.

The Defense Documentation Center provides technical information services for DOD contractors, for DOD itself, and for other qualified users. DDC in the main performs a library function. It is intended to service information requests only upon demand though it does distribute an announcement journal twice a month. To obtain any contractor developed know-how, the requester would usually have to be a DOD prime contractor, have the necessary clearance, and establish a need-to-know. Even subcontractors working on weapons systems contracts have difficulty in obtaining technical information since they must go through the project office of the prime contractor or higher tier subcontractor, or both, and obtain approval on requests for technical information. The request must then be approved by the Service Agency contracting officer. "Need-to-know is usually narrowly construed. Out of ten thousand prime and associate contractors and 300,000 subcontractors, only 1,700 obtain any information from ASTIA."[7]

---

on the TU Program. He did somewhat better in the 1965 authorization hearings, but not much.

6 *1967 NSF Report on R & D Funding,* p. 56.

7 Robert Solo, *Studies in the Anatomy of Economic Progress,* Report prepared for the National Planning Association (Washington, D.C.: NPA, 1965), p. 258. See Senator Humphrey's U.S. Congress, Senate, Committee on Government Operations, Subcommittee on Reorganization and Internal Organization, *Coordination of Information on Current Federal Research and Development Projects in the Field of Electronics,* 87th Congress, first session (Washington, D.C.; U.S. Government Printing Office, 1960) (Committee Print), survey of DOD electronics contractors, most of whom were not satisfied with existing mechanisms for obtaining information from DOD, particularly when cast in the role of a subcontractor.

Personal interviews with over 25 smaller R & D firms in the Greater Boston area indicated that they had been generally unsuccessful at obtaining technical information from DOD even within their subcontract terms, or, if the information was forthcoming, it was often too late to be useful.

DDC is not responsible for the collection of data from contractors; that is the responsibility of the contracting office. DOD has a policy of limiting its requests for technical data from contractors "to that which is essential for government purposes."[8] DOD is mission oriented and has little or no interest in promoting technology transfer.[9] DOD's program of technical data dissemination is limited at the input side by its mission orientation, and at the output side by security requirements, overzealous concern for private firm proprietary data rights, and a general lack of concern over the dissemination of technical information.[10] Of the small amount of technical information that is reported from its many prime contractors and subcontractors, little is disseminated outside the DOD or its major contractors, and none is professionally evaluated for its value outside the interest profiles of the DOD or its prime contractors.[11]

The position of DOD has always been that only by providing maximum protection to its contractors for their company know-how could it expect to get the "best" contractors and the "best" technical talent of those "best" contractors.[12] A like policy has been urged in the patent area for similar reasons.[13] Why this policy

---

[8] ASPR, section 9-202.1 (a) (1963). But see the discussion of the Army's breakout efforts on the Honest John rocket procurement in Frederick Scherer, *The Weapons Acquisition Process* (Boston: Division of Research, Graduate School of Business Administration, Harvard University, 1964), pp. 114–17.

[9] NASA claims to obtain 15 percent of its aerospace magnetic tape file from DOD and its contractors. See footnote 5 in Chapter 6.

[10] Major complaints have been raised even by major DOD contractors over this proprietary blockage and overclassification. See Solo, *op. cit.*, p. 259. No method of evaluating those reports that are received is provided (p. 258). But see President's Science Advisory Committee (PSAC) *Science, Government, and Information* (Washington, D.C.: U.S. Government Printing Office, January 1963), pp. 41–42, commentary on DOD classification and proprietary data policies.

[11] But see *Background, Guidelines* pp. A-99–A-101, for a complete gloss over the problems of DOD reporting and dissemination. DOD patent policies and overhead R & D (IR & D, PI, and BP) data policies provide additional blocks to transfer, since they in effect allow the DOD prime contractor to either fail to disclose information at all or to retain title on almost any patentable items reported, whether or not the contractor intends to commercialize the given technology.

[12] ASPR, section 9-202.2 (April 1965, rev. 10).

[13] See for example the statement of John M. Malloy, Asst. Sec'y of Defense (Procurement)—U.S. Congress, Senate, Committee on the Judiciary, Subcommittee on Patents, Trademarks and Copyrights, *Government Patent Policy,*

should apply to contractors without established commercial positions as well as to those with such positions to protect is difficult to discover. It appears that there is little or no communication between the space/defense division (s) and commercial divisions of the same corporation.[14] Thus, it seems that those best contractors with a substantial commercial business do not bring the technical expertise developed by their commercial divisions to bear on DOD projects in any case. Further, Project Hindsight (a recent DOD study to determine the utility of various types of R & D for weapons-systems development) results indicated that technical expertise developed in the commercial-industrial context plays a very minor role in weapons-systems development.[15]

Still there is no single way to test the consequences on contractor performance of a different policy. DOD has succeeded in resisting major changes in its contractor data or patent policies since World War II on the basis of a "mission first" argument.[16] Nevertheless, superiority in weapons systems has been maintained. The real issue is whether the costs, direct and indirect, have been too high and whether this policy is realistic for an extended cold-war period since it was formulated to meet U.S. needs during World War II and the Korean War.[17]

HEW—National Library of Medicine

The Department of Health, Education and Welfare has established as part of the National Library of Medicine a very elaborate and sophisticated computerized information file and retrieval system for biomedical information of all types. It is likely that it provides the largest automated file of scientific information available in any one area of the natural sciences. The system is largely a

Hearings, 89th Congress, first session, S. 789, S. 1809, and S. 1899 (Washington, D.C.: U.S. Government Printing Office, 1965), part 2, pp. 401–19, and similar statements before similar patent policy hearings from 1960 to the present.

[14] See Merton Peck and Frederick Scherer, *The Weapons Acquisition Process: An Economic Analysis* (Boston: Division of Research, Graduate School of Business Administration, Harvard University, 1962), pp. 128–30.

[15] Chalmers Sherwin and Raymond Isenson, "First Iterim Report on Project Hindsight" (Washington, D.C.: Office of the Director of Defense Research and Engineering, June 30, 1966, revised October 13, 1966).

[16] See DOD policy statement in ASPR, section 9-202.1 (a) (1963).

[17] See Frederick Scherer, *op. cit.*

library operation and limited to one discipline. This Medical Literature Analysis and Retrieval System (MEDLARS) provides scientists, medical practitioners, and educators with rapid bibliographic access to the world's biomedical literature. Five field centers are at present in operation and more are planned.

Department of Commerce—Clearinghouse for Federal Scientific and Technical Information

The Clearinghouse for Federal Scientific and Technical Information was established in 1964 in response to a recommendation by the Federal Council for Science and Technology.[18] It is located organizationally within the National Bureau of Standards. It is largely a library operation, providing copies of unclassified and nonlimited documents resulting from federal R & D projects. It also provides some literature searching and referral services in the physical sciences and engineering.

The Clearinghouse disseminates whatever the large procurement agencies furnish it; there is little or no professional evaluation of agency inputs, though some reports are examined in a cursory way and packaged for industrial use. Not only are classified materials not supplied to the Clearinghouse, but also any information deemed to contain contractor proprietary information or otherwise thought inappropriate for public dissemination is likewise not sent to the Clearinghouse. The term *limited* is apparently used to denote both contractor information considered proprietary as well as other data deemed inappropriate for dissemination by the given agency. Although reports are presented through local Department of Commerce field offices, no attempt is made to provide transfer agents at the local level capable of providing any coupling to local technology needs.

The Science Information Exchange (SIE)

The Science Information Exchange, a part of the Smithsonian Institution, provides a referral service of current and ongoing R & D tasks funded by federal agencies. It is paid for primarily by NSF. SIE obtains detailed copies of work statements or proposals from

[18] Established in 1964 in response to FCST recommendations in PSAC, *op. cit.*, pp. 46–47.

various agencies, writes descriptions of tasks to be performed, and categorizes the tasks by functional or disciplinary areas.

SIE was established in 1949 to assist other agencies in avoiding duplicate R & D funding. Any qualified engineer or scientist can obtain information about the projects in a given scientific field. SIE differs significantly from a library or technical information center. It receives no progress or technical reports from its catalogued list of agency programs and is purely a referral service. Inputs are voluntary and it has no statutory basis for the functions it performs. Further, inputs are limited to unclassified, nonlimited projects and coverage appears to be poor outside the life sciences.

Small Business Administration (SBA)

The Small Business Administration has some formal responsibility in the area of technology transfer, because of its responsibility for assisting small businesses in obtaining the benefits of government R & D and in obtaining federal agency contracts.[19] Thus, it receives numerous requests for technical data. Sometimes these data are requested in order to prepare a bid proposal for a federal contract, and on other occasions merely because the small businessman has heard of some innovation developed under federal funding and wishes to obtain more information.[20] These requests for informa-

[19] Aid to Small Business—Research and Development Act of 1958, Public Law 85-536, 15 U.S.C.A. 638 (as amended 1964).

[20] Based on my interviews with New England SBA personnel and with 25 small R & D contractors in the Greater Boston area during the fall and winter of 1966. Apparently many small businessmen turn to an SBA Field Office because it is near at hand and because of contacts with local SBA personnel. Data from the NERAC survey of New England industry disclosed that Greater Boston "Route 128" type small companies were almost five times as likely to have had some contact with the local SBA field office than less technologically oriented firms. More than 80 percent of these "128" type firms had had contact with the regional SBA representatives, while less than 20 percent of the less technically oriented firms had shown interest in SBA assistance. The percentages stated are the results of preliminary data reduction work as of April 1, 1967, from over 100 personal interviews conducted by NERAC during its feasibility study. These interviews were conducted between September 15, 1966, and March 15, 1967. They are discussed at length in New England Research Application Center, *NASA Technology Utilization Project—Feasibility Study for the Establishment of a Regional Dissemination Center for New England* (Springfield, Va.: Clearinghouse for Scientific and Technical Information, April 1967), pp. 45–52.

tion are rarely filled, whether for proposals or for commercial development. There are apparently at least two reasons for this poor record: SBA field offices are sparsely staffed, and the SBA representatives at the various NASA/DOD procurement offices are not able to bring sufficient pressure to bear to overcome contracting officers' reluctance to disclose technical data.[21]

The SBA can, however, assist materially in technology transfer by providing "seed" money in appropriate circumstances. The degree to which it does assist the transfer process can be determined only from data and studies not presently available.

NASA and the AEC conducted joint experimental transfer programs with the SBA to provide a better understanding of how to cope with the seemingly special needs of smaller business;[22] one of these programs, however, has been dropped for lack of OTU support. The other two very small-scale programs do not appear to have been as fruitful as they might have been since little attention was given to selecting smaller firms capable of using the highly sophisticated NASA-AEC technology.

Atomic Energy Commission (AEC)

The Atomic Energy Commission early in its existence established a vigorous program for disseminating unclassified R & D information that might have industrial applications.[23] This AEC dissemination program, like those sponsored by NASA and the Department of Agriculture, were motivated in part by their respective enabling legislation.

Since the amendments to the AEC enabling act in 1954, a stronger

---

[21] Hypothesis formed on the basis of the interviews described in the preceding note and U.S. Congress, Senate, Select Committee on Small Business, *Fourteenth Annual Report,* 88th Congress, second session, S. Report No. 1180 (Washington, D.C.: U.S. Government Printing Office, July 1964), pp. 52–54.

[22] *Assessing Technology Transfer,* p. 52.

[23] *Ibid.,* p. 59. The AEC as a technology-oriented agency has always had an interest in making available scientific and technical information about atomic energy. In its early years this dissemination program was primarily for the benefit of research scientists. Only later, when emphasis on weapons diminished, was an extensive program created to encourage the application of atomic energy outside the weapons area, particularly for industrial application. The cynical might call this self-perpetuation, the analytical, a technology transfer orientation.

emphasis has been placed on the dissemination of technical information relating to atomic information for peaceful application and the AEC has worked hard in several areas, notably those of radioisotopes and atomic power, to promote the peaceful uses of atomic energy.[24]

As the source of all relevant technology in this area of technology, it is not surprising that private industry has looked to the AEC for technical assistance in the transfer process. The AEC has not only provided technical assistance in the transfer process, but it has also established numerous mechanisms for promoting transfer such as providing professional referees at each AEC laboratory to evaluate contractor and AEC employee reports for declassification.[25] However, the AEC program has been limited primarily to vertical applications of atomic energy and selective dissemination to physical scientists and engineers. Nevertheless, a recent AEC study of the problems of horizontal transfer recommended that a system be established to provide for personal contact to enhance transfer.[26]

There are several limitations to the AEC program:

1. No effort has been made to coordinate its input-output function with a flexible license/patent policy. Part of the problem is the patent provisions of the enabling act (requiring the AEC to take title to any patents concerning atomic energy) and another part a relatively inflexible administrative policy.[27]

2. Little attention has been paid to horizontal transfer, but the Industrial Cooperation Program initiated in 1966 promises some improvement in the future.[28]

---

[24] Compare Section 1 of the Atomic Energy Act of 1946 with Section 1 of the Act as amended in 1954, Public Law 79-585, 42 U.S.C.A. 1801, to see the increased emphasis placed on technology transfer in the revised enabling act.

[25] PSAC, *op. cit.*, p. 40. See *Assessing Technology Transfer,* pp. 59–64 for a discussion of AEC transfer activities and U.S. Atomic Energy Commission, *Transference of Non-Nuclear Technology to Industry,* Committee Report to Oak Ridge Operations Office (Oak Ridge, Tennessee: U.S. AEC, July 1965).

[26] *Transference of Non-Nuclear Energy to Industry,* p. 25.

[27] U.S. Atomic Energy Act of 1946, as amended 1954, 42 U.S.C. U.S. Atomic Energy Commission Procurement Regulations, section 9-9.5003 (January 1966).

[28] But see William Gough, *The Relation of Controlled Fusion Research to American Science and Industry* (Washington, D.C.: AEC, 1965) for a discussion of some horizontal transfer in the area of capacitor energy storage.

3. Until the recent cooperative effort with NASA on joint Tech Briefs, no effort has been made by the Agency for industry-wide dissemination through local field centers.

4. No effective system to provide feedback on the usefulness of the information has been provided.[29]

Department of Agriculture—The Cooperative Extension Service

The Department of Agriculture goes out into the field directly to the consumer to "sell" new technology.[30] The Department of Agriculture provides a fully integrated operation whose primary mission is assisting the farmer to improve his productivity through incorporating new technology.[31]

This program includes basic and applied research at land grant colleges (matched by state funds), development of new products sponsored intramurally and extramurally, field demonstrations, and a continuing program of local assistance to the farmer.[32] The total program is many times the size of any other transfer program. Over 35 thousand federal and state employees were working under the program in 1960. Total program funding in 1960 was over $420 million. R & D funding totaled $278 million in 1960, $167.5 million

---

29 U.S. Congress, Senate, Select Committee on Small Business, Subcommittee on Science and Technology, *Policy Planning for Technology Transfer,* prepared by Richard Carpenter of the Science Policy Research Division, Legislative Reference Service, Library of Congress, 90th Congress, first session, S. Doc. No. 15 (Washington, D.C.: U.S. Government Printing Office, May 1967), p. 128.

30 There is some question of just how dynamic the field program has been. It has been contended that the more affluent, larger farmer has received most of the benefit of this program. But, it appears that there are few hard data that would either prove or disprove this contention.

31 Robert Solo in discussing various federal transfer programs remarked: "The best prototype government organization for the systematic transmission of research results, far removed from the Department of Defense, the Atomic Energy Commission and the National Aeronautics and Space Administration, remains the old-line Department of Agriculture."

Compare this statement from "Gearing Military R & D to Economic Growth," *Harvard Business Review,* XL, No. 6 (November-December, 1962), p. 49, with Don K. Price, *Government and Science* (New York: Oxford University Press, 1962), pp. 75–78, noting that the DOA program tends to be "relatively static" and lacking in "bold, ambitious national planning."

32 See H. C. Sanders, *et al.,* eds., *The Cooperative Extension Service* (Englewood Cliffs, New Jersey: Prentice-Hall, Inc., 1966), for a history of the Extension Service, its legal basis, and methods of operation.

in federal funds and $111.8 million in matching state funds. The Extension portion itself spent over $142 million in 1960.[33]

The program is vertically integrated and is intended to serve only one industry. It has benefited from considerable field experience in the transfer of technology and has in effect become a part of the farming community and farming industries in the United States.[34] It is difficult to ascribe an exact quantitative value to effects on agricultural productivity, but net output per man-hour is said to have risen twice as fast on the farm over the last 25 years as it has in United States industry generally.[35]

Research, development, and application have been coupled to the ultimate consumer by a host of local community devices. The local land grant college is brought into contact with the farmer in a variety of ways,[36] but the county agent still remains the primary coupling mechanism. Private enterprise also plays an important part in acting as an intermediary between some applied research and the farmer. It is estimated that private industry spent almost 54 percent of the funds expended for agricultural R & D in fiscal 1965, with public funding covering the other 46 percent.[37] Thus the three-way symbiosis of government, industry, and the farmer provides a key element in the success of the agricultural transfer programs. The State Technical Services Program is likewise an attempt to provide a locally integrated technology transfer mechanism for the industrial community.

Department of Commerce—State Technical Services (STS) Program

Unlike the Agricultural Program, the State Technical Services

---

[33] *Ibid.*, p. 5, for fiscal data.

[34] The enabling act was enacted in 1914. Smith-Lever Act, 38 Stat. 372, 7 U.S.C.A. 341 (as amended 1953).

[35] David Allison, "The Civilian Technology Lag," *International Science and Technology*, No. 24 (December 1963), pp. 24–34.

[36] Sanders, *op. cit.*, pp. 111–260.

[37] The report, *A National Program of Research for Agriculture*, sponsored jointly by the Association of State Universities and Land Grant Colleges and the U.S. Department of Agriculture (Washington, D.C.: U.S. DOA, October 1966), discusses the relative roles of government, industry, and the universities in agricultural R & D.

This study estimated that private industry spent $460 million in FY 1965 on a variety of R & D projects including new developments in seeds, insecticides, fertilizers, farm equipment, processing equipment, etc. (P. 6.)

Program is very recent.[38] Unlike the Agricultural Program, too, the STS Program has very little funding to study the transfer process or for transfer programs or for local industrial transfer agents.[39] The purpose of the program is comprehensively stated to be:

> . . . a national program of incentives and support for the several states individually and in cooperation with each other in their establishing and maintaining State and interstate technical service programs designed to . . . [provide for the] wider diffusion and more effective application of science and technology in business, commerce and industry. . . .[40]

The technical services are to be provided by state nonprofit institutions or public agencies.[41] Services include:

> 1. Preparing and disseminating technical documents and materials and may include establishment of a state or interstate technical information center;
> 2. Referral services;
> 3. Sponsoring industrial workshops, seminars, training programs . . . to encourage the more effective application of scientific and engineering information.[42]

The act requires each participating state to prepare and submit a five-year plan and an annual program plan.[43] The overall program is to be administered and state plans approved by the Secretary of

[38] State Technical Services Act, Public Law 84-182, 79 Stat. 679 (September 1965).

[39] $1.5 million was available for the first 3 months and about $5.5 million for the first full year. The states must match most of the federal funds. See State Technical Services Act, 79 Stat. 682, sec. 10 (1965). The Act does authorize $10 million for FY 1966, $20 million for FY 1967, and $30 million for FY 1968.

[40] State Technical Services Act, 79 Stat. 679 (1965).

[41] "Institution" is defined as nonprofit institution or public agency. Funds cannot be paid to a profit-making corporation (or individual or partnership) to assist in the program. 79 Stat. 679, section 8 (1965). The Administrative guidelines preclude use of the funds to hire profit-making organizations of any kind.

[42] State Technical Services Act, 79 Stat. 679, sections 2 (a) (1), (2), (3) (1965).

[43] State Technical Services Act, 79 Stat. 680, section 4 (a), (b) (1965).

Commerce.[44] The act provides for broad, sweeping programs with very little money to implement them, and the result thus far is a highly fragmented series of programs in over 30 states.[45] It is difficult to understand why such a minimal program has thus far been approved. However, it is still too early to foresee whether the program will grow and what tangible results may occur.

The bill intends to place "the benefits of federally financed research, as well as other research, more effectively in the hands of the American business, commerce, and industrial establishments."[46] A program with specific statutory authority to promote technology transfer from federally funded R & D has been enacted. With time and sufficient funding, this new program may evolve a useful industrial transfer program.

---

[44] State Technical Services Act, 79 Stat. 680, sections 5, 6 (1965).

[45] State Technical Services Newsletter, Vol. II, No. 5, November 1966, listing STA programs approved in fiscal 1966.

During an interview at one university RDC, it was mentioned that the state received $180,000 under the Act for FY 1966 and with matching and planning funds had over $360,000. It apportioned the money among the 10 state universities in roughly equal amounts, about enough to support one man plus a secretary at each school. Other state programs examined also appeared to be quite diffuse and to lack any unifying theme.

[46] State Technical Services Act, 79 Stat. 679 (1965).

PART II
Case Study of the NASA Technology Utilization Program

As a citizen—perhaps I should say as a moral man—I have been very gravely concerned about the relationship of the space program to other national goals and purposes. I think we have needs which far outweigh the need for exploration of space.

Polykarp Kush in Ralph Lapp,
The New Priesthood (New York: Harper & Row, 1965), p. 200.

NASA programs since 1958 have stimulated almost 3,000 inventions, most with industrial potential. "Every dollar spent for space research in the U.S. ten years ago," estimates German Finance Minister Franz Josef Strauss grimly, "is worth four times that much in economic value today."

"The Great American Purchase,"
Newsweek (Feb. 27, 1967), pp. 36–37

Chapter 6

The NASA Technology Utilization Program

With the exception of the Department of Agriculture Program, the NASA Technology Utilization Program is the most ambitious federal program to promote technology transfer. Unlike the transfer programs of the DOA and AEC, which are vertically oriented, it is primarily concerned with *horizontal* transfer to the commercial-industrial community. It stands in sharp contrast to the mission-oriented DOD's failure even to make its R & D results generally available, let alone to establish an active program for dissemination. It is not nearly so large, so well integrated with local institutions, nor so well executed as the Agricultural Program, but has a somewhat similar emphasis on local, university-based dissemination centers.

General Framework of the TU Program

The NASA Technology Utilization (TU) Program consists of two major functional elements: an Acquisition or Input Operation and a Dissemination or Output Operation. As may be seen from Chart 1, which shows the organization of the TU Program, the Program contains several other Branches or elements, but they merely supplement the two major functional elements, the Acquisition Branch and the Dissemination Branch. While important for day-to-day internal operation, these supplemental Branches are not significant for an analysis of the TU transfer operation.[1]

[1] This conclusion as to the functional importance of the Operations Branch and the Publications Branch was the result of several interviews with OTU personnel during the summer and fall of 1966 and an analysis of TU Program operation. The Biomedical Application Program is a very specialized operation and will not be discussed in detail.

Chart 1

Organization Chart—Office for Technology Utilization

Assistant Administrator for Technology Utilization
Deputy Assistant Administrator for Technology Utilization

TECHNOLOGY UTILIZATION DIVISION
Director
Program Management Officer
Branch Chiefs
- Acquisition Branch
- Dissemination Branch
- Operations Branch
- Publications Branch
- George Washington University—Biomedical Applications

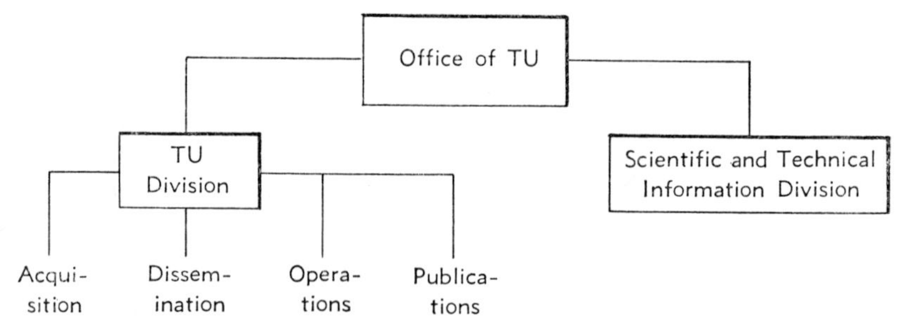

ASSISTANT ADMINISTRATOR FOR TU

The Assistant Administrator for TU is the focal point for all technical information activities, both extramural and intramural, within NASA. The responsibility of the administrator is defined in a 1966 NASA Management Instruction as follows:[2]

> The Assistant Administrator for Technology Utilization is responsible for:
> a. Planning, directing, and evaluating activities for obtaining the widest practicable and appropriate dissemination and utilization of technological and other scientific innovations and information resulting from NASA's research and development activities.
> b. Exercising agency-wide functional management responsibility and authority in accordance with reference (a) in the areas of technology utilization and scientific and technical information.

[2] NASA Management Instruction (NMI) No. 1134.8 (June 1, 1966), designated a new Assistant Administrator, solely for the TU Program, reporting directly to the NASA Deputy Administrator.

c. Performing assigned functions in conformance with the fundamental responsibilities and operating relationships prescribed for all Headquarters Program and Staff Offices in reference (b) recognizing the specific responsibility and authority of other officials and insuring that actions taken by him are in accordance with NASA policies.

After carefully upgrading the OTU operation so that it reported directly to the Deputy Administrator responsible for all NASA R & D activities, a later reorganization placed the OTU under a new Deputy Administrator whose functions are administrative rather than scientific, apparently indicating a downgrading of its status with regard to actual R & D functions which hampers its intra- and interagency effectiveness.[3]

TECHNOLOGY UTILIZATION DIVISION (TUD)

As may be seen from Chart 1, all TUD personnel report administratively as well as functionally to the Assistant Administrator for TU. TUD is functionally responsible for insuring contractor compliance with "New Technology" reporting requirements. These are to be distinguished from the specific technical reports required by the contract, which are the responsibility of the contracting officer administering the given contract.

TUD personnel are also functionally responsible for insuring NASA employee "New Technology" reporting. TUD has no direct authority to enforce the reporting provisions of the New Technology Clause. Whatever authority TUD possesses is functional and derived from the powers given the Assistant Administrator for TU. TUD personnel may, in addition, scan contractor or NASA employee work products to see whether relevant new technology is buried therein and not reported.

TUD had limited manpower with fewer than 25 employees at NASA Headquarters, including clerical help and fewer than 38 TUO's in the field to handle the work product of over 70,000 scientists and engineers in fiscal 1967.[4]

---

[3] Compare NASA Management Instruction No. 1134.8 (June 1, 1966), with NASA News Release No. 67-50 (March 8, 1967) creating the new position of Deputy Administrator for Organization and Management and placing the OTU under this purely administrative arm of NASA.

[4] U.S. Congress, House of Representatives, Committee on Science and Astronautics, Subcommittee on Advanced Research and Technology, *1968 NASA*

SCIENTIFIC AND TECHNICAL INFORMATION DIVISION (STID)

The other major Division under the Assistant Administrator for TU is the Scientific and Technical Information Division (STID). STID is responsible for collecting, indexing, abstracting, and storing on magnetic data tapes, for ready retrieval, all relevant NASA contractor and NASA employee technical reports.[5] Thus it serves much the same function for NASA as ASTIA does for DOD, that of librarian. STID likewise collects, indexes, abstracts, and stores on the same magnetic tapes such other agency aerospace information as these agencies make available to STID; it also collects international aerospace information. The over 250,000 technical reports on all aspects of aerospace technology are probably the largest automated abstract collection in any one area of technology. STID thus supplies

---

Authorization, Hearings, 90th Congress, first session, H.R. 4450 and H.R. 6470 (Washington, D.C.: U.S. Government Printing Office, 1967), part 4, p. 698.

[5] At present magnetic data tapes are obtained from two major sources: (1) federal agencies and their contractors and from foreign countries as a result of reciprocal information exchange; and (2) the American Institute of Aeronautics and Astronautics. This professional society scans over 900 domestic and foreign journals monthly for NASA. The first source is called STAR (Scientific and Technical Aerospace Reports) and the second IAA (International Aerospace Abstracts). The range of document origin is shown in the following table.

Origin of Documents*

STAR	Percentage of STAR	Approximate Percentage of Total File
NASA and Contractors	21	10.5
DOD and Contractors	30	15.0
Other Government Agencies (incl. AEC) and Contractors	6	3.0
Other U.S.	12	6.0
USSR and Soviet Bloc	19	9.5
Other Foreign	12	6.0
	100	50.0

IAA	Percentage of IAA	Approximate Percentage of Total File
United States	58	29.0
USSR	15	7.5
Great Britain	10	5.0
Germany	3	1.5
France	3	1.5
Other Foreign	11	5.5
	100	50.0

* Data supplied by NASA TUP, August 1967.

both NASA and its contractors with an excellent automated library system. Likewise, TUD draws upon STID as its sole supplier of general aerospace technical reports. These STID magnetic tapes are available to most NASA Centers, to a few major NASA contractors, to six NASA Regional Dissemination Centers (RDC's), and to several international organizations, but to no one else.[6] Other NASA contractors can have tape searches performed by applying to STID or by paying a fee to an RDC. However, these other NASA contractors usually cannot obtain copies of the magnetic tapes for their own in-house use.

STID COMPARED WITH TUD

STID is the general technical librarian while TUD is concerned primarily with innovation reporting, evaluation, and dissemination. This is not to imply that many innovations may not be found in the reports processed by STID, but that is not the focus of STID activities. Little more will be said of STID below except as its activities directly affect TUD operations.

TUO. The NASA field agents responsible for insuring both contractor and NASA employee compliance with New Technology identification and reporting do not report to the Assistant Administrator for TU. Rather, these Technology Utilization Officers (TUO's) are located at each NASA Field Office or Center and report to the Technical Manager of that Office or Center or to one of his subordinates.[7] These TUO's also perform preliminary screening of disclosed new technology prior to transmission to TUD, and attempt to promote reporting by visits to contractors and discussions with NASA employees. In short, each TUO is the focal point for all reporting under the contracts let by his particular Field Office or Center.[8]

The major criterion used in evaluating disclosures is commercial

[6] See NASA, *The Technology Utilization Program* (Washington, D.C.: NASA Headquarters, 1967), p. 12, for a list of the 31 tape recipients: 6 NASA Centers, 6 RDC's, 16 large NASA contractors, and 3 special users.

[7] At present there are 13 NASA Field Centers and Offices that let and administer R & D contracts besides Headquarters itself. See NASA, *Technology Utilization Program,* NASA No. N65-36350 (Washington, D.C.: U.S. Government Printing Office, 1965), p. 20, for a list of these Centers and Offices.

[8] Some Centers or Field Offices have more than one TUO. The number appears to be a function of workload at any given Center or Field Office.

potential not their value to the scientific or technical community in general. This emphasis on direct transferability is a variant on the Weinberg Report recommendations for insuring that technical information relevant for scientists, technologists, and students be made readily available.[9] Typically, TUO's are engineers with some business or commercial experience not topflight technical-referees.[10]

Acquisition Branch. The Acquisition Branch of the OTU is primarily responsible for new technology reporting as required by the New Technology Clause;[11] that is, it is concerned with the reporting by NASA employees, contractors, and subcontractors of innovations conceived while working under NASA-sponsored R & D projects. This reporting is not limited to specific innovations and may include some broader areas of technology, hardware or software. These innovations may not be needed to fulfill the project requirement but may be subsidiary results of the project work product.[12] This Branch is also responsible for evaluating these disclosures for commercial potential as well as evaluating STID reports for potentially valuable innovations that were reported by the usual contract reporting method.

The mechanism used to require innovation reporting by contractors and subcontractors is the New Technology Reporting Clause. The New Technology Reporting Clause is a special clause inserted in all prime R & D contracts and provides in very broad terms for contractor reporting of all innovations discovered under NASA contract funds in whole or in part and is a distinct reporting requirement in addition to that provided by the contract for specified

[9] U.S. President's Science Advisory Committee, *Science, Government, and Information* (Washington, D.C.: U.S. Government Printing Office, January 1963). The focus of this report is on technical information *per se,* not new transferable technology. The report recommends a professional referee system similar to that used in refereeing articles for the archival literature in the natural sciences (p. 40).

[10] Discussions with the TUO's at the NASA Electronics Research Center indicate that TUO authority is largely a function of the status given the TU Program at the Field Center by the Director of that Field Center.

[11] See NASA PR, section 9.101-4 (June 1966).

[12] See Robert Solo, *Studies in the Anatomy of Economic Progress,* Report prepared for the National Planning Association (Washington, D.C.: NPA, 1965), pp. 205–44, for an excellent discussion of the problems of identifying relevant innovations for commercial transfer where there is little motivation for the individual project technologist to record any but project requirements.

technical reporting, usually the specific work product of the contract.[13]

Dissemination Branch. After disclosures arrive at Headquarters, they are further evaluated for commercial-industrial potential. Subcontractors are employed to do more detailed evaluation and to reduce the more promising innovation disclosures to the one- or two-page Tech Briefs. Where a disclosure or group of disclosures covers a wider area of Technology, a Technology Survey or other Special Report may be contracted for.

The Dissemination Branch is charged with the responsibility of promoting transfer of aerospace technology, primarily, to the commercial-industrial market. The primary vehicle is the Regional Dissemination Center (RDC), which accounted for more than 90 percent of the Dissemination Branch budget in fiscal 1966.[14] Other forms of dissemination are also sponsored by TUD, in conjunction with the RDC's or independently: for example, regional demonstrations or conferences, motion pictures, interagency assistance programs, other experimental dissemination programs, and distribution of NASA technical reports by TUD for various federal regional technical report mailing lists.[15] Most of the money and effort of the Dissemination Branch, however, is concerned with making the RDC's effective local switching mechanisms for promoting the transfer of aerospace technology to the commercial-industrial market.

Innovation Reporting Policies

Related to both the acquisition and the dissemination operation is an elaborate set of patent/license regulations which regulate con-

13 NASA PR, section 9.101 (June 1966).

14 See Chapter 8, footnote 1.

15 U.S. Congress, House of Representatives, Committee on Science and Astronautics, Subcommittee on Advanced Research and Technology, *1967 NASA Authorization, Hearings,* 89th Congress, second session. H.R. 12718 (Washington, D.C.: U.S. Government Printing Office, 1966), part 4, pp. 664–65. The list given in the Committee report is said to represent areas where additional monies could profitably be spent by the OTU; however, all these areas have already received some funding by the OTU. See also Denver Research *Institute, Channels of Technology Acquisition in Commercial Firms and the NASA Dissemination Program,* NASA-sponsored Report (Springfield, Va.: Clearinghouse for Scientific and Technical Information, June 1967), pp. 63–77, for an enthusiastic description of NASA's document dissemination programs.

tractor rights in inventions discovered under NASA R & D funding and the rights available to commercial-industrial firms interested in developing a NASA-owned invention. There is also detailed in the New Technology Clause a NASA policy requiring general disclosure of innovations, whether patentable or not, to NASA, subject to certain limitations to be discussed. This general NASA policy for disclosure is extended to many subcontractors by requiring prime contractors and higher tier subcontractors to include portions of the New Technology Clause in their subcontracts.[16] Further, NASA employees are required to disclose innovations made while working for NASA. They are encouraged to do so by a well-publicized policy of rewarding quality innovations subject to the recommendations of the NASA Inventions and Contributions Board (ICB).[17] However, neither the formulation nor administration of policy regarding the patent/license area, the New Technology Clause, or the reward of NASA employees for disclosures is under the Assistant Administrator for TU,[18] and therefore neither is as effective as it might otherwise be.

In summary, NASA has established an integrated acquisition-dissemination program under a single, responsible, highly placed Administrator. It has likewise tried to assist both the acquisition and dissemination operations by a comprehensive set of regulations covering the control of intellectual property, whether generated by contractors or NASA employees.

History of the OTU

NASA is the first major science procurement agency to establish an agency-wide program to promote the transfer and application of its area of technology outside its own institutional setting.

This program was not established as an agency focal point for scientific and technical transfer, but to justify, in part, large NASA expenditures.[19] When little tangible spin-off was found to have

16 NASA PR section 9.101-4 (d) (1) (June 1966).

17 NASA, *Patent Program—A Review Document* (Washington, D.C.: NASA, Office of the General Counsel, April 1966), p. 5.

18 See NMI 1134.8, which defines the limits of his authority. None of these areas is mentioned except by inference to his functional agency-wide responsibilities.

19 This rationale for the TU Program does not appear in the literature; it is based on interviews with present and former OTU personnel, and study of the

occurred automatically, it was hoped that an expanded TU Program would not only measure spin-off but also promote secondary usage.[20] Another reason for the establishment of the TU Program was the growing concern as to the value of technical information created by the large federal expenditures for R & D in the early 1960's.[21] Shortly before the time that NASA formally inaugurated the TU Program, the Executive branch and the Congress had shown increasing concern with the poorly coordinated technical data acquisition, evaluation, and dissemination activities of the federal agencies. PSAC was commissioned to undertake a comprehensive investigation of the problem and to make recommendations for such changes as were necessary to correct the inadequate agency programs. The result was the Weinberg Report.

NASA appears to have adopted several of the Weinberg Report recommendations in the TU Program. The literature does not indi-

---

Congressional hearings since 1958. See statement by Senator Keating in U.S. Congress, Senate, Committee on Aeronautical and Space Sciences, *NASA Authorization for Fiscal Year 1965, Hearings,* 88th Congress, second session, S. 2446 (Washington, D.C.: U.S. Government Printing Office, 1964), p. 329; speaking to Mr. Webb of the recent tenor of NASA testimony, Senator Keating noted: "Your stress this year (in NASA testimony) is not so much on the manned space flight, but on the subsidiary gains from the space programs in technology and so on."

As Senator Keating observed, there was a shift in emphasis in NASA Congressional Hearings (from about 1962 on), trying to justify continued high spending by reciting spin-off gains to the economy or at least the promise of such gains with an expanded NASA transfer program.

[20] Starting in 1963, criticism of large space expenditures mounted; see, for example, "Is the Moon Race Hurting Science?" (a critical article in the) *New York Times Magazine,* May 26, 1963; "Is the Moon Project a Waste of Brain Power?" *U.S. News and World Report,* July 29, 1964; Amitai Etzioni, *The Moon Doggle; Domestic and International Implications of the Space Race* (Garden City, New York: Doubleday, 1964).

[21] See for example, PSAC, *op. cit.*; Arthur D. Little, Inc., *Centralization and Documentation* (Washington, D.C.: Clearinghouse for Scientific and Technical Information, 1963); U.S. Congress, House of Representatives, Select Committee on Government Research, *Documentation and Dissemination of Research and Development Results,* Study No. 4. 88th Congress, second session, H.R. 504 (Washington, D.C.: U.S. Government Printing Office, 1964); U.S. Congress, Senate, Committee on Government Operations, Subcommittee on Reorganization and Internal Organizations, *Coordination of Information on Current Federal Research and Development Projects in the Field of Electronics,* 87th Congress, first session (Washington, D.C.: U.S. Government Printing Office, September 1961) (Committee Print).

cate whether some of the mechanisms adopted by the TU Program were consciously borrowed from the Report. Nevertheless, the Weinberg Report did conclude that NASA had accepted the responsibility for information activities in fields that are relevant to its missions.[22]

The earliest group formed to implement the dissemination mandate of the Space Act was the Office of Technical Information and Educational Programs formed in May 1960. But an action transfer program was not initiated until June 1962 when Morton Stoller was placed in charge of what later grew into the Technology Utilization Program.[23] In August 1962, an Industrial Applications Advisory Committee (IAAC) was established at NASA "to devote its attention to the problem of accelerating the transfer of government R & D knowledge to industry."[24] In April 1963, the Technology Utilization and Policy Planning Group was officially established and placed under the Deputy Administrator.[25] This flurry of activity (in late 1962 and early 1963) appears to be directly related to increasing concern over the very low contractor reporting rates and public criticism. The mission of the Advisory Committee was primarily to accelerate the transfer of government R & D to industry not to study the problem and evolve an experimental program.[26] Instead the program was early committed to a policy of horizontal transfer and tangible results, even to the extent of impressing on "NASA contractors that the most important thing to their survival is the transfer of the results of their work."[27] Dr. Simpson, Director of the TU Program, felt that NASA contractors should be impressed with the importance of reporting and transfer. The low level of contractor reporting, until recent direct payment to contractors was

---

22 PSAC, *op. cit.*, pp. 39–45.

23 U.S. Senate, Senate Committee on Aeronautical and Space Sciences, *NASA Authorization for Fiscal Year 1963, Hearings,* 87th Congress, second session (Washington, D.C.: U.S. Government Printing Office, 1962), p. 623. From an interview at NASA Headquarters on October 1, 1968, it appears that James Webb suggested a technical information dissemination program of some sort be established shortly after he took office in January 1961.

24 See Minutes of the Meeting of the NASA Industrial Applications Advisory Committee (IAAC), January 1963, p. 3.

25 Robert Rosholt, *An Administrative History of NASA, 1958–1963,* NASA SP-4101 (Washington, D.C.: U.S. Government Printing Office, 1966), p. 346.

26 See Minutes of the IAAC Meetings, January 1963, September 1963, and January 1964.

27 See Minutes of the IAAC Meeting, September 19, 1963, p. 3.

initiated, might indicate that the contractors were not impressed with Dr. Simpson's argument.

Statutory Basis for the TUP

The statutory basis for the TU Program is primarily found in section 203 (a) (3) of the National Aeronautics and Space Act of 1958, although other sections do imply that the Administration should provide for the diffusion of NASA-developed technology. Thus section 203 (a) (3) states:

> [The Administrator shall] provide for the widest possible practicable and appropriate dissemination of information concerning its activities and the results thereof.[28]

Section 102 (c) (4) also provides some basis for the program:

> The aeronautical and space activities of the United States shall be conducted so as to contribute to one or more of the following objectives:
> . . . . (4) The establishment of long-range studies of the potential benefits to be gained from, the opportunities for, and the problems involved in the utilization of aeronautical and space activities for peaceful and scientific purposes.[29]

Legislative hearings both before and after the enactment of the Statute indicated a Congressional belief that NASA-developed technology would provide valuable economic spin-off and, therefore, that provision should be made to disseminate the results of NASA-sponsored R & D.[30] It is not clear that NASA was expected to do

[28] National Aeronautics and Space Act, 42 U.S.C.A. 2451, section 203 (a) (1964).
[29] 42 U.S.C.A. 2451, section 102 (c) (1964).
[30] "[Section 203 (a)] was not explicitly included in draft legislation." Rosholt, *op. cit.* However, it is found in part in an early House version offered by Congressman Lane, U.S. Congress, House of Representatives, Committee on Science and Astronautics, H.R. 9847, 85th Congress, second session, sections 2, 4 (Washington, D.C.: U.S. Government Printing Office, 1958).

There is little in the hearings explicitly dealing with mechanisms or institutions for dissemination or technology transfer. However, Congressional interest was clearly not wanting in the "great" benefits to the economy to be expected from space R & D.

more than act as a sort of collection agency and conduit, with spin-off or fall-out to the civilian industrial sector to occur spontaneously. Suggestion for an affirmative program to promote spin-off does not appear in the Space Act, though it may be inferred that the standing House and Senate Committees favored the actions taken by Mr. Webb to counter the criticisms of the high-cost space expenditures by establishing a group specifically responsible for promoting transfer to the civilian-industrial sector.[31]

The first written order specifying the functions of the TUP, appears to be NASA General Management Instruction 2–1–6, April 29, 1963. Specific internal authority for the present organization came on June 1, 1966. Administrative authority over the various functional elements is fragmented, with the TU Program administrator having administrative authority over information only after it has been collected from the NASA laboratories and little authority in formulating or enforcing patent or contract provisions. A liaison officer for the NASA General Counsel's Office was, however, appointed in 1966.

The statutory and regulatory bases for the OTU are vague, consisting of the general language in the enabling act and several management directives. Several of the functional elements of a transfer program are, however, provided for in the enabling act,[32] and

---

See U.S. Congress, House of Representatives, Committee on Science and Astronautics, Subcommittee on Advanced Research and Technology, *The Practical Values of Space Exploration,* 86th Congress, second session (Washington, D.C.: U.S. Government Printing Office, 1960), pp. 17–28 (Committee Print).

[31] See, for example, Robert Solo, "Gearing Military Research and Development to Economic Growth," *Harvard Business Review,* XL, No. 6 (November-December, 1962), pp. 44–60; "Will Space Research Pay Off on Earth?" *New York Times,* May 26, 1963.

See also U.S., Congress, House of Representatives, Committee on Science and Astronautics, Subcommittee on Advanced Research and Technology, *1965 NASA Authorization, Hearings,* 88th Congress, second session (Washington, D.C.: U.S. Government Printing Office, 1964), part 4, pp. 2163–2224; *1967 NASA Authorization, Hearings,* 89th Congress, second session (Washington, D.C.: U.S. Government Printing Office, 1966), pp. 634–67; see particularly Congressman Hechler's comment—"I congratulate you on the progress that has been made in technology utilization" (p. 648); see Senator Keating's comment in footnote 20. Of course, Congress has been approving specific budget requests for TU since 1963 and none have been altered significantly.

[32] NMI 1134.8, now modified by NASA News Release No. 67–50, March 8, 1967.

regulations have been promulgated in the Federal Register covering the patent/license provisions,[33] and NASA Procurement Regulations have been promulgated covering New Technology Reporting requirements.[34]

Part II presents a case study of this NASA Technology Utilization Program. This case study is intended as an analysis of the program, not a historical commentary. It will concentrate on those elements of the program that seem relevant to such questions as the following: Why was such an elaborate program established in a major federal science agency with little specific statutory basis in the enabling act?[35] What may be learned for future federal programs aimed at technology transfer?

[33] Patent and licensing authority is conferred by 42 U.S.C.A. 2451, sections 305 and 203 (b) (3) (1964).

[34] 14 C.F.R., sections 1245.100, 1245.200 (1962, 1964).

[35] NASA PR section 9.101–4 (June 1966).

Chapter 7

The Mechanics of Acquisition and Evaluation in the Technology Utilization Division

The acquisition or input function plays an important role in the NASA Technology Utilization Program, providing much of the material specifically tailored for commercial industry such as the Tech Briefs or Technology Surveys. The focal point for new technology reporting is the Technology Utilization Officer (s) located at each NASA laboratory or field office. One of the major problems for the NASA Program has been a continuing failure to acknowledge the necessary conflict of interest between the TUO and the mission-oriented contract administrator and technical supervisor. The interest of the TUO is to promote contractor new technology reporting while the interest of the contract administrator and technical supervisor is to fulfill the technical requirements of the contract.

The TUO's who report to the various project officers are, in the first instance, responsible for insuring contractor and subcontractor reporting at all levels. In any given case, however, it is the contracting officer who decides whether monies will be withheld from the contractor, not the TUO, and still less the Assistant Administrator for TU.[1]

The TUO is consulted to determine whether there has been compliance with the new technology reporting requirements, but his interests and those of the contracting officer necessarily conflict to some extent since the contracting officer's main concern is a successful project, not new technology reporting. Further, his relationship with the contractor can cause him difficulties out of all proportion to the new technology problem.

The theory is that NASA Project Managers will be motivated

[1] Gathered from interviews with various TUO's and with OTU personnel between July 1966 and March 1967.

to enforce the reporting requirements imposed by the New Technology Clause in order to curry favor with the NASA Administrator and to enhance their position with the Congressional committees at Authorization Hearings. However, reporting is a staff function at each center and not part of technical management. It is also relevant that technologists tend to regard personnel engaged in reporting and monitoring as second-class citizens.[2] There is no uniform policy about the organizational level at which each TUO stands. At some of the laboratories, he reports directly to the laboratory director; at others the TUO ranks considerably lower in the administrative scale.[3] It is clear that the organizational rank and technical status play some role in the effectiveness of the TUO, but how much has not been determined.

There is another organizational problem caused by the TUO's necessarily divided loyalties since he reports administratively to the laboratory director or his designees, but he is functionally responsible to the Assistant Administrator for TU. The major type of promotion for a TUO is an appointment that takes him out of the laboratory TU Office to a different administrative position. Further, his performance is presently determined by laboratory or field office administration, not by the OTU.

Once an innovation has been identified by the TUO, he acts as the first filter to determine, in general, whether it should be passed on to the TUP for further evaluation. The Acquisition Branch Chief at Headquarters then sends those that pass his filtering to the Illinois Institute of Technology Research Institute (IITRI) for detailed evaluation as to commercial potential.[4] The result of this

---

[2] See U.S. President's Science Advisory Committee, *Science, Government, and Information* (Washington, D.C.: U.S. Government Printing Office, January 1963).

[3] Interviews with TUO's at the NASA Electronics Research Center, Cambridge, Mass., December 1966.

[4] The yield of promising flash sheets was reported to be low. Arthur D. Little reported that about 25 percent of the flash sheets sent to them by IITRI were considered promising. Arthur D. Little, Inc. *Technology Transfer and the Technology Utilization Program,* Report to the NASA OTU (Washington, D.C.: NASA Headquarters, April 1966), pp. 2–3. In interviews with the Acquisition Branch Chief during the fall of 1966, it was stated that IITRI was said to screen out about 60 percent prior to transmission to the other reviewing institutions. Thus, only about 10 percent of all flash sheets submitted were later issued as Tech Briefs.

further evaluation is the Tech Brief, generally a one- or two-page summary of the innovation containing some information so that interested persons can pursue the matter in more detail.

The New Technology Clause seeks to make the disclosure of innovations made in the course of NASA R & D contracts a part of the fulfillment of the contract, not a subsidiary by-product.

To offset basic institutional barriers existing both within the Agency and among NASA contractors, the OTU needs more effective administrative control of those responsible for insuring that contractors comply not only with the form but also the substance of NASA policy. The TUO's should be placed under the direct control of the OTU. Men with a high degree of technical competence and experience should be selected so as to command the respect of their technical peers. These reforms would give the TUO's the added prestige they badly need and provide for direct, rapid communication and control between the Assistant Administrator for TU and each of the NASA Centers.

Evaluation Criteria

As in appraising any evaluation scheme, the criteria in use must be determined and their appropriateness to the result sought must be judged. In appraising the work of the TU, a question arises as to whether the end product sought is appropriate to the ways in which aerospace technology is likely to be transferred.

The NASA TU Program was primarily established to effect technology transfer to the commercial-industrial sector. This notion is echoed in public announcements,[5] and even in RDC contracts which appear to limit the scope of the Centers' activities to industrial applications.

---

[5] An example may be found in a statement by James Webb on the inside cover of NASA, *Technology Utilization Program,* NASA No. N65–3650 (Washington, D.C.: U.S. Government Printing Office, 1965).

> It is our objective, in accordance with the directions given by Congress and the President in creating NASA, to insure that developments resulting from NASA's scientific and technological programs be retrieved and made available to the maximum extent for the nation's **industrial** benefit in the shortest possible time, thus strengthening the bridge between technical research and marketable end use.

Or see any NASA Authorization Hearings 1963–1967.

NASA should first identify specific industrial requirements for new technology and then evaluate their disclosures in terms of these specific industrial needs. At present some vague standard of commercial-industrial applicability is used to evaluate contractor or employee disclosures. Although it is not possible to identify commercial-industrial technology needs precisely in all areas of technology, still, general forecasts are possible which would provide a framework for the evaluation process.[6] Under the present evaluation system, the TUP appears to be providing a large number of answers to unrecognized industrial needs. It appears, however, from studies performed for NASA by Arthur D. Little, Inc., that where an entrepreneurial approach is combined with a detailed knowledge of local market requirements and local company capabilities,[7] the "answers" discovered by NASA may be fitted to some specific industrial needs.

Transfer may also occur in ways other than specific item transfer, including the transfer of broad areas of new technology, particularly vertically as in the case of radioisotopes, atomic power, and weather satellites.[8]

The method of evaluation appropriate for specific items may be less appropriate for more generalized areas of technology. Transfer of generalized areas may take place by more circuitous routes, perhaps starting with a university scientist acting as an industrial consultant. Thus, criteria other than immediate market application are required to assist transfer at various levels and at various rates of diffusion.

Another difficulty arises in evaluating a specific innovation for market potential soon after conception. The mistakes in this area

---

[6] See Brian Quinn, "Technological Forecasting," *Harvard Business Review,* XLV, No. 2 (March-April 1967), pp. 89–106, or James Bright, ed., *Technological Forecasting for Industry and Government* (Englewood Cliffs, New Jersey: Prentice-Hall, 1968), for a discussion of the state of the art in technological forecasting and the use of such forecasting as a tool in meeting corporate needs for new products and services.

[7] Arthur D. Little, Inc., *Technology Transfer and the Technology Utilization Program,* Report to the NASA OTU. (Washington, D.C.: NASA Headquarters, June 1965). (Hereafter cited as *1965 A. D. Little OTU Report.*)

[8] Arthur D. Little, Inc., *Transfer of Aerospace Technology in the United States —A Critical Review,* Report to the Subcommittee on Technology of the Committee of Enquiry into the Aircraft Industry, United Kingdom (known as the Plowden Committee) Cambridge: A. D. Little, Inc., July 1966), p. 10 (hereafter cited as *Plowden Report*).

are classic, for example, Kodak's rejection of Xerography.[9] The Arthur D. Little study indicates that the Tech Brief is too brief. Too little information has been furnished a business on which to make a judgment, and if the innovation was developed by a contractor rather than by NASA,[10] it has often not been possible to obtain enough detail. Although NASA has recently undertaken to provide back-up data packages for Tech Briefs, the adequacy of these back-up data packages has not yet been determined.

Part of the problem in the evaluation process arises from political pressure to insure that there are large numbers of tangible results, even if they are only minimally useful Tech Briefs. The diffusion of technology does not appear to be a simple function. The transition time from conception to actual use may not be predictable. The first application may be as a laboratory instrument in a university laboratory, and gradually diffuse down to use in factory check out, finally finding its way into the consumer market. The cathode-ray tube is a good example of this diffusion process. The area of application may vary widely from original conception to actual end use. Thus the first application of a NASA innovation may not be for an industrial use. Advance evaluation even with highly competent business technologists is at best a risk.[11] It would appear, therefore, that at least two general standards may be needed:

1. Specific innovations that appear to fill an industrial need should continue to be reported as Tech Briefs but with a file containing sufficient additional detail that an interested businessman could obtain without a great deal of red tape and wasted time.

2. Most of the flash-sheets (contractor reporting forms) should not be discarded but collected into general areas of new technology and made available to the RDC's for experimental transfer. They might also be sent to applied science departments in universities and technical institutes. Most important, they should be available to

[9] See John Jewkes, David Sawers, and Richard Stillerman, *Sources of Invention* (New York: St. Martin's Press, 1961), pp. 116–200, 220–25.

[10] *1965 A. D. Little OTU Report,* pp. 5, 16.

[11] See Jewkes, Sawers, and Stillerman, *op. cit.,* pp. 225–35, and Rupert MacLaurin, "The Process of Technological Innovation: The Launching of a New Scientific Industry," in James Bright, *Research, Development and Technological Innovation* (Homewood, Illinois: Richard D. Irwin, 1964), pp. 69–91, for discussions of the unexpected applications often found for innovations.

places high enough up in the hierarchical chain of diffusion so that a match may be made between the sophistication of the technologist and that of the technology to be transferred. This new technology that has not reached an appropriate level for commercial-industrial transfer should be made easily accessible to technologists further away from industrial application.

It is suggested that if the transfer process is viewed as many-faceted, not easily predictable, and subject to transfer in a more-or-less hierarchical fashion, then evaluation criteria may be made more experimental and less tied to the production of given quantities of Tech Briefs or Special Reports.

The New Technology Clause

The New Technology Clause was derived from similar sections of the Armed Services Procurement Regulation (ASPR), section 9.[11] The purpose of this reporting requirement under the ASPR is defensive, to protect the government from infringement suits by later inventors and to provide the government with an irrevocable license for use in other government work. It has never been the purpose of the DOD regulations in this area to promote disclosure for the purpose of transferring innovations to other sectors of the economy outside the defense-industrial complex.[12]

Starting in 1962, NASA, in order more fully to comply with its mandate under section 203 (2) (3) of the enabling act, issued NASA Circular No. 260 to amend the "Property Rights in Inventions Clause" and to add a "Reporting of New Technology Clause."[13] With the addition of this Clause NASA started actively to promote spin-off by contract, so that a new dimension was added to NASA

---

[12] ASPR, section 9.200 (April 1965, revision 10), covers rights of DOD to contractor technical data.

[13] *Plowden Report*. Discussing the transfer objectives of DOD with respect to NASA, the Report noted (p. 5):

> The DOD portion of this funding (aerospace R & D funding) is considered to be that amount necessary to assure the maintenance of the present position of the U.S. vis-a-vis the U.S.S.R. in aircraft and missile technology. This purpose is not questioned, nor has it been suggested that DOD has any deliberate objective of transferring any of the results of this research to civilian sectors of the economy.

contract requirements. Since 1962 the Clause has gone through several variations, with new versions becoming effective in September 1964 and June 1966.

The substance of all versions is that the contractor "shall furnish to the contracting officer a report concerning each reportable item promptly. . . ."[14] where a "reportable item means any invention, discovery, improvement or innovation whether or not the same is susceptible to protection under this contract. . . ."[15]

The method of enforcement is specified in Part V, which provides for withholding of 5 percent of the amount of the contract or fifty thousand dollars, whichever is less, and a reservation of this amount after 85 percent of the contract has been paid to insure enforcement.[16] With the exception of the withholding provisions, this same Clause is applicable to R & D subcontractors.[17] The discussion will focus first on the prime contractor. Later the application of the Clause to subcontractors will be discussed.[18]

The effectiveness of a standard contract clause and nothing more to motivate reporting of inventions arising out of government-supported R & D is questionable in view of NASA experience and various studies concerning agency reporting rates. (A detailed analysis of agency reporting will be deferred until Chapter 10.)

Some improvement in reporting rate may be expected purely as a result of the present campaign to educate contractors as to the importance with which NASA views the reporting function. With the publication of *NASA Management Guidelines for New Technology Reporting* in October 1966 and the more vigorous program at Headquarters, a higher rate of reporting was to be expected.[19]

In 1965 NASA initiated direct payments to contractors for establishing a New Technology Reporting function. North American Aviation, as the largest NASA contractor, was chosen as the first

---

14 Effective date of this first version of the Clause was December 30, 1962. Now cited as NASA PR, section 9.101–4 (June 1966).

15 NASA PR, section 9.101–4, Part II (b) (June 1966).

16 NASA PR, section 9.101–4 Part I (a) (i) (June 1966).

17 NASA PR, section 9.101–4, Part V, Paragraph (r) (i), (2) (June 1966).

18 NASA PR, section 9.101–4, Part II, Paragraph (d) (1), (June 1966).

19 The clause is generally applied to nonprofit corporations but is generally omitted from contracts with university grantees (but was left in university RDC contracts).

recipient.[20] Their rate of reporting rose by a factor of 8 in the first year after payment, but there is no indication of the commercial potential of this increased reporting.

It should be noted that there are several problems associated with direct payment for contractor reporting.

1. The funds for this payment are taken directly from the Project Office funds, not from TU Program Funds, so that any monies allocable to new technology reporting are subtracted from funds otherwise available for project R & D. In the first allocation, the North American Aviation Corporation case, additional funding not part of the project funds was made available from Headquarters contingency funds. Since the Administrator considers that this function is so important, however, the Project Offices successfully complying with this finding requirement will probably find it easier to obtain the administrator's approval for future budget submittals. They will also find Congressional hearings easier if they can point to substantial new items of transferable technology. Thus far this argument has induced only one or two contractors to request specific funding.[21]

---

[20] Contractor reporting went up by half in 1966, but employee disclosures were down slightly from 1965 (382 to 367). Thus it appears that the TU Program efforts had a noticeable effect on contractor reporting, but whether more "quality" (that is, commercially useful) innovations were being reported is not apparent from the NASA figures. NASA, *A Review of NASA's Patent Program* (Washington, D.C.: NASA, Office of the General Counsel, March 1967), p. 13.

In 1966 for the first time official Guidelines were published by the Acquisition Branch. NASA, *Management Guidelines for New Technology Reporting to NASA,* NASA Handbook No. 2170.1 (Washington, D.C.: NASA OTU, October 1966). NASA, *Reportable Items Under the New Technology Clause,* NASA Handbook No. 2170.2 (Washington, D.C.: U.S. Government Printing Office, October 1966). Recently the Technology Utilization Division circulated a draft of detailed documentation to be required for new technology reporting. NASA, *Documentation Requirements Handbook* (Washington, D.C.: NASA TUD, 1968). Some informal guidelines had been circulated prior to October 1966, but they did not carry the administration's signature nor were they advertised as "Official Guidelines."

[21] See North American Aviation, Inc., *Technology Utilization Program Management and Operation Plan* (Washington, D.C.: NASA OTU, September 1965), for a discussion of their program.

The first official NASA Directive allowing specific funding for New Technology Reporting was issued in March 1966. NASA Procurement Regulation Directive No. 66–5 Para. II, pp. 2–3 (March 10, 1966). Guidelines indicate 0.5 percent of contract funding is "a reasonable cost of new technology report-

2. There is some question about the propriety of paying contractors for starting what amounts to an incipient internal commercial diversification operation paid for with government funds. The North American Aviation Corporation's *A New Technology Reporting Plan* provides specifically that one of the functions of the Corporate Director for Technology Utilization shall be that he promote commercial utilization of the reported innovations for the benefit of the company.[22]

Since subsidies are provided by the federal government to many private firms in many areas as an accepted practice today, it would be surprising if the spending of such small sums of money to promote reporting and, indirectly, spin-off were to be viewed as improper.[23] Still, conversations with TU Program personnel indicate that they are somewhat sensitive in this area.

The more fundamental problem is that the efforts of larger aerospace contractors in commercial diversification have for the most part not been notably successful and their willingness to report has always been low.[24] It is therefore unlikely that such a small monetary incentive will be an effective spur to the reporting of quality innovations, particularly if there is a possibility that space/defense contractors may hurt their competitive position in bidding on future government contracts.

Thus far, discussion has been primarily limited to aerospace contractors. Should the firm that already does substantial business in the commercial market be able to receive funding at the same

---

ing . . ." and "one qualified professional with secretarial help should be adequate to monitor . . . the activities of 125–300 engineers, scientists, and other professional personnel engaged in creative work" (Paragraph II (d), (c)).

[22] It appears that only two contractors had requested this New Technology funding after publication of the guidelines (interviews with OTU personnel during fall 1966).

[23] See NAA, *op. cit.*, p. 2. The NAA Plan provides for identifying technology with commercial potential, providing documentation of this technology to their Commercial Marketing Office and International Office. Costs of this liaison and initial marketing are included in the NASA-funded program.

[24] During the panic created by reduced DOD R & D spending in the early 1960's, suggestions were made for federal support of company diversification efforts. See for example, U.S. Arms Control and Disarmament Agency, *The Implications of Reduced Defense Demand for the Electronics Industry,* prepared by Battelle Memorial Institute (Washington, D.C.: U.S. Government Printing Office, September 1965), pp. 106–23.

rate and for the same purposes as its aerospace peers? NASA procurement regulations make no distinction and, as a matter of administrative ease or fairness, it is not clear why one type of firm should be favored over the other. The only argument that might be made is that a company with commercial business already has more incentive to report in order to insure its claim to waiver of commercial rights. But quality reporting rates to December 1965 do not bear out this hypothesis (see Table 7).[25] Although over-all reporting

Table 7

Quality Disclosures by Groups of Contractors for Contractors with Four or More Quality Disclosures to December 31, 1965[26]

Group	Disclosures	Quality Disclosures	Ratio in Percent
Aerospace Companies[a]	2,105	208	10.0
Other Large Companies[b]	921	89	10.0
Other Companies[c]	110	51	46.0
Universities and Nonprofit Organizations[d]	408	155	38.0
Total	3,544	503	14.0

a Aerojet General, Avco, Bell Aerospace, Bendix, Douglas, General Dynamics, Hughes, LTV, Lockheed, McDonnell, North American, United Aircraft, and TRW.
b Companies in 1965 Fortune Directory: Ampex, Collins Radio, General Electric, General Mills, Honeywell, IBM, Monsanto, RCA, Sperry Rand, and Westinghouse.
c Barnes Engineering, Beckman Instruments, Electro-Optical Systems, GCA, Hazelton Laboratories, Peninsular Chemical Research, and Varian Associates.
d California Institute of Technology, Illinois Institute of Technology, Midwest Research Institute, MIT, Southern Research Institute, Stanford Research Institute, University of Arizona, and University of California.
Sources: Files of AGP, ICB, NASA.

---

[25] See Arms Control and Disarmament Agency, *Defense Industry Diversification,* prepared by John Gilmore and Dean Coddington of the Denver Research Institute (Washington, D.C.: U.S. Government Printing Office, January 1966), for a discussion of defense firm difficulties in diversifying into the commercial market. See also Arthur D. Little, Inc., *Strategies for Survival in the Aerospace Industry,* prepared by Thomas Miller (Cambridge: A. D. Little, Inc., 1964), pp. 26–43, for a discussion of diversification problems for aerospace firms.

[26] Table 7 is from Donald Watson and Mary Holman, *Evaluation of NASA's Patent Policies* (Washington, D.C.: George Washington University, Economics Department, 1966), p. 54. "Quality" disclosure is defined as one on which a patent application has been filed or a patent granted.

See Appendix B for a complete listing of prime contract awards for the 100 largest NASA Contractors together with a list of their patenting activity.

by large nonaerospace contractors is somewhat higher, as a function of total funding, than that of large aerospace corporations, a detailed analysis of the type of work performed by each type of contractor would be required to evaluate these somewhat higher reporting rates.

3. Another difficult problem is the allocation of payment for reporting to a prime contractor and his subcontractor or to a subcontractor and his subcontractors. The *NASA Management Guidelines* say that "account should be taken of cost to be transmitted to subcontractors"; however, no method of allocation nor guideline is provided.[27] The issue is wholly theoretical thus far since there has been no subcontractor reporting to NASA.[28] The easiest method would be merely to allocate on the same percentage basis as for the prime contract. As the size of the subcontracts decreases, it may cost more to report per innovation so some adjustment may be needed. A more difficult question is: If lower tier subcontractors report more quality innovations, should they receive a proportionately higher percentage payment?

The evaluation of disclosures would present more serious problems if substantial reporting did result from TU Program pressures. Should the firm that produces the innovation also do the initial evaluation, or should it be done by a higher tier subcontractor, or by the prime contractor himself prior to transmission to the Acquisitions Branch? The Clause itself provides for direct reporting and evaluation bypassing the higher tier contractor. This practice of going directly to NASA headquarters is contrary to general project management hierarchical control and may result in duplication of reporting and inadequate evaluation. The magnitude of the potential problem area is noted by Rosenbloom, when he poses the question of what the OTU would do if substantial reporting at all levels occurred and at a rate comparable to that experienced by one

[27] NASA, *Management Guidelines for New Technology Reporting,* p. 11.

[28] No subcontractor reporting was reported by the Acquisition Branch Chief during fall 1966 interviews and verified by a former TUD Director. The question of subcontractor reporting is one that disturbs the Acquisition Branch Chief and TUD, in general, especially since the smaller firms, who generally appear not as prime contractors but as "subs," tend to be more innovative and subcontractors tend to do more hardware development and less systems management and control than the prime contractors.

private R & D contractor.[29] Under the present minimal field screening provided by the TUO's, thousands of reports could be sent to the OTU each month.

In sum, the monetary incentive provided by the Clause may increase the rate of innovation reporting, but the problem of using project funds for contractor new technology reporting and evaluation, of paying contractors for their own marketing evaluation programs and allocation of payments between prime contractors and their subcontractors will have to be resolved. If the monetary incentive itself accomplishes nothing else, it does make the contractor aware that NASA attaches some importance to the reporting function. It is analogous to company payment for employee disclosure, which appears to have the effect of making the employee aware of the importance the employer attaches to reporting innovations.[30]

Payment for reporting should, however, be controlled by the OTU. For the same reasons that it is appropriate for the OTU to control the withholding-of-funds provision in the New Technology Clause, it is also appropriate to place the authority for determining which contractor and subcontractor should receive payment for reporting and on what basis with the OTU, rather than as at present with the contracting officer.

Allocation procedures under the Clause should be specified as between the prime or higher-tier subcontractor and his subcontractors. *Management Guidelines for New Technology Reporting,* the first and only elaboration of methods of compliance with the New Technology Clause provisions solves the problem of allocation of funds to subcontractors for reporting by noting that "account should be taken of costs to be transmitted to subcon-

---

[29] Richard Rosenbloom, *Technology Transfer—Process and Policy* (Washington, D.C.: Special Report No. 62, NPA, July 1965), p. 25. Rosenbloom notes that Westinghouse Electric Corp. reported an average disclosure rate of 0.5 per engineering man-year, varying of course as to functional area. All these disclosures were said to be potentially patentable. Thus, if the TU Program experienced anything like this kind of reporting rate they would have about 35,000 disclosures a year to evaluate since NASA employed about 70,000 engineers and scientists in 1966. The maximum number was reported to be 3,310 in 1966. NASA, *A Review of NASA's Patent Program,* p. 13.

[30] Assuming all R & D contractors applied, under FY 1967 NASA funding, about $21 million would have been expended annually (0.5 percent of $4.2 billion).

tractors," nothing more.[31] Some formula should be evolved that would not leave to the prime contractor alone the determination of how to allocate reporting funds. The formula should be based on the size of the subcontract and the quality of disclosure. This latter criterion could be simplified administratively by equating quality disclosure with patentable items. This method is admittedly crude, but it would help minimize administrative burdens on prime contractors in disbursement of funds. If the prime contractor is to be reimbursed for reasonable costs, it appears equitable to reimburse subcontractors likewise.

Withholding under the Clause

Theoretically, contractor reporting under the New Technology Clause is to be enforced, as needed, by Part V, which provides:

> (r) (1) . . . if the contractor fails to comply with the provisions of this clause after receipt of a written decision of the Contracting Officer, . . . there shall be withheld from payment unless such failure has been corrected within the time limit set, either five percent (5%) of the amount of this contract . . . or fifty thousand dollars ($50,000), whichever is less.
> (r) (2) . . . after payment of eighty-five percent (85%) of this contract . . . payment shall be withheld until a reserve of either five percent (5%) of such amount, or fifty thousand dollars ($50,000), whichever is less, shall have been set aside, such reserve or balance to be retained until the Contractor shall have complied with the provisions of this clause. . . .
> (r) (3) The maximum amount which may be withheld under this paragraph (r) shall not exceed five percent (5%) of this contract or fifty thousand dollars ($50,000). . . .[32]

NASA does not require that this withholding provision be included in subcontractor contracts at any level.[33]

NASA TU personnel are reluctant to discuss how often this withholding provision has been invoked against a prime contractor, except to say that it has been invoked several times.[34] Even if

---

[31] *Management Guidelines for New Technology Reporting,* p. 11.
[32] NASA PR, Section 9.101–4, Part V, paras. r (1), (2) (3) (June 1966).
[33] NASA PR, section 9.101–4, Part II, para. d (1) (June 1966).
[34] The TUD Director did indicate during an interview in December 1966 that the witholding provisions had been invoked several times but declined to be any more specific or to provide any data.

invoked, it is hardly likely to have much more than a psychological effect on large prime contractors since it is only maximally effective against contracts of $1 million or less (i.e., 5% of $1 million = $50,-000). Roughly 70 percent of NASA R & D funds during fiscal 1965, 1966, and 1967 was spent on one project, Apollo, and much of it through one contractor, North American Aviation (NAA).[35] Thus, the effect of the withholding section appears to be diluted by the pattern of NASA spending.

The enforcement of the Clause is in the hands of the NASA Contracting Officer; the TUO at that site will usually be consulted as to the adequacy of contractor reporting, but the TUO has no direct power to invoke the withholding provisions. Recently, formal guidelines have been published, but prior to this publication in October 1966, neither the Contracting Officer nor contractor management had formal standards as to the quantity or quality of reporting expected.[36] The rate of reporting suggested in the guidelines is probably unrealistically high, being about twenty-five times higher than the rate up to mid-1966.[37]

Unless the withholding amount is substantially increased, it will continue to have little effect on the rate of disclosure from large prime contractors. If enforced vigorously against the smaller prime contractors, it would no doubt be arbitrary and discriminatory. Further, so long as the Project Office, not the OTU, controls withholding, it is unlikely that it will be used, except in cases of flagrant

[35] The first 28 NASA prime contractors received $3.3 billion of $4.2 billion spent by NASA on R & D in FY 1966; data obtained from NASA list of 100 largest prime contractors, Appendix B. However, a number of different contract instruments may have been involved and the provisions of the regulations do not define the term contract where it may in fact be part of a larger contract or an add-on.

[36] *Management Guidelines for New Technology Reporting.*

[37] Watson and Holman, *op. cit.,* p. 32, reported that 54,000 technologists employed by NASA industrial contractors disclosed 2,094 items in FY 1965 or about 1 disclosure per 25 engineering man-years. The guidelines speak of one reportable item per design engineer per year. Since many of the 54,000 contractor technologists are engaged in activities less likely to result in reportable items, such as test and evaluation, the guideline goals appear wholly unrealistic either in terms of previous NASA experience or of other federal agency experience. See Federal Council on Science and Technology, *Annual Report on Government Patent Policy* (Washington, D.C.: U.S. Government Printing Office, June 1967), pp. 40–57, for a tabular view of all major procurement agency disclosures and R & D spending for fiscal year 1963–66.

disregard of the reporting requirement or when extreme pressure is applied by the administrator. The standards set now by the Guidelines are not realistic; even a conscientious Contracting Officer will find little guidance in them.

The New Technology Clause in the Three-Party Relation

Enforcement of new technology reporting when a subcontractor is involved presents the classic third-party beneficiary problem. For simplicity, it will be assumed that only a first-tier subcontractor is involved. NASA stands in the position of the third-party beneficiary; the prime contractor exacts a promise from the subcontractor (the promisor) to report new technology for the benefit of NASA.[38]

Subcontractors report directly to the NASA Contracting Officer.[39] The responsibility of the prime contractor is not spelled out in the provisions of the Clause, other than the requirement of "frequent periodic reviews of the work performed by the Contractor to assure that all reportable items have been reported to the Contracting Officer."[40] The mere fact that there is an additional organizational layer between NASA and the contractor-inventor increases the difficulty of identifying innovations to the point that NASA TUO's and Contracting Officers have simply refused to consider enforcement.[41]

The next question is whether it is worth the effort to promote reporting below the level of the prime contractors; that is, are there any significant number of quality subcontractor innovations to be reported? Another way of phrasing the question is: How much R & D money is expended below the prime contract level, and is it expended in the type of R & D work that would be likely to yield innovations compared with the R & D activities of the prime contractor.

---

[38] NASA PR, section 9.101–4, Part I, para. (d) (June 1966).

[39] In reading NASA PR, section 9.101–4, Part V, para. (a) (iv) together with Part II, para. (b), it appears that the subcontractor is obliged to report each "reportable item" directly to the NASA contracting officer, and no provision is made for reporting such item (s) to the prime contractor. However, the prime contractor is subject to the withholding requirement for failure to comply and compliance appears to include a review of reporting under the entire contract (including subcontractor reporting).

[40] NASA PR, section 9.101–4, Part II, para. (c) (June 1966).

[41] Interviews with TUO's and OTU officials indicate that debates in this area are not only continuing but acrimonious, with little or no headway made in evolving methods of identifying subcontractor innovation and inducing compliance.

There is no direct evidence of the innovative value of new technology produced at the subcontractor level. There is in fact very little detailed data below the level of first-tier subcontractors on just how the money is diffused.[42] Since the bulk of R & D funding by NASA supports just one project, lack of subcontractor reporting is probably an important item in explaining the small number of reported innovations.

Several types of evidence are available as to the value of subcontractor technology. First, prime contractors on larger contracts usually expend a great deal of their effort in project management functions rather than in R & D itself. Software innovations may result from the large prime contractor's problems of control, management, and administration. Much of the hardware design apart from the airframe itself is often performed by subcontractors.[43] Medium and smaller companies rarely bid on large prime contracts since they do not have the resources to write the very elaborate proposals.[44]

The data tend to substantiate both the hypothesis that smaller and medium companies produce more valuable innovations and the hypothesis that there is little difference between a large aerospace contractor and the aerospace division of a large diversified corporation. The data are limited, for they are derived only from prime contracts; and the equation of quality with potential patentability is not altogether satisfactory since only a small number of valuable innovations are likely to be patentable. The data do not indicate relative cost of these "quality" innovations, nor do we know whether medium and smaller firms receive more dollars for R & D as prime

---

[42] The assumption is that a substantial portion of NAA and other large Apollo prime contract monies are subcontracted. It appears from data collected by Merton Peck and Frederick Scherer, *The Weapons Acquisition Process: An Economic Analysis* (Boston: Division of Research, Graduate School of Business Administration, Harvard University, 1962), p. 150, that the large defense prime contractors they studied paid out 50% of their funding in subcontracts, for both materials and parts purchases as well as subsystem development.

[43] Much of the electronics component and material development appears to be subcontracted. On Apollo, such areas as guidance, communication, and telemetry development have been subcontracted.

[44] A NASA-supplied list of their 100 largest contractors revealed that no firm classified as "small" received a prime contract larger than $6.4 million. (See Appendix B.)

contractors on small contracts or as Nth tier subcontractors on large contracts. (See Table 7.)

Withholding Enforcement against Subcontractors

Though NASA stands in the position of a third-party beneficiary, it is not clear that this creates an enforceable legal right of action in NASA against the subcontractor, since no sanctions for nonreporting need be included in the subcontract, nor are liquidated damages provided. It is not clear that a court would be willing or able to fix damages since the loss suffered by NASA from a failure to disclose would be extremely difficult for a court to place a value on. The loss really affects the overall economy in a not easily determinable manner. Thus the New Technology Clause has the effect of creating a right in NASA with respect to each subcontractor that is probably not enforceable by NASA against the subcontractor unless the prime contractor has himself provided for liquidated damages in his contract with the subcontractor, which he is not obligated to do by the New Technology Clause itself.[45] Given these conditions, NASA must depend on the good faith efforts of the prime contractor to motivate subcontractors to report, unless subcontractors are specifically granted a portion of the reporting fee mentioned in the Management Guidelines.[46]

In sum, it is suggested that control over withholding provisions, formulation of the policy, and enforcement should rest with the OTU. Discretion over the withholding provision should rest with the organization that is best able to judge contractor performance and motivated to insure contractor compliance, not with the contracting officer. At present, some Centers require the OTU to sign off before all contracts funds are released, others do not. There is very little motivation for the contracting officer to trouble himself over the withholding provisions when he is strongly mission oriented.

The amount of withholding should be increased. As noted previously, the present withholding provision is only of maximum effectiveness against contracts totaling one million dollars or less.

---

[45] NASA PR section 9.10;–4, Part II, para. (d) (1) (June 1966).

[46] However, the prime contractor is not legally bound to allocate any reporting funds made available to him either under the Clause or the Guidelines.

The provision should either be eliminated or extended so that larger contracts are equally subject to a withholding penalty.

The withholding provision should be extended to include subcontractors. The present withholding provision would not typically be included in subcontracts, no matter how large. It is not certain that, even if this type of liquidated damage provision were included, it would be convenient or appropriate in the project management context for NASA as a third-party beneficiary to enforce the withholding provision since it might tend to undermine the authority of the private firm project manager. Typically the project manager has the primary responsibilities in controlling his subcontractors under a NASA prime contract. But it would provide another visible symbol of the importance NASA attached to reporting. It would also put the higher-tier contractor on notice that NASA attaches a minimum dollar value to proper reporting and that there is always the possibility of litigation. It is also equitable to require inclusion since the dollar value of many subcontracts exceeds that of many prime contractors.

Chapter 8
The Dissemination Function

This section will discuss the dissemination or output portion of the NASA TU Program. More specifically it will concentrate on the institutions known as the Regional Dissemination Centers (RDC's): first, because they constitute the largest portion of the dissemination operation, both quantitatively and functionally (approximately 90 percent of the \$2.0 million allocated for dissemination in fiscal 1966 was spent by the RDC's)[1] and second, because they constitute a novel institutional arrangement for the transfer of technical information to the nonagricultural sector of the economy, employing university-based "field offices" to act as the linking mechanisms.

Certain basic themes and tacit assumptions have affected the operation of these RDC's. These will be examined in an attempt to understand some of the problems the RDC's have had in becoming effective transfer mechanisms and to see how this part of NASA's transfer system interacts with the acquisition portion.

---

[1] This 90 percent figure was obtained from the number given in U.S. Congress, Senate, Committee on Aeronautical and Space Sciences, *NASA Authorization for Fiscal 1966, Hearings,* 89th Congress, first session (Washington, D.C.: U.S. Government Printing Office, 1965), p. 1000, and from interviews with personnel at 4 RDC's and various OTU personnel. Roughly the same proportion of dissemination funds appear to have been allocated to the RDC's in fiscal 1967. Some of the money given to the RDC's is in addition to the basic contract so that one Center with a contract calling for \$300,000 in 1966, actually received in excess of \$450,000 when additional funding for special OTU projects was included. And, of course, these figures do not include any client fees or other local contributions.

Total OTU funding for FY's 1965 and 1966 was set at \$4.75 million per year. A good breakdown of these figures for FY's 1965, 1966, and 1967 is given in the U.S. Congress, House of Representatives, Committee on Science and Astronautics, Subcommittee on Advanced Research and Technology, *1967 NASA Authorization, Hearings,* 89th Congress, second session (Washington, D.C.: U.S. Government Printing Office, 1966), Part 4, p. 635 (hereafter cited as *1967 House NASA Authorization*).

The RDC's, General Description

The Regional Dissemination Center has been labeled by NASA as a "special coupling mechanism at the local level."[2] The RDC approach is to find industrial clients who believe that aerospace technology is relevant to their technology needs or to convince them that it is. Having paired a fee-paying client with a technology requirement, RDC personnel then try to find relevant information. Most often the STID tapes are used, but other sources of information are commonly available to the RDC's, such as AEC documents, chemical abstracts, and the situs university's resources. In general each Center provides applications engineering services, retrospective searches by computer to search the STID tapes,[3] dissemination of new information as it arrives at the Center (selected to match an interest profile of each client), and such other services as each Center believes will serve the unique needs of its locale, including referral services based on acquired knowledge of local resources.

In theory these Centers are to serve industrial clients only on a fee basis. Eventually the fees are to cover the entire cost of the industrial services, with NASA supplying only the aerospace information free of charge and providing only such additional monies as are needed to cover other than industrial services, if any. The OTU theory is "if this type of service is truly worthwhile, industry will eventually provide the financial support for the effort."[4]

There are now seven RDC's in existence. Until January 1967, most of the Centers were in the Midwest or Southwest. (See Chart 2 for a list of centers and dates they were established.)[5] One contract

---

[2] Richard Lesher and George Howick, *Assessing Technology Transfer,* NASA SP–5067 (Washington, D.C.: U.S. Government Printing Office, 1966) p. 67.

[3] Retrospective searches may be done manually or by computer program. Typically a group of key words are used as a guide to the relevant technical documents. Searches may go back in time one or more years, depending upon the particular field of technology.

[4] George Howick and James Mahoney, "Technology—A Resource," *Research/Development,* XVII, No. 9 (September 1966), pp. 18, 20.

Rosenbloom suggested in 1965 that the amount that users might be willing to pay would be some indirect measure of its worth. Richard Rosenbloom *Technology Transfer—Process and Policy* (Washington, D.C.: Special Report No. 62, NPA, July 1965), pp. 33–34.

[5] A short description of each RDC established prior to January 1967 and of the OTU output operation is contained in George Howick, *et al., Research/Development,* XVII, No. 9 (September 1966), pp. 18–46.

Chart 2

List of RDC's and the Dates of Establishment	
Midwest Research Institute (ASTRA) (now closed)	January 1962
Indiana University (ARAC) (partially closed)	January 1963
Wayne State University (CAST) (now closed)	January 1964
University of Maryland (Discontinued as of July 1967)	April 1964
University of Pittsburgh (KASC)	May 1964
North Carolina Science and Technology Research Center (STRC)	June 1964
Southeastern State College (TUSC, Okla.)	February 1964
University of New Mexico (TAC)	May 1965
Newer Centers	
University of Southern California (WESRAC)	January 1967
University of Connecticut (NERAC)	April 1967

was let to establish a quite different type of Center at the University of Maryland; its main function was to follow up requests for technical information from NASA by private firms in order to establish how the information was to be used. This Maryland Center was not an RDC as defined above but really a study project to determine the utilization of NASA inventions as delineated in NASA Tech Briefs or other Special Reports.[6] There are in addition, two newer Centers at the University of Southern California and at the University of Connecticut.[7]

---

[6] The Center at the University of Maryland was not funded by the OTU but by the Goddard Space Flight Center, Greenbelt, Maryland. Thus, the OTU appeared to exercise at most functional, not line, supervision. Office of Industrial Application, Univ. of Maryland, *Final Report of 1964 Activities,* NASA Contract No. NAS 5–3566 and *Final Report of 1965 Activities* (Greenbelt, Maryland: NASA, Goddard Space Flight Center, 1965, 1966). This contract was terminated in mid-1967.

[7] See Samuel Doctors, "Technology Utilization: NERAC Service," *Industry,* XXXII, No. 11 (November 1966), pp. 33, 89, for a brief description of the Center for New England at the University of Connecticut. This Center was the first to be required to perform an extensive feasibility study prior to initiation. With the exception of the New Center at the University of Southern California, all other Centers merely submitted short, solicited proposals generally indicating what services they would offer. NERAC was required to perform an analysis of its region's industrial community and their technology needs. NERAC, *NASA Technology Utilization Project, Feasibility Study for Establishment of Regional Dissemination Center for New England* (Springfield, Va.: Clearinghouse for Scientific and Technical Information, April 1967).

These Centers are said to be experimental efforts established by NASA in response to the mandate granted under the enabling act.[8] Each Center is said to be established because of its unique approach to technology transfer,[9] but in fact there are more similarities than differences in the actual services offered. From interviews at four Centers, it was apparent that the Centers operate in virtual isolation from each other. There are semiannual OTU meetings, to which only Center Directors are invited. But there is no sharing of client profiles or interests; there is no inter-Center referral.

All the Centers except one have been located at Universities; the remaining Center was at the Midwest Research Institute (MRI). None of the Centers is located at a university that would be classified in the top rank of academic institutions. These Centers are established by means of a contract, similar to that used for making grants for university research projects, but the terms, conditions, and administration are different from the average university grant in that they are usually subject to much closer supervision by the contracting agency.

The RDC's were established when centralized document distribution from Headquarters failed to produce any noticeable results. They have numerous shortcomings but also have the potential to accomplish effective coupling, although possibly not in the way nor by the means articulated by NASA. For instance, RDC's could be used to facilitate vertical transfer by assisting smaller R & D companies to obtain bid-proposal information more expeditiously from NASA Laboratories or Field Offices, but thus far little or no effort has been made in this area of transfer.

Many of the problems experienced by these Centers have stemmed from the close OTU organizational tie with the Administrator and their political use by NASA.

---

[8] Howick and Mahoney, *op. cit.* Also see The National Aeronautics and Space Act of 1958, 42 U.S.C. 2451, section 203 (as amended 1964).

[9] This "uniqueness" norm does not appear in any contract as a criterion but has been used by the OTU as justification for funding additional Centers. The difficulty with the term is that, in fact, most RDC's are very much alike in their approach to transfer and the OTU has nowhere established standards for its application. Further, OTU norms appear to militate against much innovation in Center operation.

The Evolution of the Dissemination Program and Political Pressures

Until very recently all Centers have been located in areas of the country without a high degree of aerospace technology as represented by both a technical university base and a high concentration of R & D firms or Government laboratories or both. (See Chart 2.) The Centers have been located in regions where there is little common ground or receptivity for the transfer of aerospace technology.[10] The rationale behind the particular locations chosen is a complex one and not one that is discussed very openly. However, the following appear to have been some of the major reasons:

1. It was felt that centers for technology transfer were not really needed in areas of highly concentrated R & D spending since transfer was assumed to be more or less automatic there.[11]

2. In order to placate some Congressional leaders over the concentration of NASA funding in the Northeastern, Southern, and Far Western states, the early centers were located in the Midwest and Southwest.[12]

3. A desire by NASA to transfer aerospace technology where it would do the *largest* amount of good, namely, by redressing the regional imbalance caused by federal R & D spending patterns and assisting depressed regions, and so on.[13]

---

[10] Roberts and his colleagues at MIT have found that the Greater Boston area, because of the combination of technical industry, a high level of federal R & D spending, and first-rate universities, has a high rate of technology transfer. Edward Roberts and Herbert Wainer, "Technology Transfer and Entrepreneurial Success," Paper presented to the Twentieth National Conference on the Administration of Research, Miami Beach, Florida (October 27, 1966). Daniel Shimshoni, "Aspects of Scientific Entrepreneurship" (Unpublished Doctoral Dissertation, Kennedy School of Government, Harvard University, 1966), also found a similar phenomenon in the Palo Alto area.

[11] This OTU theory is not found in NASA literature but was discovered in interviews with OTU and RDC personnel.

[12] See discussion between Congressman Rumsfield and Dr. Simpson in U.S. Congress, House of Representatives, Committee on Science and Astronautics, Subcommittee on the Space Sciences and Applications, *1965 NASA Authorization, Hearings,* 88th Congress, second session (Washington, D.C.: U.S. Government Printing Office, 1964), part 4, pp. 2163, 2214–16, and similar discussion in 1963 and 1965 House Hearings about the rationale for Center location. Also, an interview with a former OTU Branch Chief confirms this NASA motive for Center location.

[13] See the "imbalance" discussion in Lesher and Howick, *op. cit.,* pp. 5, 14–15.

4. A covert intent to establish centers in institutions that would be more susceptible to NASA control since one of their primary uses was to be as a political ploy in Congressional Authorization Hearings.[14]

5. Chance friendships and acquaintances that created the kind of bond Roberts suggests as a key element in letting government R & D contracts.[15] All of the Centers were actually established by single-source OTU-solicited proposals although numerous unsolicited proposals are said to have been received by the OTU.

Of course, many of these reasons lie behind many government contract awards. There should be no onus attaching to the TU Program because it is in part politically motivated. Nevertheless, these reasons do explain some of the problems the RDC's have had in becoming fully effective local transfer agents.

Another problem area has been the OTU's continuing need of document distribution statistics or other quantifiable data to establish the amount of transfer accomplished. Somehow, these numbers are thought by the OTU to be a measure of technology transferred. Requests from Headquarters tend to be particularly numerous about the time of Congressional Authorization Hearings.[16] The result has been some disruption in day-to-day RDC operation.

Another common problem is the need to work closely within the norms established, informally, by OTU fiat. There is a strong incentive to play safe and stay well within OTU guidelines, since pressure may be brought to bear directly or indirectly to enforce

---

Distribution of federal R & D may be symptomatic of regional imbalances, not necessarily the cause.

14 This is a difficult hypothesis to substantiate. But from conversations, interviews, and discussions with a score or more RDC personnel, MIT and Harvard faculty members, other professionals at NPA, George Washington University and the OTU, it appears that NASA did choose to locate Centers at schools where control would be facilitated. The best indication of the validity of this hypothesis may be the close, continuing degree of supervision exercised by the OTU over Center operations.

15 Edward Roberts, "Marketing and Engineering Strategies for Winning R & D Contracts," Paper presented at the 4th Annual Conference on Marketing in the Defense Industries, Boston, May 27, 1965.

16 Information derived from interviews with RDC personnel, OTU personnel and inferences drawn from Congressional Hearings. All the House NASA Authorization Hearings from 1964 on contain many pages of RDC document statistics, testimonials from RDC clients, and miscellaneous local color.

compliance. Innovation in transfer techniques outside these guidelines is discouraged, with the result that several RDC's perform little more than selective library functions,[17] sending out computerized abstracts, NASA Reports, Tech Briefs, and miscellaneous other technical information. Prior to January 1967, only one Center appeared to be pursuing a variety of different techniques for technology transfer. This Center had worked on projects with other nonprofit organizations as well as state and local government units and in the process had neglected its mandate to transfer to commercial-industrial clients, much to the chagrin of the OTU. This Center received a sizable amount of criticism from the OTU, and its funding has quite recently been discontinued for failure to solicit sufficient industrial funds. In short, almost any activity that is in conflict with pre-New Deal notions of the relative roles of government vis-à-vis private industry tends to be suspect as do projects outside the commercial-industrial ambit, unless approved in advance by the OTU. One of the newer Centers suggested an approach employing entrepreneurial activities by Center personnel, market surveys of NASA innovations, detailed client profiles, and other marketing assistance for clients. The OTU refused to fund any such efforts and further required the personnel to refrain from any such activities.[18]

The Effect of Type of Institution Housing an RDC on Its Methods of Operation

RDC's have been placed in universities and in a nonprofit institute. Thus far, no RDC has been placed in a profit-motivated firm,[19]

[17] There is no correlation between quality transfer experimentation and OTU approbation. Pure literature dissemination is favored over any transfer activities involving participation in any relevant market.

[18] The Arthur D. Little OTU project personnel recommended an entrepreneurial approach to the transfer of specific NASA inventions to industry. Arthur D. Little, Inc., *Technology Transfer and the Technology Utilization Program,* Report to NASA OTU (Washington, D.C.: NASA, January 1965) pp. 11–15 (hereafter cited as *1965 A. D. Little OTU Report*). Arthur D. Little, Inc., *Technology Transfer and the Technology Utilization Program 1965,* Report to the NASA OTU (Washington, D.C.: NASA, April 1966), pp. 13–17 (hereafter cited as *1966 A. D. Little OTU Report*).

[19] However, A. D. Little did perform a trial study of the transfer of specific NASA inventions, *1965 A. D. Little OTU Report,* pp. 1–17, and it appears that three of these inventions were produced by industrial firms (pp. 7–8).

although the growth of a knowledge transformation industry to act as intermediary between government agencies and the potential users has been suggested as a real possibility.[20]

There are significant real and theoretical differences between the university-based RDC's and the RDC located at a nonprofit corporation, in their approach as to technology transfer and in the problems and opportunities created by the two different types of situs institution.

ADVANTAGES OF A NONPROFIT RESEARCH INSTITUTE SITUS

1. A relatively stable group of experienced, industrially oriented technologists are available in most areas of interest to local industry. The universities, in contrast, must depend for technical consulting for the most part on part-time faculty help, often comparatively unfamiliar with local industrial needs.[21]

2. A nonprofit research laboratory is likely to have greater rapport with local industry because of its experience in providing consulting services to this industry. Since much of this consulting is in highly sensitive areas such as new product development, the nonprofit research institute is accustomed to protecting its corporate clients' proprietary information. Universities may enjoy local industrial support, but most of the RDC universities have not done extensive research involving proprietary industrial data. Thus communication in many sensitive corporate areas may, in theory, be easier for an RDC situated in a nonprofit research corporation.

ADVANTAGES OF A UNIVERSITY SITUS

1. It is easier to obtain student help, which not only reduces costs but also considerably enhances transfer since the mobility of technical personnel is a key element in transfer, whereas the staff of a nonprofit research laboratory would tend to be much more stable. The MRI Staff appears to have been highly stable, with a very low turnover rate.

---

[20] Rosenbloom, *op. cit.*, p. 32. Rosenbloom attributes this notion of a "knowledge transformation industry" to Werner Hirsh of the University of Southern California, "Transformation of New Knowledge for Economic Growth," NASA-UCLA Symposium and Workshop, June 1964.

[21] MRI, as a practical matter, has apparently made little use of its technical staff for consulting to determine client technology requirements.

2. Universities have a lower overhead rate and they typically are unable to obtain a fee for capital expenditure on their contracts.[22]

Of course, with a more stable full-time staff, nonprofit institutions should be able to offer different and perhaps better services than their university counterparts. It would be a worthwhile experiment in transfer to place an RDC at another nonprofit research corporation which is not so dependent on NASA R & D contracts as was MRI, to see whether new approaches to the transfer process could be evolved which would justify the higher relative costs. It would also be worthwhile to establish an RDC in a profit-making firm, under reasonable controls as to practices and profit margins, to discover whether such a profit-oriented organization could evolve different useful transfer techniques. The small transfer project at Arthur D. Little for the OTU seems to have been a more imaginative, innovative, and successful approach to transfer of aerospace technology than any at an RDC.[23]

Placing an RDC in a profit-making firm or even in a competitive, aggressive nonprofit corporation may present problems of competition with local consultants. Additional problems may be raised by NASA policies of allowing RDC's exclusive use of the STID tapes and of permitting an RDC to solicit clients in any geographic area. These potentially troublesome policies have not yet created problems for the present RDC's.

The RDC institutional setting may have a direct effect on the entrepreneurial activities of a given RDC since a conservative university setting may militate against assumption of an active role as a champion of aerospace innovations. The assumption of such an activist, market-oriented role may be partially obviated by the values of the situs institution. One could imagine an RDC located at MIT or Stanford as being quite aggressive in selling technology whereas a Center located at a more traditional university is more likely to consider such business activities as inconsistent with academic tradi-

[22] In an interview with John Dinwiddie, Contracts Manager MRI on February 23, 1967, he indicated MRI overhead rate ran about 100 percent plus 4 percent of total contract cost as a fund for capital expenditures. University RDC'c had about a 50 percent overhead rate in fiscal 1968, and no additional allowance for facilities or equipment purchase has been made in present contracts.

[23] *1965 A. D. Little OTU Report* and *1966 A. D. Little OTU Report.*

tion. In sum, those universities that have played an active role in breaking down the traditional divisions between universities, business, and government are likely to be more cognizant of the variety of institutional interactions possible between the university and the business community and more tolerant in their use.[24]

The Market Theory Approach to the Existence of the Centers

The OTU emphasis has been on the direct transfer of aerospace technology to the commercial-industrial market, with very little work on transfer to other institutions such as universities, colleges, and nonprofit research institutions located in the regions contiguous with the various RDC's.[25] However, as already noted earlier, technology transfer appears to be a stratified diffusion process, so that a match must be found between the sophistication of the transferee and that of the information to be transferred. Aerospace technology, although applicable at more than one level in the hierarchy, nevertheless requires a good deal of technical sophistication on the part of both the agent-transferor and the recipient-transferee.

Trying to channel new technology so as to minimize regional in-

---

[24] The variety of roles that leading U.S. universities have assumed in government R & D has run the gamut from the more traditional pure research grant to managing large R & D projects, even assuming supervision over numerous industrial firms. By placing RDC's at universities that have had little experience or understanding of these changing institutional patterns, NASA may well have built in a barrier to innovation in the transfer process. See Don K. Price, *The Scientific Estate* (Cambridge: Harvard University Press, 1965), pp. 21–56, and *Government and Science* (New York: Oxford University Press, 1962), pp. 65–94, for a discussion of the various roles assumed by universities in federal R & D programs since World War II.

[25] Recently some attention has been directed to biomedical applications, attempting to link aerospace technology with hospitals and medical research people in a few universities; however, success has been limited by the imposition of norms which restrict the degree of permissible activity to problem definition, identification of relevant aerospace technology, if any, and dissemination of this information. No evaluation or adaptation is allowed for the new area of application. Thus, several of the transfers claimed by the OTU have been merely identified areas of application; no manufacturer has in fact agreed to evaluate them or to adapt them for manufacture. Information based on interviews with RDC and OTU personnel during 1966–67. See Quentin Hartwig and David Bendersky, "Guidelines to the Application of Space Technology to Medicine," *Research/Development,* XVII, No. 9 (September 1966), pp. 44–46 for a general but romanticized description of the NASA biomedical applications program.

dustrial imbalances in technological sophistication appears premature when data are lacking for even partial understanding of the transfer process. One way to establish the value of aerospace inventions is to find companies willing to try them, but the OTU may believe it easier to defend a program which shows *x* publications distributed by *y* individuals each year than to defend what may in some instances amount to NASA-sponsored assistance to businessmen in areas of the country where large sums of federal R & D money are already being spent and where results may take some years to measure.

The OTU has maintained that the worth of the Centers will be proved by the renewal rate of fee-paying clients. There is no explanation or rationale offered for this market justification for Center operation. It is not clear why RDC's should have to justify their existence when Department of Commerce Field Offices or SBA Field Offices are not likewise required to support themselves. Also, the Agricultural Cooperative Extension Service is subsidized at a rate 20 times as great and is likewise not self-supporting. Such Centers might have a chance of self-sufficiency in regions where many businessmen are accustomed to buying and selling intangibles such as aerospace systems design and consulting.

The RDC is likely to become more like a local Agricultural Extension Office than a university research grantee. As such, it may in time create reliance interests not only in local industry but in the situs university and with other participating organizations and individuals. In spite of the repeated assertions that NASA will be able to withdraw support from the Centers eventually, it is not clear what criteria should be used to withdraw funds from a Center that did not become self-supporting through industrial subscriptions. These criteria are not articulated in Center contracts except that specific amounts to be generated by industrial subscription fee have been included in some RDC contracts. Of course, an argument can be made that if the RDC is truly a local resource, then local funding should support it. But, this is a poor argument in view of the variety of federal field offices in existence, which are essentially local resources. In theory, it was hard to imagine an RDC being discontinued by NASA, lacking some overt misuse of funds or other gross mismanagement. Discontinuing an RDC would, arguably, be more difficult than closing an arsenal or shipyard, since technical information dissemination is hardly likely to become obsolete or noncost effective in any objective sense. However, recently two Centers have had their NASA funding cut off for failure to obtain sufficient industrial sales, and the funding of a third has been curtailed.

Congressman John W. Wydler conducted a mail survey of all fee-paying clients of the RDC's as of June 30, 1965 (87 companies). "Out of 71 replies received [to a questionnaire sent to Regional Dissemination Center subscribers], only 10 could be described as enthusiastically in favor of the NASA programs to which they subscribe . . . 51 out of 71 said that the program was worthwhile, but 41 offered reservations." Of the 71 responding, 18 firms indicated they would continue, 5 said they would discontinue, 38 did not say, and 10 were "unfathomable." Only 2 firms expressed an opinion that the program should be self-supporting. Fewer than 15 percent of the client firms were buying RDC service in the hope of near-term benefits. Whether in fact any of the other 85 percent of the firms used the information distributed by the Centers was not indicated in the survey.[26]

The requirement that each RDC be experimental in the transfer process and try unique approaches, coupled with the requirement of self-sufficiency within a fixed period of time (usually three years) seem to be incompatible goals. The most innovative Center visited appeared little concerned about industrial clients but was trying new approaches to technology transfer. If the program is truly experimental, then surely renewals of fee-paying firms are only one form of evidence of success. Even if an innovative RDC should fail to become self-supporting, however, this may be a poor reason to apply continuing pressures or to withdraw support.

As noted in the House hearings, reasons other than satisfaction with RDC services could induce renewals for indefinite periods, especially when the fees are nominal (ranging from $100 to $15,000). Many larger firms might renew merely as cheap insurance against overlooking any aerospace data in their in-plant libraries; firms may renew to have their names appear favorably in Congressional hearings and for the national publicity they receive; almost half of the

---

[26] *1967 House NASA Authorization Hearings,* p. 646.

firms are government contractors and may feel their good faith participation may assist them in future contract awards; and some firms may consider their fee a donation to a local university.[27]

MRI had had 920 industrial clients when it gave the information away free. When it began charging fees in 1965, it dropped to 45. Further, the fee was only a flat $500 per year, regardless of the amount of services rendered. This Center dropped below 45 clients when the OTU required that it charge fees nearer to actual costs.[28]

Another justification often given for this market-theory test is that if a firm pays for services, it is likely to use them. This hypothesis is no easier to prove than the general market-renewal theory. It suffers from another infirmity. Merely because a patient must pay a large fee to a psychiatrist does not insure that he will work harder at the analysis; it may only be a species of conspicuous consumption or serve some other subsidiary motive.

One main criticism of market justification is that it may cause Centers to become less innovative, not more. More client renewals may be obtained by working with a company librarian or within existing corporate institutions so that the company library becomes chock-full of NASA documents, but little may actually be transferred to working technologists or entrepreneurs within the company. Not rocking the boat may in many larger corporations be the best way to insure continued client fees but one of the poorer methods of transfer.[29] Personal contact appears to be a key element in transfer. Finding methods of identifying entrepreneurs within the corporate structure and vigorously advocating some new area of aerospace technology to these individuals within the company may be a far more effective method of transfer than merely working through one individual or one functional group within the company. Innovation in transfer methods is as important in stimulating in-

---

[27] Most of these reasons for industrial support were discussed in U.S. Congress, House of Representatives, Committee on Science and Astronautics, Subcommittee on Advanced Research and Technology, *1964 NASA Authorization, Hearings,* 88th Congress, first session (Washington, D.C.: U.S. Government Printing Office, 1963), part 4, pp. 3430–60.

[28] Information gathered in an interview at the MRI RDC, February 1967.

[29] See Roberts and Wainer, *op. cit.,* and Richard Rosenbloom and Francis Wolek, *Technology Information and Organization: Information Transfer in Industrial R & D, Report* prepared by NSF (Boston: Harvard University Graduate School of Business Administration, June 1967).

dividuals within the corporation as the technical innovations that are being transferred.[30]

While there is some common sense plausibility to market justification for an RDC, it appears that it may be premature at this time. Market justification is probably too crude a measure since the technology transfer process is so poorly understood. Renewal frequency may obscure meaningful transfer results outside the commercial-industrial sector. In any case, the NASA RDC programs may be justified because at a cost of less than .15 percent of the fiscal 1967 NASA budget, about $7.5 million compared with $5 billion, they represent an innovative approach for the dissemination of federal R & D results which may have a long-term payoff potential.

Need for RDC to Provide a "Champion" for Innovations

Since the TU Program is attempting to transfer technology horizontally, the "champion" must be found in the transferor organization. Just as industrial organizations must provide champions to promote the development of an innovation or a new area of technology, so an RDC must provide a champion until one can be identified within the transferee organization.

Though NASA has advertised some dozen or so specific item transfers to commercial industry, most have been low-cost development, low-risk items, and some have never received more than an expression of interest by the industrial concern.[31] This failure is probably due not only to the typically high development costs and difficulty of horizontal transfer of aerospace technology but also to a failure on NASA's part to support experimental programs designed to try different methods of transferring specific inventions.

Granted that many inventions resulting from aerospace R & D are unlikely to find a near-term use in commercial industry, still,

---

[30] Rosenbloom has observed "[k]eeping the R & D professional informed is more than a mechanical information retrieval task and is very sensitive to organizational policies." Richard Rosenbloom, "Product Innovation in a Scientific Age," Paper presented before the 49th National Meeting of the American Marketing Association, June 14, 1960, p. 13.

[31] Interviews with A. D. Little TU group, leading RDC personnel, and the continual repetition of the same specific items in Congressional hearings further confirm this conclusion. For example, the "Lunar Walker," the "Wireless Cardiac Sensors," "Fused Amorphous Silica," etc., appear over and over again in Congressional hearings, NASA publications, and the trade press.

if contractor reporting can be stimulated, there should be numerous items capable of transfer.

The NASA TU Administrator in public statements indicates the need to encourage an entrepreneurial approach for transferring specific inventions. In a 1966 NASA publication the Assistant Administrator for TU and the TUD Director observed that:

> A wealth of experience on a variety of fronts documents the assertion that the odds on a technology being employed are greatly enhanced if it is championed by the inventor, the man who visualizes the application, an intermediary, the management of the firm that might use the concept, or by a person or group responsibile for identifying or using new technology.[32]
>
> The effective channeling of new technologies, then, demands more than document dissemination, and even more than communication of information. . . .[33]

Contrast the preceding quotation with the response by the same OTU Administrators to a concrete proposal by Arthur D. Little to implement an entrepreneurial approach to transfer.

> For some time we have been advocating entrepreneurial activities as the key to success in achieving meaningful application of new technology. You [NASA OTU] have agreed in principle, but have pointed out (1) that such activity is expensive per unit transfer, and (2) that transfer activities go beyond NASA's legal charter. The economic burden, you have stated, should be borne by those industrial firms which hope to gain additional profits through use of publicly available knowledge and art.
>
> . . . [But] the primary responsibility for showing the validity of the concept that economic value may be derived from space or other natural scientific endeavors rests with NASA and ultimately with the TU Program.
>
> The key concept is entrepreneuring, by which we mean pursuit of new business opportunities with inventiveness and flexibility.[34]

---

[32] Lesher and Howick, *op. cit.,* pp. 100–101.

[33] *Ibid.,* p. 35

[34] *1965 A. D. Little OTU Report,* pp. 8, 13. The actual cost to transfer three NASA inventions to four companies by one A. D. Little technologist working on this experimental program for NASA was $15,000, or $5,000 per invention, including initial learning by the A. D. Little "entrepreneur" and report writing. No data have been obtained on the actual value of these inventions to the transferee companies. Three is a very small sample, but the general result

As noted, a champion for new invention in this type of transfer operation appears to be a key element. The OTU admits it. The Arthur D. Little studies have shown that NASA inventions can probably be sold to industry at a nominal cost per sale, yet the TU Program is firmly committed to a program primarily concerned with document dissemination. Of course, some selection of the documents is made so that value is added to the information. Several of the RDC's do perform some applications engineering tasks; that is, they give technical advice on specific questions that client firms may ask. However, any suggestion such as that in the Arthur D. Little report is met with the reply that it is beyond the NASA Charter.[35]

Is it valid to argue that it is beyond the OTU Charter to provide some marketing assistance to promote transfer? Probably not, since the OTU charter of operation is based on the enabling act provisions for the "widest practicable and appropriate dissemination."[36] The Administrator exercises wide discretionary power in the administration of the space program. The provisions granting this authority are very general and do not appear to preclude funding experiments and programs reasonably related to the technology transfer process. It seems strange that at a time when so many sectors of the United States economy receive subsidies, direct and indirect, that assessing of market potential for a given NASA innovation, identifying specific firms that would have an interest match, working with these firms to acquaint them with the innovation, and obtaining additional technical information for them where needed to develop the innovation should be viewed as somehow inconsistent with the aims of NASA and the OTU. [37]

---

is in agreement with my interviews with Massachusetts businessmen during 1966–67.

See also Donald Schon, "Champions for Radical New Inventions," *Harvard Business Review,* XLI, No. 2 (March-April 1963), pp. 49–60, for a forceful argument that in the absence of an entrepreneur, new inventions will usually languish.

[35] Information obtained in a number of interviews with NASA TUD Director and Arthur D. Little OTU project personnel, September 1966 to December 1966.

[36] U.S. National Aeronautics and Space Act of 1958, 72 Stat. 426, 42 U.S.C.A. 2451, sections 203 (2) & (3) (as amended 1964).

[37] See U.S. National Aeronautics and Space Act of 1958, 42 U.S.C.A. 2451, section 203 (only three functions for the Administrator are enumerated); and see section 205, giving the Administrator authority upon his own initiative

One of the more difficult problems in trying to transfer technology from publicly funded R & D is the fact that there is not even the possibility of a champion in the transferee firm, unless one is identified from the outside. Inventions generated within a company on company funds, or even on federal funds, just by the contiguity of the inventions and company personnel stand a far greater chance of finding a "champion" with little or no "outside" assistance. Assuming that someone with an interest in seeing the invention promoted is essential to start the ball rolling, he probably must be found outside the company until a champion is identified within the company.

It might be possible to assume that companies seeing the *great* potential worth of NASA inventions might have individuals within their organizations instantly motivated to champion the invention, but this has seldom been the case. In fact, such instantaneous motivation would be more likely if several NASA inventions were sold and proved commercially successful and were sufficiently publicized.

Arthur D. Little has shown that NASA inventions could be transferred by an entrepreneurial approach at a relatively low cost, surely an order of magnitude smaller than the cost of NASA TU literature dissemination. Then, if such an entrepreneurial program is recognized by the OTU as essential in technology transfer, recommended by Arthur D. Little (after four years of work with OTU in all phases of TU activity), and has been shown successful (in limited field experiments) where other RDC transfer techniques

---

to explore international cooperation in space. With the complex program established by NASA under this very general language, it is difficult to imagine that anyone could argue that the Administrator would not be held to have such powers as are reasonably necessary to effectuate the policies of the act, including all reasonable methods for technology transfer. Surely, the aerospace/weapons systems industry is itself highly subsidized. The government is the risk taker, even company product improvement and independent R & D is 80 to 90 percent funded by the government. It is a paradox that while the primary mission of the Agency is carried out by firms, not part of the traditional market economy, the OTU should be so preoccupied with traditional notations of the separation of business and government. See U.S. Bureau of the Budget, *Government Contracting for Research and Development: A Report to the President* (Washington, D. C.: U.S. Government Printing Office, 1962), for a discussion of the role played by the newly developed space/defense industry in our economy.

have elicited only nominal success and support, why has the OTU successfully foreclosed this avenue of attack? The reason is apparently fear of Congressional criticism. A reading of the Congressional hearings on TU since 1962 reveals that great stress has always been placed on the fact that NASA would not subsidize the benefits of transfer for private industry nor would they compete with private consultants in new product development.[38]

The RDC as a champion of new innovations is not a panacea for all transfer problems. As was discussed in Chapter 4, space/defense inventions are only likely to be transferred in a locality where there is a high degree of technical sophistication coupled with a group of companies possessed of a high degree of entrepreneurial zeal.[39] In other areas, the elements of the transfer process suggested in Chapter 4 would appear to require less emphasis on specific item transfer to commercial industry and more generalized technology transfer to institutions capable of using aerospace technology for other than commercial purposes.

This is not to say that highly motivated entrepreneurs, possibly even with sufficient technical sophistication, are not to be found in all parts of the country, but if one has limited resources and a need for successful transfer models, one should try where the probability is highest not lowest to obtain data to understand the transfer process better.

In sum, the following suggestions have been made:

1. Horizontal transfer requires a champion in the transferor organization until such a champion can be identified and motivated in the transferee organization, since the invention was not developed within the transferee company.

2. The OTU has frowned upon such activist behavior despite its acknowledgment that it is essential in the transfer process. This pol-

---

[38] See for example U.S. Congress, House of Representatives, Committee on Science and Astronautics, Subcommittee on Advanced Research and Technology, *1965 NASA Authorization, Hearings,* 88th Congress, second session (Washington, D. C.: U.S. Government Printing Office, 1964), pp. 3181–95; *1967 NASA House Authorization Hearings,* pp. 637–67.

[39] The very high success rate of the spin-off companies studied by Roberts and his colleagues at MIT and their great success in transferring very sophisticated technology indicate that this type of firm may be the most promising with which to try specific invention transfer. Roberts and Wainer, *op. cit.*

icy position appears to be based on a very narrow reading of the enabling act, on a fear of Congressional criticism, and on an excessively conservative view of the proper role of the government with respect to private industry in the transfer process.[40]

3. Some specific aerospace inventions can be transferred to industry successfully and at a not very high per unit cost.

4. Specific aerospace invention transfer is only appropriate, in terms of resource allocation, in areas having a large number of technically sophisticated, innovative, entrepreneurial firms. In other areas the transfer of aerospace technology is likely to be more efficient if based on more general information transfer, primarily to universities, colleges, and nonprofit research organizations.

5. The RDC's, as the existing field transfer agents of the OTU program, are the natural places to locate the needed entrepreneurial-transferor agents, but only where RDC's are located in appropriate regions such as WESRAC in Los Angeles or the Boston Regional Office of NERAC (now closed).

Measuring the Results of the Transfer Process

Most observers agree that significant improvement in transfer methods will depend on establishing effective feedback methods to provide data for modifying present transfer methodology. Rosenbloom has observed:

> Given the lack of satisfactory operational approaches to the establishment of feedback mechanisms, we would stress the importance of experimentation in this regard as well as with the primary activities in a program of technology utilization. Although the desirability of explicit definition of objectives and criteria and of the development of effective means for obtaining feedback on results would seem to be almost self-evident, regrettably little attention has been paid to this subject to date.[41]

The Arthur D. Little OTU project personnel have been concerned about the operational difficulties in obtaining feedback data as to the Program effectiveness:

---

[40] Rosenbloom, *Technology Transfer: Process and Policy,* pp. 28–32.
[41] *Ibid.,* p. 32.

> [An] intractable problem concerns obtaining evidence of industrial utilization of NASA technology. The safest procedure for any manufacturer to follow is to keep the nature and source of his new developments confidential, particularly when that source is readily available to his competitors. Well-established working contact between the transfer agent and the manufacturer can partially mitigate the problem.[42]

One of the most difficult but most important problems in technology transfer is that of measuring the results of the process. The NASA OTU is aware of this very difficult problem. It is attempting to use the RDC's as feedback mechanisms. In each RDC contract there is now a requirement to develop evaluation programs which will allow a better assessment of such transfer as occurs. Thus far, however, little feedback other than document statistics has resulted from RDC transfer programs.

It is clear that NASA must establish more effective feedback mechanisms to improve RDC transfer capability. The following items should be included in any OTU planning to establish such a feedback program:

1. Effective technology transfer must work in areas of industrial sensitivity, such as new product development, diversification, and strategic planning.

2. The uncertain nature of NASA RDC funding does not allow for long-term planning in this area, thereby making the problem even more intractable.

3. However, a university situs may provide some advantage in obtaining feedback from profit-oriented organizations since they may view such transfer agents as relatively neutral. But university personnel are unaccustomed to the problems associated with maintaining fiduciary relationships with industrial clients, since free interchange of ideas is a norm among university faculty.

4. Successful well-publicized transfer would partially mitigate the problem of trust and materially assist in establishing viable feedback mechanisms.

5. The stress on commercial transfer may hinder effective feedback in many regions for two reasons.

a. Transfer may be difficult where the industry-transferees are un-

---

[42] *1966 A. D. Little OTU Report,* p. 8.

able to appreciate aerospace technology even if spoon-fed.

b. Transfer to nonprofit research laboratories, local universities, and colleges might provide more feedback in many regions.

6. Finally, transfer is in general a very slow process. The politically imposed need for rapid results may inhibit feedback. Transfer of advanced technology may prove to be a multistep process; that is, it may go through several noncommercial applications before it reaches a commercial channel.

RDC's often deal with private firms in very sensitive areas, such as new product development, possible diversification, bid proposal formulation for federal, state, or local contracts or the referral of appropriate consultants or subcontractors. However, none of the RDC's contacted reported any significant difficulty in working with client firms to obtain sufficient data to establish technical interest profiles either for computer search strategies or for referral services. It appears that if there are few reported problems in obtaining sufficient information to establish corporate technical interests, then the RDC's may not be materially assisting their client firms. Both the Arthur D. Little study and the NERAC study indicate that most technically oriented firms in the Greater Boston area feel that establishing effective communication in any of these sensitive areas is one of the major barriers to effective communication.[43] Assuming that there is a problem of effective communication in these sensitive areas, then the question arises as to what can be done to mitigate the problem.

The most sensitive role at the RDC's is that filled by the applications engineer, whose job it is to establish and maintain customer contact and design the client-interest profile. This profile includes not only technical information requirements but should include enough information about the firm's organization, internal communication, and marketing information to allow him to assist the firm in applying aerospace technology to corporate new technology needs.

---

[43] Over 75 percent of the (Boston area, science-based) "Route 128" type firms contacted in personal interview during the NERAC feasibility study thought that potential problems might occur in this area. Many of the firms engaged in more traditional industrial areas were less concerned.

The *1966 A. D. Little OTU Report,* p. 8, likewise indicates that this was a serious barrier during their study.

The present university-based RDC's make some use of graduate students in the applications engineering area. The client firms are or should be aware that these students may shortly be employed by their competitors. None of the Centers uses a long-term appointment like the one used by MIT for its personnel working in the Industrial Liaison Program (three years). The more extensive use of long-term personnel as applications engineers would help. In order to do this, however, the Centers must be able to offer these applications engineers mutually rewarding contracts. With the present uncertainty and funding vagaries surrounding the OTU program, this is not possible.

A university situs may provide an advantage in dealing with a profit-making organization since it may be less likely to impute commercial motives to university personnel. On the other hand, it may think of university personnel as ivory tower types. Thus the selection of application engineers is most important. Also, the university operation must be conducted in a businesslike manner, which may not be consistent with the academic requirements of a university. One situs university will not allow its RDC to write contracts with client firms, regarding them as inconsistent with the ethics of the university; another will not permit reimbursement for the printing of business cards. However, if the situs university can be convinced that an RDC is a social science experiment and as such will provide valuable research information, then some of the university problems may be alleviated. And if the industrial clients can be convinced that the RDC does run a businesslike operation, then this barrier may be partially overcome.

Another problem in the university environment is unfamiliarity with establishing and maintaining a fiduciary relationship with a client.[44] The academic environment generally encourages the freest possible interchange among its members and with the outside world. An accommodation must be reached in the RDC context or the RDC's are likely to prove ineffective in many areas of transfer.

The Arthur D. Little studies indicated that successful transfer

---

[44] The faculty members of the situs universities thus far chosen have apparently done little consulting, nor are the university administrators very familiar with dealing with industrial firms in a continuing business relationship except in the area of university fund-raising activities.

may help mitigate feedback problems, "if only because the manufacturer who has profited from one NASA development would like to hear of others."[45] Thus, initially RDC's should attempt to structure their transfer, not where the occasional transfer will make headlines but where it is most likely to succeed. It seems likely that a few very successful transfers would be worth far more than large numbers of transfers of only marginal worth.

Finally, technology transfer is usually a slow process. Attempts to obtain quick feedback, that is, document dissemination statistics, obscure the problem and have at some RDC's diverted personnel from the task of transfer. Long-range planning is vital. Less OTU interruption in day-to-day RDC operation and more "bold, ambitious planning,"[46] in establishing feedback mechanisms is a vital need; another is some form of long-term funding which allows the RDC's themselves to work at the problem on a time-base compatible with the dimension of the feedback problem, perhaps 10 to 15 years. The contract device currently used to establish, maintain, and control the RDC's may not be the proper vehicle for this type of project.

---

[45] Center personnel at one RDC indicated that calls from the OTU for document distribution numbers were numerous and disruptive and the OTU emphasis had always been on short-term feedback results.

[46] Professor Don Price feels that the flexible contract device has been far more successful in providing imaginative centralized agency planning with little interference in day-to-day contractor/grantee work than the longer term Cooperative Extension Service. But, he does note that the smaller contractor/grantees might have more reason to complain of interference than the larger ones. Price, *Government and Science,* pp. 65–76. The maximum single RDC funding by the OTU appears to be $450,000; most of the others are considerably less.

Chapter 9
The Contract as a Control Device

An RDC is established through a cost reimbursement contract, subject to a fixed upper limit on costs, between NASA and the situs institution. The NASA Office of Grants and Research Contracts, which formally administers all RDC contracts, conducts a continuing program to assist in improving agency-university relations. Technical supervision is provided by the Technology Utilization Division of the OTU. The OTU has also been interested in improving RDC contract terms. However, the changes have been peripheral to the main issue, that is, the essentially social-scientific, experimental nature of the RDC.[1]

Typical of many government R & D contracts, the RDC contracts are subject to renegotiation yearly and/or cancellation upon the initiative of either party. NASA has recently failed to renew several RDC contracts because of the institutions' failure to solicit sufficient industrial fees.[2]

Contracts and grants have become the hallmark of extramural R & D in this country.[3] Originally sanctioned by Congress in the First War Powers Act of 1941 and later made permanent,[4] the cost-

[1] The information presented in this section was obtained from three RDC contracts, interviews with RDC personnel at four RDC's and with OTU personnel at Headquarters and in the field. See NASA, *Proceedings of the University Program Review Conference* (Washington, D.C.: U.S. Government Printing Office, March 1965), for a discussion of NASA/university research relations. This document, however, is mainly concerned with physical or life science research projects.

[2] "NASA Cuts Back Spin-off Program," *Electronics* (September 30, 1968), p. 63.

[3] Although there are formal differences between contracts and grants, these differences may disappear in practice. It has been suggested that a loosely administered contract may even be preferable to a restrictively administered grant. George Glocker, "The Contract Versus The Grant Approach to Basic Research Activities," *Federal Bar Journal,* XVII (July-September 1957), pp. 265–80.

[4] Stephen Dupré and Sanford Lakoff, *Science and the Nation* (Englewood Cliffs, New Jersey: Prentice-Hall, 1962), p. 17.

reimbursement contract was an ingenious adaptation of the classic government procurement contract to the peculiarities of R & D. In a situation where the government was uncertain about the nature and value of the end products authorized and where the contractor had no prior experience upon which to base his estimate, the conventional fixed-price contract simply involved too much risk to be workable. The cost-reimbursement mechanism proved admirably suited to eliminate these risks, and the phenomenal growth of extramural R & D began quickly after its inception.

The cost-reimbursement contract assumed even greater importance after the end of World War II, when the civil service salary ceilings and the desire of some scientists to return to the academic environment threatened to undermine the nation's substantially increased commitment to R & D. The contract device not only permitted the continued growth of the country's R & D effort, it established a new relationship of interdependence between the government and the universities.[5] Since the government had long been short of talent and the universities of funds, it is not surprising that both were enormously pleased with their new partnership in research. Nor is it surprising that little critical attention was paid to the mechanism that made it all possible.

Historically, however, the contract was rooted in the concept of *quid pro quo*, with both the *quid* and the *quo* clearly defined. Since the typical R & D contract contains only a broad definition of the research to be performed[6] and since neither party has a clear idea of the exact results of the project, the contractor's obligation probably rests in his promise to perform services and the government's obligation in its promise to pay for these services. The formal similarity of this contractual arrangement to the typical employment contract may not be desirable in a situation where the sponsoring agency objects to the methodology or subject emphasis of its con-

[5] *Ibid.*, pp. 15–19.

[6] Charles Kidd, *American Universities and Federal Research* (Cambridge: Harvard University Press 1959), p. 108.

> The general trend has been toward the adoption of contract and grant terms providing for progressively broader definitions of research, partly in response to representations from universities, and partly because the federal agencies have gradually seen that their objectives are more effectively attained by broad definitions of research.

tractor's services. If X agrees to pay Y in return for Y's promise to perform services, the fact that Y is a university engaged in research must overcome the natural reaction that X, not Y, ought to decide what methodology or subject emphasis will be.

Some distinction must be made, of course, between "sponsored research" and "purchased research" in that the former is intended to be less mission oriented and to act more in the nature of direct subsidizing of university research, while the latter is intended primarily to further the sponsoring agency's mission. But, in either case, university researchers are employed because of their independence and objectivity. Any attempt to determine what degree of control the agency should exercise over either sponsored research or purchased research is necessarily qualitative and subjective, but it is clear that agency attempts to control university research which impinge on the researcher's independence do undermine academic freedom and the ultimate value of the research results for the agency.

Another aspect of the contract which deserves attention here is also rooted in its historical development. At one time, most contracts were probably the result of clause-by-clause negotiation between two parties of roughly equal bargaining power. With the advent of giant corporations and federal agencies, however, this balance of power disappeared and "boiler plate" (standard contract clauses) began to replace negotiated contracts whenever there was substantial inequality of bargaining power. The possibility of abuse inherent in these boiler plates is not confined, however, to private industry. In the government-university R & D relation, inequality of bargaining power can also result in the substitution, for negotiated contracts, of boiler plate with objectionable terms.

Notwithstanding these possible disadvantages, the contract device seems, by and large, to have worked well in the more common physical science contracts. Only a few commentators have discussed government control at all, and their conclusions support the view that government contracts have not restricted the scientific independence of the university contractor.[7] Since there has been little serious research on this matter, it is impossible to judge the accuracy of these conclusions.

---

[7] Lewis Mainzer, "Scientific Freedom in Government Sponsored Research," *Journal of Politics,* XXIII (1961), pp. 212–30.

The Contract and the Operation of RDC's

In contrast, however, to its adequacy for funding physical science R & D, the contract device and its administration in the RDC's have led to numerous problems of excessive control. NASA has been ambivalent about the status of the RDC's as an R & D project, characterizing them as "research" in Congressional appropriations hearings while withholding from them the degree of independence usually associated with university research. The reluctance of NASA to grant this independence may perhaps have arisen because of several of the more unusual features of the RDC project.

The first of these features is the high degree of visibility in the RDC's; that is, the RDC must work not in the confines of a university or government laboratory but out in the market place. If such a program is to be effective, it will have to interact with and affect social and economic interests directly, unlike the usually more remote space/defense R & D physical science project.[8] Indeed, one measure of the success of an RDC may be the number of companies made aware of its existence and functions.

The visibility of the project assumes importance also because of a second characteristic of the RDC's, the familiarity of the phenomenon under investigation. The layman may be able to make judgments about means and ends where the intent is to transfer aerospace technology to the commercial sector. He can decide that the use of aggressive selling techniques is inappropriate for a govern-

[8] In this regard it is interesting to note the problems Project Camelot had in undertaking to perform policy-oriented, social science R & D and to contrast it with those experienced by the NASA transfer program (even though the Camelot project never achieved operational status), both for the project and for those performing the research. Both projects raise the question of whether contractual policies appropriate for physical science or nonpolicy-oriented social science will ever provide an effective framework for this type of visible, policy-oriented social science research. Irving Horowitz, ed., *The Rise and Fall of Project Camelot: Studies in the Relationship Between Social Science and Practical Politics* (Cambridge: The M.I.T. Press, 1967). The issue of unduly restrictive agency contract terms is briefly discussed in U.S. Congress, House of Representatives, Committee on Government Operations, Research and Technical Programs Subcommittee, *The Use of Social Research in Federal Domestic Programs, Report.* 90th Congress, first session (Washington, D. C.: U.S. Government Printing Office, April 1967), part 4, pp. 486–658 (Committee Print). This document is particularly relevant to agency restrictions on publication.

ment-sponsored project or he can become disturbed at what may appear to be government involvement in new product design for a private firm, whereas the same layman would be unwilling or unable to make a judgment about the appropriate means used to conduct research in solid-state physics or to perform an experiment employing a linear accelerator. A social-engineering experiment that moves out into the market place is accessible to criticism by almost anyone, professional, layman, or agency administrator.[9]

Naturally, NASA is interested in maintaining close supervision over such a highly visible, highly political, social science experiment; on the other hand, a university is interested in preserving its academic freedom. In the context of their potentially competing interests, the contract device has not proved a satisfactory institutional arrangement for the RDC's. Conflicts about the methodology or subject emphasis of the services rendered have been frequent, and NASA's greater bargaining power has usually allowed it to resolve these conflicts in its own favor, either in the terms of the contract itself or through close supervision under the contract.

The participation of a university in a project which involves objectionable restrictions on academic freedom is of questionable propriety: Dupré and Lakoff in discussing the role of federally funded research for Universities observed that:

> Universities . . . exist for the dissemination and accumulation of knowledge—more plainly, for the teaching and research that together make up higher education. . . . To the extent that Government support of research . . . comes close to the universities' ideal, it contributes to the public service of higher education. But to the extent that it forces universities to deviate from their goal, higher education will be sacrificed in favor of other public functions.[10]

---

[9] In an analogous context, John Rubel notes that our attitudes toward federal spending vary widely, depending upon the area of expenditure, so that a federal near-monopoly of R & D funding is much less likely to come under critical examination than a 10 percent participation in some area considered private, even though the former may have a far larger impact on the economy than the latter. John Rubel, "The Impact of Government Research and Development on Industrial Growth: Trends and Challenges in Research and Development," Paper presented before the Research and Development Symposium of the National Security Industry Association, March 13, 1963.

[10] Dupré and Lakoff, *op. cit.*, pp. 44–45.

Ideally the university ought to be willing to reject or terminate a project rather than accept or continue it under objectionable conditions. The ideal, however, ignores the competitive pressures on universities to maintain the large-scale R & D efforts which have become necessary to attract talented faculty and graduate students. These competitive pressures have placed the less prestigious universities in the position of needing government funds more than the government needs their facilities or staff. Given this imbalance of bargaining power, it is not surprising that restrictions on academic freedom have been accepted all too often.

Harold Orlans in discussing restrictions imposed by federal agencies on university researchers noted that:

> The list of administrative restrictions that have led individual investigators and, at times, institutions, to shun various Government programs is long but not nearly long enough, for complaints have come more readily than action, the private action of individuals has been more frequent than their united public resolve, and rarely have many institutions jointly refused to participate in a program until designated restrictions were removed.[11]

The one-year contract with a university which does not have large amounts of R & D funding can be a powerful lever in the hands of an overzealous, politically attuned project office. The overt or unspoken threat of cutback or cancellation hangs over each conflict about the course of the experiment and may generate institutional pressures to avoid antagonizing confrontations with the sponsoring agency. Less prestigious universities may be particularly vulnerable to this pressure,[12] since they typically have fewer opportunities for R & D funds and may have become dependent upon only a few federal patrons. As noted earlier, all RDC's except the one formerly located at MRI have been located at less prestigious institutions.

[11] Harold Orlans, "Ethical Problems in the Relations of Research Sponsors and Investigators," in Gideon Sjoberg, ed., *Ethics, Politics, and Social Research* (Cambridge: Schenkman Publishing Company, 1967), p. 9.

[12] See *Report on the Use of Social Research in Federal Programs,* pp. 493–95, 509, for firm university policies (Harvard and Stanford) declining any research contracts placing restrictions on time or place of publication. This attitude is to be compared with the RDC situs universities which regularly accept contract clauses containing restrictions on publication and even respond to coercion relative to staffing assignments.

For some of these universities, this contract either represented their first sizable federal R & D contract or supports a substantial part of the school or department's R & D activities.[13]

Current RDC Problems

In general, in the NASA TU Program, there has been continuing close supervision by OTU administrators over day-to-day RDC operation. Often, instructions have come down from the OTU to perform specific tasks for the OTU, such as collecting document distribution statistics or providing special reports; sometimes the OTU has issued detailed RDC personnel policies.

The OTU has also commonly changed the norms of operation with little or no discussion with Center personnel. The latest set of proposed contract changes includes as a new standard clause a prohibition upon "public announcement of any part of the subject matter of this contract or any phase of any work thereunder" without approval of the Technology Utilization Division.[14]

By the terms of the contracts, the OTU, as technical supervisor, has very wide latitude in supervising the operation of the RDC. Don Price has noted that, "The contractual system makes it theoretically possible, of course, for the contracting officer to dominate completely the decisions of the contractor."[15] The theoretical possibility has become the practice in many Center operations. Monitoring of the RDC's has been continual, often harassing and demoralizing. Appeal from an OTU fiat is difficult in view of the very general work statement and broad administrative discretion usually afforded technical supervision in administering smaller R & D projects.

The TU Program makes an interesting study in Administrative Procedure in the university-federal nexus, where a less than top-flight university is involved. It appears that an informative study might be conducted to see what correlation there is, if any, between

[13] For one of the universities visited it represented the first substantial federal R & D funding outside the Medical School, for another it was the first large R & D contract received by the school.

[14] See NASA Memorandum, Concerning Selected Provisions for Inclusion in Technology Utilization Division Contracts as Appropriate (Washington, D.C.: NASA OTU, October 15, 1967), p. 3. Such a provision had been included in the NERAC Contract, p. 3 (NSR 07-002-029, April 1967).

[15] Don K. Price, *Government and Science* (New York: Oxford University Press, 1962), p. 73.

the degree of federal agency control over university grantees or contractors and the quality of the university or department. It may have some relation to the apparent built-in concentration of federal R & D funds in just a handful of universities since topflight researchers at a lesser school may be discouraged not only by the lack of funds for R & D but also by the degree of control over their activities. This effect may be quite subtle since it may well influence the administration and faculty chairman, though not overtly.

Not only has the day-to-day supervision of RDC contractors been unduly restrictive, but the type of control imposed has varied widely with the different OTU administrators. Aside from the boiler plate, these contracts have fewer than 20 operative clauses, each consisting of several general sentences, the total occupying no more than four pages. With such simple contract devices, much of the control is exercised by the technical supervisor acting in his self-interest in interpreting the general work statement. Norms and values of the technical supervisor, in fact, control the working out of the terms. Shifts in OTU personnel have resulted in 180-degree shifts in contract work statement definition. Successors in interest are a difficult problem in this context; whenever there is a change in OTU administration, quite different requirements have been imposed on RDC operation. In one case an initial contract to start an operational RDC was turned into a very "iffy" feasibility study.

The generalized supervisory language also makes appeal through channels likely to fail. On the other hand a very specific work statement could hardly avoid being unduly restrictive in such an experimental program.

In addition to the insecurity created by the one-year contract, its lengthy renegotiation cycle each year has apparently precluded long-term appointments for key personnel without tenure, such as applications engineers. Renegotiation periods average six months, making an accurate accounting system difficult and imposing a financial strain on university funds. Some Centers have had the full-time equivalent of twenty or more professional staff members, a strain for a school that is not wealthy. Interest charges have not been an allowable overhead expense. In fact, overruns of any type have been difficult to collect even to cover additional OTU-imposed requirements. More important than the directly measurable monetary effects may be the more intangible effects on Center morale.

A number of clauses in some of the RDC contracts have proved quite troublesome. One such provision is the requirement to produce a predetermined amount of client fees. One contract provided that over $170,000 of client fees, generated "primarily from industrial sources," was to be procured during the given contract year.[16] Other contracts are silent on this issue, but RDC's have been informed orally that they will be expected to produce a given amount of client revenue as proof of their "experimental" efforts.

Another clause provides that particular emphasis should be placed on investigating and initiating transfer methods which can be made routine. Since the problem of transfer is so poorly understood, any attempt to create routine transfer methods seems inappropriate.

Some contracts contain provisions requiring clearance by the OTU before any material concerning the project may be published or even discussed publicly, despite the fact that no classified or restricted data are involved in the project and that the project is to be conducted at an academic institution, one of whose primary aims is the publication of research results, subject only to critical review by peer-referees.

This is a term in one RDC contract that I read and is to be applied to most of the others.[17] Enforcement is by way of renegotiation difficulty and other veiled administrative threats. The protection of academic freedom appears to be a continuing battle in the context of federal grants or contracts to a university despite Price's optimistic projections.[18]

OTU rationale for imposing this censorship requirement is said to be a concern that only *factually* correct reports be published. Why OTU Administrators should be any better judges of factual accuracy than RDC experimenters is not clear.

---

16 NASA Contract NASr-175, Amendment No. 2 (with Wayne State University), Article I, section B (3) (b) (1966) requiring the RDC to "establish a fee/subscription program which will result in a total of $170,000 income for CY 1966. . . ."

17 The new contract terms to be included are discussed in NASA Memorandum, *op. cit.*

18 Don K. Price, *The Scientific Estate* (Cambridge: Harvard University Press, 1965), pp. 53, 71–72.

In sum, the contract device has allowed the OTU to prescribe many norms of operation directly in the contract terms or indirectly through close and continuing supervision. The result has been a conservative operation with little bold or imaginative planning at the national level and a similar lack of imagination in experimentation at the RDC. More important the freedom of the host institution has been infringed upon, yet fear of cancellation has prevented appeal from arbitrary terms and conditions.

Suggested Contract and Administrative Changes

Many of the potential problems inherent in the contract relationship between the government agency and the university researcher have become actual problems for NASA and the RDC's. Some of the problems have been due to a failure by both sides to discuss the mutual problems openly. Dupré and Lakoff in analyzing the difficulties inherent in the government-sponsor-university-researcher relationship observed:

> . . . [A] research partnership between public and private institutions does not necessarily work easily and automatically. In order to perform its tasks effectively, it must be the object of thoughtfully constructed policies and of mutual accommodation between the partners. Its smooth functioning is a major organizational challenge.[19]

The establishment of what amounts to an experimental field office for technology transfer by a simple contract device is a slightly different use of the contract than the usual government R & D contract or university grant. The use of the cost reimbursement contract should materially assist in allowing for an experimental approach to technology transfer since the transfer process is as much of an unknown as many areas of physical research. It is important for this reason that both contracting parties realize that the methods that must be tried are experimental, that results may be obtained only slowly, and that norms and methodology should be determined as results are compiled and analyzed.

The RDC contract should be viewed as a method of funding an

[19] Dupré and Lakoff, *op. cit.*, p. 19.

R & D project since the RDC is an experiment in social engineering; that is, it attempts to increase the diffusion of aerospace technology through the use of a new institutional system, the TU Program. Little is known about the horizontal transfer of aerospace technology.[20] There are few data indicating how much transfer has taken place or by what means. Further, the RDC has many of the characteristics of the more usual R & D project in the physical sciences, in that the outcomes of the various transfer activities are uncertain. It is very difficult to place a monetary value on this type of operation until such time as there is sufficient reliable feedback. Such feedback may come only indirectly and slowly.[21]

Routine methods prescribed in advance should not, in the first instance, be part of RDC investigations; rather, the Centers should have freedom to try many different transfer techniques and to devise effective and meaningful feedback mechanisms. Center contracts should, therefore, allow and encourage freedom to experiment in this feedback area as in the transfer process itself. Emphasis should not necessarily be placed on transfer to commercial-industrial clients since in some regions other institutions may be more appropriate vehicles for transfer. Specific fee-subscription requirements should not be imposed. If the Centers are able to generate revenue, that may be one indication of successful transfer, but concentration on this indicator to the exclusion of others may be detrimental to what should be a primary goal of the RDC's, a greater understanding of the transfer process.

OTU interference in RDC operation should be no greater than federal agency supervision and control of R & D projects in other areas. Since so many university and nonprofit R & D projects are supported with limited technical direction by the major procurement agencies, there should be no more need for this close supervision of the RDC's than of other R & D projects.

In summary, contract terms should provide for an experimental

---

20 Robert Solo contends that ". . . the transmission of the results of space/military research into industrial application [should be viewed not] as a happy instance of spillover. . . [but] as part of an immensely difficult job of social engineering." "Gearing Military R & D to Economic Growth," *Harvard Business Review*, XL, No. 6 (November-December 1962), p. 49.

21 Richard Rosenbloom, *Technology Transfer—Process and Policy* (Washington, D. C.: Special Report No. 62, NPA, July 1965), pp. 33–34.

program in technology transfer with the same number of financial and technical reports as other R & D projects. More important, technical supervision should be maintained at a level no greater than in an R & D program in any other area. The challenge here is to use the OTU to shield the RDC's from close agency or Congressional scrutiny or both, rather than to use it as a highly visible political device to enhance the agency's position.

Alternative Approaches

The difficulties encountered with the contract device lead to questions about the feasibility of alternative methods of support. Perhaps the nearest analogy to the RDC system is the Agricultural Cooperative Extension Service, which is administered through federal-state relationships of a semipermanent nature.[22] As Price has noted, this close tie with local interests is likely "to keep appropriations up, but is discouraging to bold ambitious rational planning."[23] He goes on to question whether any institution such as the Extension Service, which is subject to so many local pressures, can compete with the federal contract system that has evolved since World War II in procuring quality extramural R & D.[24] In view of the administrative restrictions already discussed, however, it seems that the advantages Price claims for the contract system, as opposed to the Extension Service's more permanent arrangement, have not come to pass.

Another alternative method would be to channel funds through an intermediary organization—the National Science Foundation or the proposed National Foundation for the Social Sciences, for example—which could act as a buffer. In Britain a fixed amount of money is given each year to a nongovernmental agency, the University Grants Committee (UGC), run by academicians, to support university research. This agency is not required to account for its expenditures to the government. The UGC provides funds directly to the institution on a *quinquennial* basis that covers all its activities—research and teaching. The researcher in turn obtains his funds from the institution and thus has no direct contact with even the

22 The operation of the Cooperative Extension Service is described in Appendix A, pp. 176–180.

23 Price, *Government and Science,* p. 76.

24 *Ibid.,* pp. 76–78.

UGC. No financial or progress reports are required. Other countries similarly differ quite extensively from the federal grant/contract approach institutionalized here. It may be that differing institutional approaches for supporting university R & D are appropriate as we move from the physical to the social sciences.[25]

If, for the time being, the contract device is to continue as the institutional arrangement of the RDC's, one answer to the control problems may be to place the RDC's in first-rank universities, provided they would accept the Centers with their past record of conflict with the sponsoring agency and publication restrictions. With greater bargaining power than the present situs institutions, perhaps these universities would be more able and willing to rebuff the OTU's attempts at control and to assert their independence as scientific investigators. With greater freedom of investigation, the RDC might prove a more meaningful experiment in technology transfer.

[25] Eric Ashby, "Science and Public Policy: Some Institutional Patterns Outside America," in Boyd Keenan, ed., *Science and the University* (New York: Columbia University Press, 1966), pp. 13–26.

Chapter 10
NASA Patent/License Policy and the Effect on Transfer

The contract form is not the only legal device that has had an effect on the NASA transfer program; another set of legal devices, the patent/license policy of NASA, also has affected the program. While patentable items form only a small portion of the total technology developed by an agency, their transfer should theoretically be more easily measured than that of nonpatentable technology since the items are documented and their use could be traced more easily. This element of measurable feedback is most important for any program of technology transfer since so little is known about the actual process of transfer.[1]

A patent policy may influence a technology transfer program in one of two ways: A liberal or "license" patent policy (i.e., one that allows government contractors to retain title to all or most patentable inventions discovered in the course of government-sponsored R & D) may act as an incentive to contractors to disclose inventions to the government. The rationale of such a policy is that if a contractor knows that he will obtain patent rights to his invention, he will report it so that he may reap the commercial profits. Such reporting may be considered the input function in a technology transfer program. A "strict title" policy (i.e., one in which the government retains title to any patentable inventions) frees the device for all

---

[1] Most government-owned patents have been considered to be in the public domain and companies have therefore often used these patents without entering into a formal agreement with the government. To use government-owned patents to establish an effective feedback mechanism would require that federal agencies adopt a general policy of maintaining control over their patents whenever used by private firms.

See Richard Rosenbloom, *Technology Transfer—Process and Policy* (Washington, D. C.: Special Report No. 62, NPA, July 1965), p. 32, for a discussion of the importance of feedback in establishing an effective transfer program.

to use since government-held patents are with few exceptions available to all for licensing.[2] Here the rationale is that if no one has a right to exclude others, the right to use the technology can be made generally available free of any rights of the contractor to exclude third party use. Thus a strict-title policy affects the output function in technology transfer programs.

This is admittedly a simplified conceptualization, but it illustrates the basic tension in the relationship of patent policy to technology transfer: The greater the patent incentive provided to contractors to disclose new innovations, the less available the device will be for transfer to and use by others. One reservation needs to be made at this point. If an inventor-contractor himself commercially develops the device to which he was accorded the patent rights, he by-passes the technology transfer system in the sense that he transfers the device to another division within his own company. Hence, the argument is logically available that not only does the contractor-take-all policy encourage reporting, but also it makes unnecessary elaborate systems to transfer technology since the contractor himself will apply the device commercially. This does not generally appear to have been the experience of the government, which implies that freely giving contractors patent rights to inventions is not a significant element in motivating commercial utilization. This chapter will therefore argue that agency policy should not favor the contractor-inventor in the grant of patent rights unless the contractor is able to show intracompany transfer.

Patent Policy and the Input Function

ADVANCE WAIVERS UNDER THE SPACE ACT

Before technology developed under government contract may be transferred to others it must first be reported to the sponsoring government agency. Beginning in 1962, NASA inserted in its R & D contracts a "New Technology Clause" requiring the reporting to NASA of every invention developed in the course of the R & D work.[3] Beyond the contractual obligation to report imposed on

[2] *Tektronix, Inc.* v. *U.S.,* 351 Fed. Rep. 2d 630 (Ct. of Claims) discusses for the first time in a litigated case the right of the government to sue a citizen for infringing a government-owned patent.

[3] NASA PR, section 9.101-4 (June 1966). The National Aeronautics and Space Act of 1958, Public Law 85-568, 72 Stat. 426, 42 U.S.C.A. 2451, section

contractors, NASA has attempted to encourage reporting by generally waiving to contractors who apply, the patent rights to their innovations. Current NASA regulations allow waivers in three situations: a blanket waiver prior to contract initiation,[4] a blanket waiver within sixty days of the execution of the contract,[5] a waiver for particular innovations after they have been identified and reported.[6]

Congressional mandate for the waiver authority may be found in Section 305 of the Space Act,[7] subsection (a) of which provides that inventions made by NASA contractors in the course of their work "shall be the exclusive property of the United States" unless the Administrator waives the government's rights. Subsection (f) states in part that the Administrator "may waive all or any part of the rights of the United States under this section with respect to any invention or class of inventions made or which may be made by any person or class of persons . . . if the Administrator determines that the interests of the United States will be served thereby."[8] It is a matter of contention between NASA and certain senators as to just what policy Congress had in mind when it passed Section 305;[9]

---

305 (a) (as amended 1964), requires that such clauses be inserted in NASA R & D contracts. NASA's original clause was patterned after similar sections of Armed Services Procurement Regulations section IX (now 9.100, April 1965 rev. 10).

[4] 14 C.F.R., section 1245.104 (May 1966).

[5] 14 C.F.R., section 1245.105 (May 1966).

[6] 14 C.F.R., section 1245.106 (May 1966).

[7] 42 U.S.C.A. 2451, section 305 (1964). Of course, the waiver rights apply only to commercial use since the government's rights to use the invention for governmental purposes cannot be waived (section 305 (f)).

[8] *Idem.*

[9] Compare the agency statement in NASA, *Patent Program—A Review Document* (Washington, D. C.: NASA, Office of the General Counsel, April 1966), p. 13, with the comments of Senators Morse and Long in U.S. Congress, Senate Committee on the Judiciary, Subcommittee on Patents, Trademarks, and Copyrights, *Government Patent Policy, Hearings,* 89th Congress, first session, part 1, S. 789, S. 1809, and S. 1899. (Washington, D.C.: U.S. Government Printing Office, June 1965), pp. 329–83.

Senator Morse commented in hearings before the Senate Small Business Committee that:

> Congress has seriously considered this matter. In 1958 when it passed the Space Act, it provided in section 305 that the Government was to take title to these patents, except in the unusual and exceptional case.
>
> NASA was apparently unhappy with this Congressional policy, however. Twice it sought changes in section 305, to come closer to the Defense

presumptively title is in the government, but the waiver authority is very broad. A well-documented study of the "property rights in inventions" provisions of the Space Act concluded that Congress neither intended presumptively to vest title in the government nor presumptively to waive title, rather, a flexible policy was intended,[10] which comes close to saying that Congress did not address itself to the problem, preferring to leave the detailed elaboration to the Administrator.

If, indeed, Congress intended a flexible title policy, it is far from clear that such flexibility is generated by blanket waivers in advance of the identification of any particular inventions.[11] One can refer to the words "or class of inventions made or which may be made" in Section 305 for support of the Administrator's authority to grant such waivers. However, a "class of inventions" does not necessarily mean anything which may be invented in the course of a large government-sponsored research project, nor are the words "which may be made" conclusive because Congress could have been referring to inventions which might be made after the Act was passed. NASA's

---

> Department's policy of handing over exclusive rights on tax payer-financed research and development to the private contractor. Both attempts failed. Now it is clear, NASA is trying to circumvent the clear Congressional mandate of section 305 by an administrative regulation.

U.S. Congress, Senate Select Committee on Small Business, Subcommittee on Monoply, *Economic Aspects of Government Patent Policies, Hearings,* 88th Congress, first session (Washington, D.C.: U.S. Government Printing Office, March 1963), p. 299.

[10] David Aaronson, "Legislative History of the Property Rights in Inventions Provisions of the National Aeronautics and Space Act of 1958." This paper appears as Appendix A in the report, Donald Watson and Mary Holman, *Evaluation of NASA's Patent Policies* (Washington, D.C.: George Washington University, Department of Economics, 1966). Aaronson's study comprises some 127 pages in the Watson and Holman report and traces the origin of the patent section of the Space Act, using original texts of Committee Prints, interviews with Committee and NASA counsel and other original unprinted materials.

[11] The National Aeronautics and Space Administration, NASA, is supposed to take the patents but they have a right to waive it and that is where we get into mischief under NASA because these people are trying to get to where they even waive the public's property rights before they know what they are waiving.

Comment of Senator Long, in the 1965 Senate Judiciary Committee Patent Hearings, *op. cit.,* p. 349.

reliance on the President's Patent Policy Statement of 1963,[12] for the right to grant blanket waivers, is equally ill-founded because while the statement by inference does contemplate blanket waivers of title at or before contract initiation,[13] surely Executive policy in general for all agencies cannot determine Congressional intent toward a particular agency, in this case, NASA. The disposal of property and patent powers of Congress makes any other conclusion untenable.[14]

In the context of this discussion, whether or not NASA has authority to grant advance waivers is less significant than the effect that such inadequate Congressional guidelines has had on agency administration of patent regulations. On the one hand, NASA continually seeks to convince its Congressional critics that, while its promulgated regulations may appear unduly liberal, its practices are much like those of the AEC.[15] On the other hand, it seeks to

---

[12] 14 C.F.R., section 1245.104 (a) (5) (May 1966), quotes the language of the Presidential Patent Policy statement. The NASA Office of The General Counsel discusses the issue of waivers in NASA, *A Review of NASA's Patent Program* (Washington, D.C.: NASA, Office of the General Counsel, March 1967) pp. 16–27.

President Kennedy's Memorandum and Statement of Government Patent Policy, 28 Fed. Rep., section 10,943 (October 12, 1963).

[13] In attempting to devise a consistent if nonuniform government patent policy, the statement deals with three different situations:

1. Cases where the best interests of the public would be served by retention of exclusive rights in the government.

2. ". . . where the purpose of the contract is to build upon existing knowledge or technology. . . .," in which case the contractor should be allowed the patent. 28 Fed. Reg. section 10,945.

3. "Where the commercial interests of the contractor are not sufficiently established to be covered by the criteria in situation 2 (above), the determination of rights shall be made by the Agency after the invention has been identified." 28 Fed. Reg. section 10,945. By implication, blanket disposition of government rights in advance of identification is contemplated in situation (2).

[14] Granted to Congress by U.S., *Constitution,* Article I, section 8, and Article IV, section 3.

[15] Examples of this dual policy may be found by contrasting the official NASA Congressional position in NASA, *A Review of NASA's Patent Program,* with a position paper delivered to NASA contractors by the Deputy General Counsel for Patent Matters, Robert Allnutt, "Recent Developments in NASA Patent Policy and Data Policies," Paper presented before a meeting of NASA contractors, February 1966.

Page 28 of the Patent Review Document states that "Of all contractor inventions reported, commercial rights have been waived in less than 4% of the cases, and advance waivers have been granted or recommended in only

convince contractors that its blanket waiver provisions are an important incentive to report their inventions to NASA. Maintenance of this dual policy has apparently failed to achieve either objective.

ADVANCE WAIVERS, WAIVERS, AND LICENSES AS INCENTIVES TO REPORT

The rationale for advance waivers is straightforward enough: "Advance waivers create a positive and self-serving incentive for the contractor to prepare and submit . . . reports,"[16] thereby making these reports available as part of NASA's technology bank for the TUP.

The same can be said for waivers granted to particular inventions after they have been identified: The incentive to report in order to obtain exclusive commercial rights exists insofar as a contractor believes that he will receive a waiver. A third incentive to report is thought to be provided by NASA's guarantee of an irrevocable, nonexclusive royalty-free license to any contractor who reports an invention whether he retains title or not.[17] The assumption here is that so long as the contractor knows that he can use the device, he will not be deterred from disclosing it.

Of course, these incentives exist only to the extent that they are made available. A contractor knows that if he reports the device, he will at least receive a license. If he files a petition for a blanket waiver, he has somewhat less than a 50 percent chance of receiving it; if he files a petition for waiver of title for a particular invention, he has about an 80 percent chance of receiving it.[18] In all cases the

---

118 contracts out of almost 13,200 contracts and subcontracts awarded by NASA since the advance waiver policy was established or in less than 1% of the cases." However, these low percentages are due to the fact that few contractors apply for waivers: of those who do, over 80 percent obtain regular waivers, 42 percent advance waivers.

The AEC is required by its enabling act to acquire title to all inventions in the atomic energy field. Atomic Energy Act of 1946, Public Law 79-585, 60 Stat. 919, 42 U.S.C.A. 2011, section 159 (as amended 1954). It also acquires rights in nonatomic fields unless the contractor has an established industrial position. Section 152.

For a general discussion see *Patents and Technical Data* (Washington, D.C.: The George Washington University Government Contracts Program, 1967), pp. 11–15.

[16] NASA, *A Review of NASA's Patent Program,* p. 22.

[17] 14 C.F.R., section 1245.113 (1966).

[18] As of June 30, 1968, NASA had acted finally on 516 individual petitions for waiver and has granted 423 and denied 93 for an 82 percent average.

contractor-inventor will receive some portion of the patent rights to any invention he reports, from a guaranteed nonexclusive license to title to a class or single invention.

None of these incentives appears to have had any noticeable effect on contractor reporting. To begin with, it should be noted that the number of patent applications arising out of government-financed R & D is generally very much smaller than arises out of that generated by private R & D in the same area of research. Christopher Freeman's study, in which he compared R & D performed by the electronics industry for DOD with R & D privately financed in the same industry, showed that a billion dollars of privately financed R & D yielded about 9,000 patent applications while a billion dollars of government-financed R & D yielded about 760 patent applications.[19] While lack of motivation in carrying an idea through to the point of commercial practice may account for much of this difference, lack of reporting is surely a large factor as well.

NASA's ratio of patents to R & D dollar investment has been lower than that of most government agencies. From 1964, when NASA began its liberal waiver policy, through 1966, contractor-reported innovations on NASA-sponsored research averaged 620 disclosures per billion dollars of R & D.[20] In 1964, NASA was receiving

Letter Gayle Parker to Samuel Doctors concerning *Minnesota Law Review* article, October 25, 1968, p. 8.

Apparently the percentage figure has varied little since 1966. As of December 31, 1966, NASA had received a total of 428 petitions for regular waiver, of which 267 were granted, 61 denied, 44 withdrawn and 56 still pending; 81 percent were granted, excluding those withdrawn or on which action had not been taken. As of December 31, 1966, NASA had received 341 petitions for advance waivers, of which 118 were granted or recommended, 162 were denied, 39 were withdrawn, and 21 still pending. NASA, *A Review of NASA's Patent Program,* p. 28.

[19] Christopher Freeman, "Research and Development in Electronic Capital Goods," *National Institute Economics Review* (November 1965), p. 73.

[20] "Disclosure" does not mean only potentially patentable inventions but all reportable inventions. NASA's disclosure rate has been rising:

Year	Contractor Disclosures	Estimated Extramural R & D Expenditures in billions of dollars	Disclosures per billion dollar expenditure
1964	1203	3.017	400
1965	2094	3.429	630
1966	3307	4.288	788
TOTAL	6604	10.734	Average: 606

610 disclosures per billion dollars while the average of all other government agencies was 990 disclosures/billion.[21] Among major R & D agencies for fiscal year 1965, the Navy ranked highest with 1,653 disclosures/billion; the number of disclosures was about the same for the Atomic Energy Commission (1,613), somewhat lower for the Army (1,400), very low for the Air Force (657), and even lower for NASA (388).[22]

The figures illustrate very clearly that there is no apparent correlation between present agency patent policies and disclosure rates. The Department of Defense, which generally allows its R & D contractors to take title to patented inventions, has both the highest and close to the lowest disclosure rates. The Atomic Energy Commission, which retains title to almost all patents on contractors' inventions, has one of the highest disclosure rates; and NASA, with a fairly liberal patent policy, is near the bottom. However, with the sole exception of NASA, these policies have not been established or administered with a view to maximizing transfer but rather to fulfill the mission requirements of the given agency, and NASA's present policies and practices have only been in effect since 1964.

NASA's lower rate of reporting might be accounted for in several ways: the rapid initiation of the NASA program, the esoteric technology of NASA, its emphasis on increments in precision rather than on new devices, and its highly mission-oriented R & D. On the other hand, NASA alone of all the agencies listed has a high-level

---

Data are from Watson and Holman, *op. cit.,* p. 36, *NASA, A Review of NASA's Patent Program,* p. 13, and U.S. Congress, Senate Committee on Aeronautical and Space Sciences, *NASA Authorization for Fiscal Year 1967,* 89th Congress, second session (Washington, D.C.: U.S. Government Printing Office, 1966), p. 4.

Experts differ on the validity of comparing the invention disclosure rates for a billion dollars of R & D in one agency with that of another agency. Many problems are involved in this type of comparison:

Some types of R & D are likely to be more productive of patentable inventions than others.

The relative value of different agency patent yields is not indicated.

There is often a reporting lag of several years between R & D spending and invention reporting.

[21] Watson and Holman, *op. cit.,* p. 34.

[22] U.S. Federal Council for Science and Technology, *Annual Report on Government Patent Policy* (Washington, D. C.: U.S. Government Printing Office, June 1967), pp. 40–57. The number of invention disclosures listed by the FCST is low particularly for NASA, because there is no allowance for the lag of several years between R & D funding and invention reporting.

policy to promote disclosure in order to disseminate inventions to others.[23] Further, if explanations are to be sought in the peculiar nature of NASA R & D, account must be taken of the fact that NASA contractors disclose significantly less often than do NASA employees.[24] It should be noted, however, that contractors have probably done more of the basic construction and systems work, out of which few innovations would come, than NASA employees.

An additional explanation stems from the fact that 70 percent of NASA's R & D is spent on the Apollo program, for which North American Aviation is the largest prime contractor.[25] While prime contractors are obligated to impose the New Technology Clause on first-tier subcontractors, there is no provision of penalties for lack of compliance by subcontractors, nor does the prime contractor have any incentive to enforce the clause against his subcontractors. By contracting for so much of its R & D through Apollo, and most of that through one large prime contractor, NASA probably has a greater proportion of its work done by the larger subcontractors, who are not oriented to reporting, than other agencies.

Whatever the causes of NASA's peculiarly low rate of reporting,

---

[23] The Department of Defense has long been indifferent to contractor reporting for purposes other than satisfying immediate mission objectives, receiving less than 40 percent of the reports that are by-products of its R & D program. President's Science Advisory Committee, *Science, Government, and Information* (Washington, D. C.: U.S. Government Printing Office, January 1963), p.41. Because NASA contractors are often also contractors with the Department of Defense, the impact of NASA's uniquely heavy emphasis on contractor reporting may have been diluted by contractor inertia.

[24] Solo found that for the period 1958–65, NASA employees reported nearly twice as many inventions per employee as did contractors' employees (where "employees" was defined as scientists or engineers). On the other hand, for 1965 itself, the rate of reporting was about the same. Robert Solo, *Patent Policy for Government Sponsored Research and Development,* Report prepared by NASA Administrator's Office (Washington, D.C.: NASA Headquarters, 1966), part II, p. 14. The Watson and Holman conclusions are similar; Watson and Holman, *op. cit.,* pp. 35–36. However, it may be that NASA employees are primarily concerned with component development while contractors are primarily concerned with system development. Without a detailed analysis of the functions performed by each, it would be difficult to pinpoint the exact reason for the disparity of reporting. However, with less than 20 percent of all NASA funds spent intramurally, contractor reporting seems quite low.

[25] Arthur D. Little, Inc., *Transfer of Aerospace Technology in the United States—A Critical Review* (Cambridge: A. D. Little, July 1966), p. 4.

the important fact is that agency patent policy has not proved relevant to the reporting function. The hypothesis that granting patent rights to a contractor will lead him to report is not supported by available data. The fact is that contractors are relatively indifferent to whether or not patent rights are granted. In the contract negotiation process, the price does not appear dependent upon whether a waiver of patent rights is granted.[26] Moreover, few NASA contractors have ever bothered to apply for waivers, either in advance of contract execution or after a particular device has been reported.[27]

This contractor indifference might be accounted for by the uncertainty of rewards: "For a contractor to acquire patent rights in an R & D contract is like getting a lottery ticket in a lottery with an unknown number of prizes of unknown value, awarded at unknown dates in the future."[28] Probably more important is the fact that NASA like the other agencies retains a nonexclusive, royalty-free license to use for government work any device to which it waives title.[29] This means that for purposes of bidding for future government contracts the patent has no value since any contractor can use the device without applying for a license or paying royalties.[30]

---

[26] Watson and Holman, *op. cit.*, p. 163. See also Solo, *op. cit.*, p. 41: "The strongest impression to be gotten from an examination of the record of waived inventions is of the indifference, the general, pervasive sometimes the absolute *indifference* on the part of the contractor to the commercial potentialities of inventions made under government R & D contracts."

[27] Of 8,065 reported inventions as of December 31, 1966, contractors petitioned for waivers on 428 items, or 5 percent of those available. Of 13,200 prime contracts or first- or second-tier subcontracts, advance waivers were requested 341 times, or 2.5 percent of the time. NASA, *A Review of NASA's Patent Program*, p. 28.

[28] Watson and Holman, *op. cit.*, p. 164.

[29] 14 C.F.R., section 1245.107 (May 1966).

[30] Abolishing this reserved license would not give the contractor much less incentive because even patents, the product of private R & D, are usually irrelevant to a contractor's bidding strategy: (The Comptroller General's construction of Court of Claims—Patent Cases Act of 1958, 28 U.S.C.A. 1498 as amended, 1960) has led government procurement agencies to disregard possible patent infringements in selecting among bids and proposals. *Herbert Cooper Co.*, unpublished division of the Comptroller General, B-136916 (August 25, 1958). Also see the discussion in Gerald Mossinghoff and Robert Allnutt, "Patent Infringement in Government Procurement: A Remedy Without a Right?" *Notre Dame Law Review*, XLII (October 1966), pp. 5–28. If the decision of the Comptroller General since *Herbert Cooper* was reversed, then it is arguable that the government-retained license should be abolished

If, on the other hand, a contractor does not report his inventions, he can reveal them in later bids and proposals as being helpful to future government work. In this way failure to report may give him an advantage over his competitors when the next government R & D contract is let.

Again, a contractor may report his invention to DOD and not NASA, where a number of inventions may have arisen partly from NASA funding and partly from that sponsored by the DOD, since contractors may obtain title to DOD-supported inventions almost as a matter of course.[31] In this way, a contractor may follow his self-interest and not report and yet still not consider he has acted dishonestly or illegally. It is often quite difficult to determine which agency funding is primarily responsible for any given invention since projects sponsored by NASA and DOD may overlap and even use the same technologists at different times.

Further, there is no reporting requirement for any inventions produced under independent or overhead R & D funding and this type of funding is apparently responsible for a significant number of inventions.[32]

To be sure, if contractors foresaw potential commercial use for

---

to provide an incentive in patent holding to report. It is unlikely that Congress will adopt such a position, however. See Appendix C for a more complete discussion.

31 But see International Economic Policy Association, *U.S. Government-Financed Research and Development: Policies and Practices in Protection and Use of Results* (Washington, D. C.: IEPA, June 1967), pp. 14–15, for a quite different interpretation of the effect of the Presidential Patent Policy Message on DOD patent policy.

32 Chalmers Sherwin and Raymond Isenson, "First Interim Report on Project Hindsight," Report to the Director of Defense Research and Engineering (Washington, D.C.: June 1966, revised October 1966). Independent research and development of other overhead R & D is funded by federal agencies (notably the Department of Defense and NASA) on the theory that higher commercial corporate profits are not available to the space/defense contractor to reinvest in "company" R & D, and that such investment is essential to maintain a competitive position in the rapidly changing technological space/defense market. U.S. Department of Defense, Letter to the General Accounting Office Explaining DOD Policy as to Rights in Technical Data Resulting from Independent Research and Development, Defense Procurement Circular #22 (Washington, D. C.: DOD or GAO, January 29, 1965). Results of this overhead R & D funding, although largely federally supported, need not be disclosed to government agencies. ASPR, section 9.200 (April 1965) and NASA PR, section 9.101-4 (June 1966). See Appendix C for further discussion.

a device, as opposed to future government use only, then they would have some incentive to report and obtain patent rights. As pointed out in the following section, however, with the exception of small, innovative firms, contractors seldom commercialize the few innovations on which they do apply for waivers.

CONTRACTOR UTILIZATION OF WAIVED INVENTIONS

As observed in the introduction to this chapter, to the extent that contractors themselves commercialize inventions on which they are given patent rights, a formal technology transfer system such as the TUP is bypassed since transfer has already been accomplished within the company. Thus, the additional factor of intracompany transfer must be weighed in determining the desirability of a liberal waiver policy.

The overall utilization rate of inventions to which NASA has waived title is thought to be about 11.5 percent.[33] But utilization is an elusive concept. If it means the number of inventions successfully applied commercially, rather than the number of inventions on which commercial development has merely taken place, then only seven inventions can be said to have been commercialized by NASA contractors between 1959 and 1965.[34] This is about 4.5 percent of the number of waivers granted in that period. These very low figures should be contrasted with the estimated 60 percent of patents resulting from private R & D which are commercially utilized.[35]

These figures must of course be received with some reservation. For one thing, NASA is of relatively recent origin, and commercial development of a device may take considerably longer than the period during which NASA has existed.[36] Also it is probably true

---

33 Watson and Holman, *op. cit.*, pp. 148–49.

34 Solo, *op. cit.*, p. 34.

35 Donald Watson, Harold Bright, and Arthur Burns, "Federal Patent Policy in Contracts for Research and Development," *Patent, Trademark, and Copyright Journal of Research and Education,* IV, No. 4 (Winter 1960), p. 377.

36 While the development rate varies enormously depending on the innovation, a rough guide would be 14 years or longer from conception to industrial applications. Frank Lynn, *An Investigation of the Rate of Development and Diffusion of Technology in Our Modern Society,* Report to the U.S. National Commission on Technology, Automation and Economic Progress. (Washington, D. C.: U.S. Government Printing Office, 1966); Edwin Mansfield, "Diffusion of Technological Change," *Reviews of Data on Research and Development,* No. 31, NSF 61-52 (Washington, D.C.: U.S. Government Printing Office, October 1961).

that government-sponsored research produces innovations which are more expensive to develop commercially than those which are the product of private research.[37] Still, the rate is unquestionably low.

It is possible that the rate would be even lower had NASA not attempted, in its advance waiver regulations, to distinguish between contractors having the potential to utilize their inventions and those lacking such potential. Only the former are likely to be encouraged to report by the incentives of patent rights and waivers, and by definition only the former are likely themselves to commercialize the invention. NASA regulations impose six conditions on the grant of advance waivers: the relevant one here is that "The work called for by the contract is in a field of technology in which the contractor has acquired technical competence . . . directly related to an area in which the contractor has an established nongovernmental commercial position."[38]

Even with this limitation of "commercial position," advance waivers are a very blunt instrument compared with waivers on particular inventions. While it is possible to assess a particular contractor's ability to develop a given invention, it is difficult to make this kind of judgment on advance waivers because there is no way to predict what inventions may start as by-products. Probably many inventions to which contractors retain title under advance waiver do not relate in any meaningful way to the contractor's "established commercial position."

Not only is this distinction not useful as applied to advance waivers, but the distinction itself is not a useful one. What, after all, is an "established commercial position"? If a literal interpretation is applied, General Electric, General Motors, and other large industrial firms will be able to show a commercial position in many fields whereas smaller companies will not. But the large corporations and the large aerospace corporations in particular appear to show a very low utilization rate whereas smaller companies appear to commercialize the technology developed under federal funding more readily. Aerospace companies and the aerospace divisions of large diversified

---

[37] National Planning Association, *Technology Transfer and Industrial Innovation,* Unpublished Report prepared for the National Science Foundation by Sumner Myers, *et al.* (Washington, D.C.: NSF, February 1967).

[38] 14 C.F.R., section 1245.104 (a) (6) (May 1966).

corporations act very much alike when it comes to utilization of NASA inventions. There appears to be very little intracompany transfer between the military/space divisions and their commercial counterparts.[39] Thus, although aerospace companies and aerospace divisions of large corporations received over 90 percent of the prime contracts with NASA,[40] by January 1, 1966, they had obtained waivers on only 97 inventions, compared to the 52 waived inventions held by smaller companies. More important, of these 97 inventions only 9 are in commercial use, or about 9 percent; an equal number of inventions is used commercially by small companies, which is about 17 percent of waivers held by these companies.[41] While the numbers are small, they substantiate in part the contention that greater commercialization is undertaken by smaller companies. Further substantiation is given by several studies which have shown that smaller companies tend to be more innovative generally, and in particular tend to have less difficulty in transferring space/defense technology to their civilian operations than do large aerospace contractors.[42]

---

39 Merton Peck and Frederick Scherer, *The Weapons Acquisition Process: An Economic Analysis* (Boston: Division of Research, Graduate School of Business Administration, Harvard University, 1962), pp. 128–37. Aside from possible physical isolation of the various divisions, the managers of large aerospace divisions or subsidiaries often act as "profit centers" in that maximum personal advancement comes from division or subsidiary profits, not from reporting new innovations to other divisions or subsidiaries of the same company.

40 NASA-supplied data indicate that over 90 percent of the R & D funding in fiscal 1965 was given to corporations listed among the 500 largest by *Fortune*: Most were among the 100 largest. See Appendix B for a list of the 100 largest NASA contractors.

41 Watson and Holman, *op. cit.*, p. 150.

42 Daniel Hamberg, *R & D Essays on the Economics of Research and Development* (New York: Random House, 1963), parts 1–3; Edwin Mansfield, "Technical Change and the Rate of Imitation," *Econometrics,* XXIX (October 1961), pp. 741–66, and "Size of Firms, Market Structure and Innovation," *Journal of Political Economy,* LXXXI, No. 6 (December 1963), pp. 556–76. Edward Roberts and Herbert Wainer, "Technology Transfer and Entrepreneurial Success," Paper presented to the Twentieth National Conference on the Administration of Research, Miami Beach, Florida, October 26, 1966, and Daniel Shimshoni, "Aspects of Scientific Entrepreneurship," Unpublished Doctoral Dissertation, Kennedy School of Government, Harvard University, 1966. The spin-off firms studied by Roberts, Wainer, and Shimshoni reported 40 percent of their sales were in the commercial market after 5 years, as compared with little or no commercialization of space/defense technology by the large space/defense contractors.

The distinction that should be drawn by the regulations should single out companies which intend to commercialize and have demonstrated commercialization capability. There need be no stipulation that smaller companies should be given a preference; rather, if my contention is correct, then smaller contractors will receive a disproportionate number of waivers simply because they appear to be more innovative and more successful in commercializing space/defense technology. The distinction should only be applied to waivers on individual inventions; advance waivers should be abolished.

An aid to making such a distinction would be the placement of Technology Utilization personnel in positions where they would render the initial decisions on applications for waivers. The petitions for waiver are currently processed through the NASA Inventions and Contributions Board (ICB). The necessary distinction between a contractor with a genuine intent to commercialize and one without such an intent is a most difficult one for the ICB to draw because it has little contact with the companies applying for waivers and because the ICB is unlikely to have the necessary expertise properly to appraise the arguments made by the contractors.

Technology Utilization personnel would bring to the waiver decision process more knowledge of company utilization and more experience with large numbers of companies; there would be a concern with technology transfer in the processing of waivers which Board members are not likely to have. With TU personnel in almost continual contact with most NASA contractors and with their interest in promoting commercialization, it is likely they would be in an excellent position to make an initial assessment of the petition subject to review by the ICB.[43]

WAIVERS AS A BARRIER TO COMMERCIALIZATION BY OTHERS

While a liberal waiver policy does not seem to encourage any significant increase in reporting or to encourage direct commercialization by the innovating contractor,[44] it does have a negative impact on the output function.

---

43 Since early 1967, the NASA TU Program has had a single representative on the ICB but little use has been made of TU field experience with NASA contractors or with commercial industry.

44 Nor does a liberal waiver policy seem to provide the basis for another justification often advanced in its favor, namely, that by waiving rights the

Whenever NASA waives its rights to an invention, the resulting patent remains with the inventing contractor and necessarily discourages others from using or developing the device. NASA has taken several steps to minimize this obstruction in the transfer system. The first, already discussed, is the NASA decision to grant advance waivers only to firms showing an established commercial position. Refusal to waive rights to any other contractors increases the number of inventions available for the use of nonaerospace firms. The same recommendations made earlier apply here also: If the distinction is drawn so that waivers are granted only to firms with demonstrated capacity and intent to utilize particular innovations, then the obstruction to transfer represented by advance or regular waivers would be removed.

Another step taken by NASA to minimize this obstruction has been to attach a number of conditions to its waivers in the form of "March-In" rights. The innovating contractor's title will revert to NASA under the following conditions:

1. The invention is not brought "to the point of practical application" within three years of the granting of a U.S. patent; or,

2. The patent is needed for public health; or,

3. The contractor has refused to license any responsible applicant, either royalty-free or at reasonable royalties, more than three years after he has obtained a U.S. patent.[45]

"best" contractors will be obtained by the government or that contractors will be encouraged to assign more creative personnel for government-sponsored work. While examination of these justifications is beyond the scope of this book, there is no evidence that the Atomic Energy Commission or NASA obtains less results from contractors than the Department of Defense, U.S. Congress, Senate, Select Committee on Small Business, Subcommittee on Monopoly, *Patent Policies of Government Departments and Agencies, Conference on Federal Patent Policies,* 86th Congress, second session (Washington, D.C.: U.S. Government Printing Office, June 1960) (Committee Print).

But see U.S. Congress, House of Representatives, Committee on Science and Astronautics, Subcommittee on Patents and Scientific Inventions, *Ownership of Inventions Developed in The Course of Federal Space Research Contracts, Report,* 87th Congress, second session (Washington, D.C.: U.S. Government Printing Office, 1962) (Committee Print), or Helge Holst, "Government Patent Policy—Its Impact on Contractor Cooperation and Widespread Use of Government Sponsored Technology," *Patent, Trademark, and Copyright Journal of Research and Education,* IX, No. 2 (Summer 1965), pp. 273–96 for a quite different view of federal patent policy.

[45] 14 C.F.R., section 1245.108 (1966).

The rationale behind these regulations is clearly sound. If the inventing contractor fails to develop his invention commercially or refuses to make it available to others after three years, then the device is freed for use by others. NASA has at the present time revoked 23 waivers on single inventions, but not one invention held under advance waiver has been revoked.[46] Since it has been only a few years since these regulations were adopted (1964), this low revocation rate, as compared to the very high nonutilization rate, is not surprising. It appears unlikely, however, that NASA will expend the necessary resources to keep track of the state of development of all its waived inventions; it seems even more unlikely that NASA will be inclined to disrupt harmonious contractor relationships with many revocations. These provisions will probably be invoked, if at all, only at the urging of a third party interested in the device.

A related question is, What happens to the license granted the inventor-contractor should his waiver rights be revoked? NASA regulations described such licenses as "irrevocable."[47] The Patent Counsel's Office interprets this as meaning that even if the patent is revoked, the contractor still retains his royalty-free, nonexclusive license. Such an interpretation presents an unnecessary barrier to utilization of the device, for NASA may later wish to grant an exclusive license to a third party as an incentive to commercialize the innovation. If the contractor has retained his nonexclusive license, the "exclusive" commercial rights granted to the third party in fact are not really exclusive, and the latter will know that if he develops the device and makes it successful, another may take advantage of his development work. Further, this license to the contractor may undercut his incentive to commercialize since he knows that even if he fails to put forth his best efforts, he retains a potentially valuable nuisance interest.

If NASA ceased to grant these licenses automatically to inventing contractors, would the advantage to the output side be overbalanced

---

[46] As of December 31, 1966, there were 267 waivers granted on individual inventions: Revocation of 23 is about 9 percent of this total. There were also as of December 31, 1966, 53 inventions held under advanced waiver. Figures from NASA, *A Review of NASA's Patent Program,* p. 28. Revocations occurred because the contractor did not file the prerequisite patent application. No waiver has yet been revoked for failure to develop the invention. Letter of Gayle Parker to Samuel Doctors, referred to in footnote 18.

[47] 14 C.F.R., section 1245.113 (May 1966).

by the disadvantage to the input side in the form of a reduced incentive to report? The answer to that question depends on the clarity of NASA's waiver policy. If NASA makes it clear that any inventing contractor who can show commercial interest and potential for one of his inventions may obtain a waiver (for that invention only), then removal of the license should make little difference. A contractor would be encouraged to report by the present license policy only if he himself wanted to utilize the device commercially; and if he could obtain the patent in that case, he would have no need of the license.

Since NASA patent policy exists in an industrial milieu created and dominated by DOD, no matter how clear NASA waiver policy is made, it is unlikely that more than marginal improvement in contractor reporting rates can be expected unless DOD adopts a policy of selective grant of title to contractors based on their intent to commercialize. Nevertheless, NASA as the leader among federal agencies in promoting technology transfer may be considered to have an implied duty to formulate and administer a policy designed to maximize transfer within its present operational structure.

ALTERNATIVE INCENTIVES TO REPORT

If advance waivers are abolished, irrevocable licenses terminated, and regular waivers administered so as to allow title to inventing contractors only where they can demonstrate commercial potential, what incentive will there be for contractors to report? The answer is that there will not be very much. The full answer is that there will not be very much less than the present incentive, for, as I have argued, the typical contractor regards patent rights as being virtually irrelevant to his disclosure strategy. Patent rights act as an incentive to report only where commercial rights are important, and it is in just those situations that the recommendations I have made would allow a waiver of those rights.

More reporting probably can be obtained but not through a more liberal waiver policy. The contractual penalties imposed by the New Technology Clause certainly do not seem to have promoted much disclosure either. While a comprehensive examination of the problems involved with each suggestion is beyond the scope of this study, I would like to indicate a few avenues as yet unexplored or only partially explored.

NASA could institute a program of payments to reward contractors' employees for making and reporting of particularly useful innovations. Thus far, NASA has not initiated such a program with any of its contractors although authority to do so exists under section 306 of the Space Act.[48] NASA has maintained an award system for its own employees, whose disclosure rate as noted above is very much higher than that of contractors' employees.

My second suggestion, related to the first, is that NASA seek to channel reports directly from contractors' employees to the NASA TUP, thus bypassing company channels. As Solo has observed, individual inventors already have an incentive to disclose inventions in that their professional prestige is enhanced; it is the recognition by higher administrative officials in the company, including patent counsel, that it is in the company's interest not to disclose whatever can successfully be hidden, that acts as a barrier to disclosure.[49]

Third, NASA could keep track of the rate of disclosure for its various contractors. Current records show that the rate varies much more than can be justified entirely by different types of R & D work.[50] As a result of keeping such records and referring to them when a contractor seeks a new government project, the incentive to report can perhaps be increased.

The alternative of direct payment to NASA contractors is being tried by NASA. The results are still insufficient for a complete evaluation, but it does appear that direct payments of nominal sums will not alone promote a large quantity of quality reporting.[51]

Patent Policy and the Output Function

NASA LICENSE POLICY

A major effect of an agency's patent policy on the output function has already been noted. A liberal waiver policy without significant contractor commercialization impedes the dissemination and use of the technology by others. Patent policy can affect the output function in a positive manner as well, provided that title to inventions is not waived. Licensing without royalties, or even in some cases

---

[48] 42 U.S.C.A. 2451, section 306 (1964). NASA recently issued regulations indicating that the award program had been extended to contractor employees. 32 Fed. Reg. section 11,262 (August 1967).

[49] Solo, *op. cit.*, part III, p. 9.

[50] *Ibid.*, part II, p. 16.

[51] See Chapter 7, footnotes 24 and 25.

exclusive licensing, may act as an incentive for third parties to commercialize government-developed technology.

NASA describes its license policy as follows:

> [NASA] regulations provided for broad royalty-free, non-exclusive licensing during the first two years after a patent is issued to NASA. After the two year period, if the benefits of the inventions have not been brought to the public, NASA will grant an exclusive license to exploit the invention. If, however, the invention has been commercially worked during the two years, the patent will continue to be available on a non-exclusive basis. This licensing policy differs from that of other government agencies in that in cases where utilization will thus be made possible, the granting of exclusive licenses will be used as an incentive to commercial working of dormant government owned patents. . . .[52]

This statement by the NASA General Counsel's Office is somewhat misleading in that the license denoted as "exclusive" has a number of significant limitations attaching to it. If the originating party was a NASA contractor, this license is subject to an irrevocable, royalty-free, contractor nonexclusive license.[53] The term of the limited exclusive license is not necessarily coextensive with that of the patent, but is a negotiable item between the applicant and the Administrator.[54] Further, the regulations provide March-In Rights; the Administrator may revoke the license if the licensee fails to use "his continuing best efforts to work the invention."[55] "Best efforts" are to be defined in the negotiations between the applicant and NASA. This limited exclusive license is also subject to a royalty-free, nontransferable right to practice the invention by or on behalf of the government.[56] Finally, the license is nontransferable except to a successor in interest of the licensee.[57]

Despite these restrictions, which are not usually associated with the grant of an exclusive license by a private party, NASA's grant of a limited exclusive license does carry with it the right to exclude unlicensed commercial practice of the device. In this respect it may offer significantly greater incentive to industry to commercialize

52 NASA, *A Review of NASA's Patent Program,* p. 32.
53 14 C.F.R., section 1245.113 (May 1966).
54 14 C.F.R., section 1245.205 (c) (3) (October 1966).
55 14 C.F.R., section 1245.205 (c) (6) (October 1962).
56 14 C.F.R., section 1245.206 (c) (4) (October 1962).
57 14 C.F.R., section 1245.205 (c) (5) (October 1962).

certain of NASA's inventions. Before this hypothesis is examined, there is the initial question of what kinds of licenses are statutorily or even Constitutionally permissible for NASA or for any government agency to grant.

EXCLUSIVE LICENSE, ALIENATION OF A NONEXISTENT RIGHT?

In descending order of generality, three questions will be analyzed: Does government ownership of a patent necessarily eliminate, for the government and for its licensees, the right to exclude others from using the device? If not, does alienation of this right to exclude amount to a "disposal of property" requiring Congressional authorization? If so, has Congress delegated such authority to NASA?

The first of these questions is a Constitutional one: On what Constitutional authority can the federal government justify granting to itself the right to exclude others from the practice of certain inventions? The question has long remained not only unanswered but for the most part unasked, largely because it has been the policy of all government agencies not to enforce their patents. The only case to date in which the government has sought to enforce a patent appears to be *Tektronix* v. *United States* (1965).[58] In this case, the government had been sued for infringement and had counterclaimed for infringement of one of its own patents. Although presented with the argument on the Constitutional issue, The Court of Claims avoided it by holding the government estopped from enforcing its patents due to its century-long policy of not enforcing them. In the absence of special circumstances justifying enforcement or some kind of notice to the public that government-owned patents would be enforced, the government was held to have implicitly licensed all users.[59] A series of opinions from the United States Attorney General has more directly faced the Constitutional issue with the conclusion that the assignment of a patent to the government is not equivalent to a dedication to the public and that the government is thus able to enforce its patents.[60]

It is difficult to find Constitutional justification for the Attorney

[58] *Tektronix* v. *U.S.,* 351 Fed. Rep. 2d 630 (1965) (Ct. of Claims).

[59] *Ibid.,* 633. The court relied on *Buford* v. *Houtz,* 133 U.S. 320 (1889) where the Supreme Court held that the custom of allowing grazing animals on government land implicitly licensed such use of the land.

[60] 39 Op. Att'y Gen. 425 (1938); 38 Op. Att'y Gen. 164 (1936). Even here, the question is merely raised and then answered by relying on an earlier opinion

General's conclusion. The Constitution grants to Congress the "power to dispose of and make all needful rules and regulations respecting the territory or other property belonging to the United States."[61] This provision is not helpful because the question is whether the government's taking title to the patent does not necessarily remove its "property" attributes. In other words, the government first has to create the property by granting a right to exclude, and it is that power of creation that is questioned.

The Constitution also states that "Congress shall have power . . . to promote the progress of science and useful arts, by securing for limited times to authors and inventors the exclusive right to their writings and discoveries."[62] Can the United States consider itself an "inventor" entitled to exclusive rights? Certainly the policies of the patent provision are not applicable to the United States as an inventor: The government needs neither the incentive to do research nor the incentive to disclose the results of that research thought to be provided by the grant of a right to exclude others for 17 years. Nor can it be argued that the government should be rewarded by the grant of exclusive rights to itself. Granting an exclusive license to nongovernmental third parties may, however, be an effective way "to promote the progress of science and useful arts," particularly when these licenses may be the only effective means to transfer government-developed inventions to private industry.[63]

It seems exceedingly strange that the government may grant to third parties a right to exclude which it does not itself possess, even though the policies behind the patent power suggest this conclusion. Indeed, it seems clear that this conclusion is not valid, for potential

---

by Harlan Stone, 34 Op. Att'y Gen. 320 (1924). Stone in the latter opinion gave his view that Executive departments could license (revocably and nonexclusively) private parties for government-held patents. The former two opinions reason that the grant of a license makes sense only if the patent has not been dedicated to general use, and do not discuss the Constitutional foundations of the power they approve.

61 U.S. *Constitution,* Article IV, section 3.

62 U.S. *Constitution,* Article I, section 8.

63 Early criticisms of government patent ownership could not foresee this beneficial use of the power to exclude because the government was not foreseen as engaging in technology transfer. Thomas Ewing, "Government Owned Patents," *Journal of the Patent Office Society,* X, No. 4 (January 1928), pp. 149–56. Frank Wille, "Government Ownership of Patents," *Fordham Law Review,* XII, No. 2 (May 1943), pp. 105–29.

licensees are not "inventors" to whom the federal government has delegated authority to grant exclusive rights. The granting of such rights to noninventors would be the kind of use of monopoly power by the sovereign so disliked by the framers of the Constitution when they passed the limited patent power.[64]

Since the most desirable policy probably cannot be recognized (i.e., allowing the government to grant the right to exclude even though it cannot exercise the right itself), the patent provision should be construed to include the United States as an "inventor." As long as the opinion in *Tektronix* is upheld, then the same distinction can in fact be drawn: Since the government possesses the power to exclude, it may grant the power to third parties but is estopped by long usage from exercising the power itself.[65]

If one assumes that exclusive licenses on government patents are Constitutionally permissible, then to whom is such authority delegated, to the Congress or to each Executive department? Does conveying the right to exclude amount to a "disposal of property" over which Congress has power? It might be argued that the true value of a patent to the government lies in its defensive capabilities, that is, the fact that it protects the government from infringement actions by other inventors holding similar patents. Indeed the longstanding policy of the government never to enforce its patents reinforces that conception. Hence, the argument continues, as long as an agency retains sufficient control over the licensee to ensure that the government-owned patent is employed in furthering a legitimate agency program, the issuance of a limited exclusive license is a proper use or exercise of government property rights rather than

[64] One cannot be certain what the framers had in mind because the patent power seems to have provoked little or no debate. Carl Fenning, "The Origin of the Patent and Copyright Clause of the Constitution," *Georgetown Law Journal,* XVII, No. 2 (February 1929), pp. 109–17. However, it does seem clear that the original proposal was always in its limited form. Max Farrand, *Record of the Federal Convention of 1787* (New Haven: Yale University Press, 1911), vol. 2, pp. 321–22, where the provisions in question are first introduced.

[65] The result is not quite the same, for under this interpretation Congress or the Executive branch could revoke the implied license by the government by giving public notice. A related problem is whether the granting of an exclusive license gives the public the kind of notice required by the *Tektronix'* rationale. Peter Berger, "Utilization or Dispensation—Suggestions for the Government's Patent Procurement Program," *Journal of the Patent Office Society,* XLVIII, No. 7 (July 1966), p. 460; Watson and Holman, *op. cit.,* p. 89.

an unauthorized disposal of these rights.[66] It is difficult to understand just what remains of the property rights inherent in a patent without the power to exclude. There is only the right to practice the invention immune from infringement suits by others, which could as easily be afforded by publication rather than by patent.[67] Surely if the government published rather than patented its inventions, there would be no property created, other than a copyright granted by a separate statute. Hence, unless patents are not to be considered property at all, alienation of the right to exclude must be a disposal of property.

This argument is implied in the leading exposition on executive power to dispose of government patent rights, an opinion (in 1924) by the then Attorney General Harlan Fiske Stone.[68] In considering the power of the Secretary of the Navy to grant revocable, nonexclusive licenses, Stone implicitly assumes first, that the federal government does have the power to exclude, and second, that disposal of all patent rights would be a disposal of property requiring explicit Congressional authorization. Proceeding from there, Stone sets forth a number of distinctions, one being that a nonexclusive license "does not dispose . . . of the patent monopoly. . . . The patentee still retains all the elements or characteristics of the property or monopoly. He can still assign, sell, exclude others from making, using, or selling, and can sue for infringement—*and these are all the rights which a patent confers.*"[69]

To say that granting a nonexclusive license does not dispose of the patent monopoly is not precise, for each nonexclusive license does reduce the patent monopoly and, given a finite number of potential users, a number of such licenses could eventually completely erode the monopoly. The distinction can nonetheless be made, and if it were, exclusive licensing would be a disposition of property whereas nonexclusive licensing would not be.

66 While some such authority to use government property in executing the laws might well be implied in Article II, Congress has explicitly assigned such authority to the head of each department over the "custody, use, and preservation of the . . . property appertaining to it." 5 U.S.C.A. 301 (Supp. 1966).

67 Publication does not afford exactly the same immunity from future infringement suits that a patent does. Solo, *op. cit.*, pp. 28–32, and Berger, *op. cit.*, p. 461.

68 Opinion of the Hon. Harlan Fiske Stone, 34 Op. Att'y Gen. 320 (1924).

69 *Ibid.*, p. 325.

Assuming that Congressional authorization is necessary, it is arguable whether NASA has the necessary power to license exclusively. Section 305 (g) of the Space Act grants very broad authority to the Administrator to "determine . . . the terms and conditions upon which licenses will be granted. . . ."[70] It might be urged either that such vague language confers the necessary authority on NASA or that long-standing Congressional acquiescence in various Executive departments' license policies has delegated sufficient authority to NASA as well as other agencies.[71] On the other hand, examination of the literature reveals that only one agency has ever licensed any of its patents exclusively, the Tennessee Valley Authority.[72] Congressional acquiescence has not extended to exclusive licensing. Similarly had Congress intended so radically to alter prevailing government licensing practice in Section 305, this would probably have been stated, for "it is clearly the intent of Congress that basic guidelines of government patent policy should be determined by Congress."[73]

---

[70] 42 U.S.C.A. 2451, section 203 (b) (3) (1964) provides that the ". . . [Administrator may] sell and otherwise dispose of real and personal property (including patents and rights thereunder)." However, this section of the enabling act is specifically tied to property as defined under the Management and Disposal of Government Property Act of 1949, 63 Stat. 378, 49 U.S.C.A. 472 (1964). This act is limited to "excess property," i.e., not needed for discharge of an agency's responsibilities and requires approval for GSA "surplus." 40 U.S.C.A. 472 (g) (1964). In view of the declaration in President Kennedy's Patent Policy statement to the effect that government-owned inventions constitute a "valuable" national resource, 28 Fed. Reg., section 10,942 (1963), such a determination that patent rights constitute "excess property" or surplus would be inappropriate.

[71] See for example *United States* v. *Midwest Oil Co.,* 236 U.S. 459 (1915).

[72] The Tennessee Valley Authority's statutory mandate to dispose of patent rights is at least as vague as NASA's; it is authorized "to grant such licenses thereunder under its patents, as shall be authorized by the Board." Tennessee Valley Authority Act of 1933, Public Law 73–17, 48 Stat. 58, 16 U.S.C.A. 831 (d) (1) (as amended 1964).

The Authority has granted one exclusive license for a term of five years to a private firm and five such licenses to employee-inventors. No test of Board authority has ever arisen, and the TVA has apparently decided not to issue any other exclusive licenses. U.S. Congress, Senate Committee on the Judiciary, Subcommittee on Patents, Trademarks, and Copyrights, *Patent Practices of the Tennessee Valley Authority,* 86th Congress, first session (Washington, D.C.: U.S. Government Printing Office, 1959), pp. 199, 210 (Committee Print). The literature I examined fails to disclose any other agency grants of exclusive licenses to third parties.

[73] Statement of Senator McClellan, in 1965 Hearings of Senate Sub-

NASA LICENSE POLICY AS A SPUR TO UTILIZATION

The visible effects of NASA patent policy on the output function have not been very impressive. As of January 1, 1967, NASA had title to 488 patents, with about 746 pending.[74] Of that number, only 365 patents and 509 applications were listed as available for licensing.[75] NASA had granted 80 nonexclusive "licenses" on 19 patent applications, and two exclusive licenses, one of which has since been terminated because the licensee (Union Carbide) could not justify additional development costs.[76] This means that about 10 percent of NASA-held available patents were licensed in 1966.[77] Of these, about 11 percent were in commercial use.[78] Thus, assuming minimal use by nonlicensees,[79] commercialization has so far been successful for about 1 percent of NASA-held patents.

With only one outstanding exclusive license, comparisons between exclusive and nonexclusive licenses would be meaningless. Still, it seems reasonable to speculate that the added incentive of exclusive commercial rights would spur on faster development. NASA, possibly unsure of its authority, has turned down several requests for exclusive licenses.[80] If given explicit statutory authorization, NASA could grant more licenses and perhaps significantly increase the utilization rate.

To be sure, the patent incentive to commercialize a device provided by an exclusive license is no greater than that offered a contractor who has been waived title to the patent. The difference is that exclusive licensees can be selected from companies more likely to commercialize, that is, those with a proven record of success in the commercial market for the given class of inventions or those who are able to demonstrate a clear intent to enter the given com-

---

committee on Patents, Trademarks, and Copyrights, *op. cit.,* part 1, p. 1.

74 NASA, *A Review of NASA's Patent Program,* p. 13.

75 *Ibid.,* p. 29.

76 *Idem.*

77 Watson and Holman, *op. cit.,* p. 68.

78 This figure extrapolates the 1965 estimate obtained by Watson and Holman, *op. cit.,* pp. 68–101, through questionnaires to licensees.

79 The assumption is quite reasonable (despite widespread knowledge that the government will not enforce its patents against nonlicensed users) because the license costs nothing and because NASA may well supply the licensee with supplementary information. Solo, *op. cit.,* p. 35.

80 Watson and Holman, *op. cit.,* p. 91.

mercial market.[81] Moreover, companies can be selected on the basis of their interest in a particular device as opposed to being granted an advance waiver whatever inventions may turn up. It is for these reasons, as well as those noted earlier, that the granting of advance waivers ought to be discontinued, and more emphasis placed on exclusive licensing to noncontractors rather than on individual waivers for contractor-inventors.

EXCLUSIVE LICENSING AS A BARRIER TO USE BY OTHERS

Just as granting a contractor exclusive commercial rights prevents others from using innovations, the grant of an exclusive license may prevent the widest possible use of technical information. NASA has taken two steps to minimize this bar to use by others. Present NASA policy is to make patents available to all potential users on a nonexclusive, royalty-free basis: If after two years, no one has "worked" the device, then it is available for exclusive licensing.[82] The reasoning underlying the regulation is clear. The greatest possible commercial use is most desirable, and if the device is attractive enough to be developed without the incentive of an exclusive license, then that goal can be achieved; if the device is not so alluring, then the less desirable alternative of offering exclusive rights is to be explored. Given an effective information dissemination program so that potential developers can learn of the device, the two-year waiting period is NASA's measurement of the appeal of its innovations.

While the rationale of promoting greatest possible commercial usage is sound, two suggestions would facilitate the realization of this goal. First, the idea that the passage of a period of time is an

---

[81] The evidence that smaller firms will be more successful in commercializing space/defense innovations is less impressive than that supporting the proposition advanced earlier, that smaller firms will utilize innovations they themselves have produced as NASA contractors. See footnote 42. Representative John W. Wydler polled subscribers to one of NASA's Regional Dissemination Centers and found a "high degree of success reported by small businessmen who subscribed to the programs. All of them commented that the availability of advanced NASA research material and information is invaluable as each of their firms is too small to maintain its own research and development department. These small businessmen constituted fully half of those 10 reporting financial gain." U.S. Congress, House of Representatives, Committee on Science and Astronautics, Subcommittee on Advanced Research and Technology, *1967 NASA Authorization, Hearings,* 89th Congress, first session. H.R. 12718 (Washington, D.C.: U.S. Government Printing Office, 1966), part 4, p. 646.

[82] 14 C.F.R., section 1245.206 (c) (October 1962).

adequate measure of the commercial potential of innovations is administratively workable but somewhat crude; nor is the alternative of evaluating each invention for commercial potential much more attractive. If, however, the waiting period were made discretionary rather than mandatory, NASA personnel could grant exclusive licenses without waiting two years in certain instances, as where only one applicant applies and he refuses to apply for a nonexclusive license, or where the device is such that a two-year wait would have the effect of diluting the worth of an exclusive license.

The official two-year period could also be shortened to one year. With a one-year period, the General Counsel's Office could begin processing an application with the understanding that it would be rejected if an application for a nonexclusive license were received.

NASA's March-In rights are also designed to minimize the bar to use by others represented by an exclusive license. As in the evaluation of waiver applications, the enforcement of such rights creates an administrative problem, although in the license situation NASA at least would not be revoking the title rights of one of its contractors. Thus far, keeping track of the one oustanding exclusive license probably does not tax NASA greatly. Should more such licenses be granted, however, as I recommended, NASA would have to devise a system for monitoring the commercial development of many devices. Assigning this monitoring task to the one body within NASA with a real interest in promoting commercialization, the Office of Technology Utilization, would materially assist in evaluating compliance with the contract terms. The Regional Dissemination Centers of OTU could do whatever field work proved necessary for the monitoring task. Moreover, their continuing contact with industrial clients should provide the expertise to evaluate contract compliance properly.

Conclusion

NASA's patent policy places more emphasis on attempting to encourage the reporting of inventions than on fostering the utilization of such inventions by other segments of the economy. However, both advance waivers and irrevocable nonexclusive licenses, two of the principal means used to induce reporting, have proved ineffective in stimulating the input function of NASA's Technology Utilization

Program. It is arguable that advance waivers have not been authorized by Congress. Second, and more important, waiver of title is valueless unless the contractor intends to commercialize the invention. Irrevocable nonexclusive licenses should not be granted because they provide little incentive to report and act as a clog on commercialization by others. Advance waivers should be abolished, and waivers on individual inventions should be granted only where NASA's technology personnel determine that the contractor has the requisite commercial position or an intent to commercialize the innovation in question. In addition, alternative and more effective reporting incentives should be used to lessen the harmful effects of the present patent policy on the output function.

NASA's patent policy would be a more effective component of the technology transfer program if it placed more emphasis on the output function. Retraction of the present liberal waiver policy would remove one of the obstacles to dissemination as would a more liberal use of exclusive licenses. However, since exclusive licenses can also operate as a partial bar to dissemination, there must be some reasonable limitations on the issuance of such licenses. A nonexclusive license could be granted for one year, with a provision for convertibility to an exclusive license if no one else had used the device during the period. In addition, Technology Utilization personnel should also monitor work being done by exclusive licensees so that NASA could utilize its March-In rights where necessary. Finally, since NASA is justifiably uncertain of its right to grant exclusive licenses, Congress should provide it with explicit statutory authorization.

Although patent policy is not the most important variable in the process of technology transfer, nevertheless it should be revised so as to be as consistent with NASA's TU Program as possible. Since it is one area in which the effects of policy changes can be measured more easily, some check can be provided on the functioning of a technology transfer program. In addition, since NASA has taken the lead in developing a comprehensive technology transfer program, a better coordinated patent policy may serve succeeding agency programs as a more workable model.

PART III
Conclusions and Recommendations

Chapter 11

Conclusions and Recommendations

With the Technology Utilization Program, NASA has taken the lead in attempting to implement an agency-wide program for making the results of its R & D available in a reasonably rapid, easily accessible fashion. This chapter will discuss the major steps taken by NASA to promote technology transfer, important problems with the present TU Program, conclusions concerning the transfer process, and recommendations for the elements of an experimental transfer program designed to provide data for useful programs. Specifically, the following conditions appear to be important for any successful transfer program within a federal science agency.

1. By establishing a high-level Administrator as a focal point for information activities within the agency, the NASA Administrator has advertised to intra-agency personnel, to other federal agencies, to contractors, and to the public that NASA considers transfer an important part of its mission.
2. By inserting a New Technology Clause in each prime contract and many subcontracts, NASA has visibly demonstrated to its many contractors that it considers new technology reporting part of their contract requirements.
3. By providing one or more Technology Utilization Officers at each of NASA's 13 Field Offices and Centers, it has provided a focal point near the source of the new technology, theoretically able to identify, collect, and evaluate this new technology. It has also set some precedent for the professional referee system advocated by the Weinberg Report.
4. By establishing separate, yet organizationally integrated acquisition and dissemination operations, NASA has gone some way toward recognizing that these two variables are functionally inseparable.

5. By doing extensive work in STID on automated data retrieval, NASA has provided a basic, easily accessible library of new technology, readily available to the commercial-industrial sector of the economy through local transfer agents, the RDC's.

6. By promulgating a comprehensive series of patent/license regulations, which attempt to balance the agency mission requirement of obtaining the best qualified contractors against that of obtaining the largest amount of transfer and application of aerospace technology, NASA has provided a visible symbol of the importance it attaches to both parts of the agency mission.

7. Finally, by establishing a series of Regional Dissemination Centers, it has established a potentially effective linking mechanism between the results of agency R & D and the public sector using the resources and capabilities of local academic institutions.

These, then, are positive steps NASA has taken to establish a comprehensive transfer program. The lack of success of this very comprehensive agency-wide program either in promoting aerospace technology transfer or in measuring the transfer that has occurred may be accounted for as follows:

1. First, the Program is very new. As discussed in Chapter 3, technology transfer, that is, the process whereby innovations are adapted for use in a new institutional setting is an exceedingly slow one. Too much has probably been expected of the TU Program in too short a time.

2. Organizationally, the TU Program is far too fragmented for effective operation. The focal point for the acquisition of information, the TUO's, are only nominally under the control of the Assistant Administrator for TU. Further, the TUO's have little authority to enforce either contractor reporting or NASA employee reporting. At some NASA Field Centers, the TUO's are many steps removed from access to the Director. Also contrary to the recommendation of the Weinberg Report, the TU Program is a *staff* not a *line* organization, an administrative not a science-oriented department. Thus, many of the powers and prerogatives accruing to a technical line organization in a science agency are not available to the Assistant Administrator for TU. He must rely almost entirely

on persuasion to achieve his ends; and since he has little status in a science agency, his powers of persuasion are quite limited.

3. NASA does not operate in a self-contained environment; that is, many NASA contractors either are concurrently DOD contractors or were DOD contractors until quite recently. DOD has a policy of very permissive reporting of new technology since it has always contended that its mission of military hardware primacy relegated all other objectives, such as promoting technology transfer, to an insignificant place within the agency. Thus, the NASA TU Program must operate in an environment hostile to reporting except as minimally needed to fulfill contract requirements. In fact, the optimum strategy for a space/defense contractor is to disclose as little as possible to the government except as needed to obtain new contracts or for performance of present contracts. Further, many NASA contracting officers are former DOD personnel; even the NASA Procurement regulations were primarily derived from those of DOD. NASA contractors and many NASA contracting officers are almost conditioned against the widest practicable acquisition and dissemination of aerospace technology.

4. The TU Program was founded primarily in response to political pressures and has continued to be used as a device for partial justification of NASA R & D funding, rather than as a technical project in its own right. Therefore, instead of being an experimental program, as so often advertised, it is in many ways an expanded library operation with regional branch libraries located in many areas that have a low interest in aerospace technology. Not only have political pressures prevented imaginative or bold long-range planning, they have tended to affect even day-to-day operations of the Headquarters Office as well as the RDC's through crisis-reporting demands and pressures to avoid potentially embarrassing experiments.

5. The emphasis on commercial-industrial transfer has limited the program in that technical information of interest to researchers in other institutional settings receives either little or no professional screening or selective dissemination. This emphasis has also forced RDC's to confine their operations almost exclusively to industrial firms whether or not, in terms of a transfer model for the diffusion

of technical information, they should have been doing so. Little attention appears to have been given to working with universities and other nonprofit institutions in regions where there is a small or nonexistent technically oriented industrial base.

6. The patent/license policy, while trying to balance mission requirements against maximum transfer has thus far received extensive criticism by contractors and very little use by third-party commercial-industrial firms. Further, this policy has not, even by federal agency reporting standards, produced a high reporting rate of patentable inventions.

7. Finally, the RDC's, while in theory excellent linking mechanisms for transferring aerospace technology to the public sector, have not been measurably successful in transferring it to the industrial-commercial sector and have been kept from much activity outside this area. Since RDC's have been primarily limited to library functions, entrepreneurial activity and market assistance to client firms have been severely limited.

This then has been one agency's answer to its perceived duty to make available to industry the results of its sponsored R & D. To transfer technology successfully, however, requires more than perception of a duty, it requires a program based on objective, experimental evidence.[1] Existing studies such as those produced by the programs at M.I.T.'s Sloan School or by Arthur D. Little must be used without regard to whether their results are consistent with

[1] Systematic studies of technology transfer from federal agency R & D results have been rare, but a number of studies have been completed recently. Denver Research Institute, *The Commercial Application of Missile/Space Technology,* NASA sponsored report (Springfield, Va.: Clearinghouse for Scientific and Technical Information, September 1963). Robert Solo, *Studies in the Anatomy of Economic Progress,* Report prepared for the National Planning Association (Washington, D.C.: NPA, 1965). Denver Research Institute, *The Channels of Technology Acquisition in Commercial Firms, and the NASA Dissemination Program,* NASA sponsored report (Springfield, Va.: Clearinghouse for Scientific and Technical Information, June 1967). Donald Marquis and Edward Roberts and their associates at MIT—a number of studies of entrepreneurial spin-off firms (NASA sponsored, 1964–67). (Available at the MIT Sloan School, Research Program on the Management of Science and Technology.) Arthur D. Little, Inc., studies of methods of motivating industrial usage of NASA technology (NASA sponsored, 1964–66).

agency political objectives or preconceptions.[2] A successful transfer program must be free to experiment, testing numerous methods and levels of transfer within the framework of a carefully designed applied social science research project. This book has often referred to the need for such a program and even noted that the NASA TU Program is actually a species of applied social science project. The TU Program apparently thinks of itself not as a social science research project but rather as a project to *do* transfer. This raises the question as to whether a mission-oriented federal agency can be expected to support a social science research project that is free to conduct experiments which may yield results prejudicial to its bases of political support. The NASA TU Program indicates that hard as an agency may strive to establish what it calls an experimental transfer program, the need to produce a given set of visible results, relatively rapidly, militates against an objective, scientific approach. It has even been assumed that American industry stood ready, willing, and able to use the results of space R & D with little or no testing of the hypothesis. Such has not been the case.

However, there still exists a *prima facie* case for a federally sponsored program aimed at increasing our understanding of the process whereby the transfer of a portion of the results of federally sponsored R & D has been effected in the past and investigate means whereby the rate and quality of this transfer process might be increased in the future. Such a *prima facie* case is based on the following facts:

1. The federal government is the primary sponsor of R & D and appears likely to remain so for the immediate future.
2. Much of the scarce resources of technical talent and risk capital is devoted to the narrow mission objectives of a few federal agencies.
3. The technology generated thereunder is theoretically part of the public domain, but without a carefully structured program to make relevant results available on a timely basis and to promote their exploitation, little of this technology is in fact available.

---

[2] It appears that both the results of the MIT studies and the smaller ones at Arthur D. Little have been ignored by NASA as somehow inconsistent with agency norms.

As discussed in Chapter 5 and Appendix A, numerous federal programs presently exist to transfer technical information to various segments of the economy, but aside from the Department of Agriculture program it appears that little thought or effort has gone into providing for interpersonal transfer of technology at the local level or to means of motivating the use of this new technology. Most of the programs to date are expanded technical library programs. Much as libraries serve a useful purpose in providing general background material and some increased receptivity for new technical development, it does not appear that they form a significant part in actually motivating the adaptation of new technology across institutional lines.[3] Perhaps more important, such expanded library programs provide little feedback to establish more effective transfer mechanisms.

The transfer of federal R & D results is a very difficult problem, requiring a change in attitude by both transferees and transferors. Thus, the transfer of federally sponsored R & D results appears to be a complex function of several interrelated variables:

1. The acquisition of the technology from federal laboratories and contractors.
2. The evaluation of reported information relative to the needs of the ultimate user, whether he be a businessman or a university research engineer or a graduate student in economics.
3. The dissemination of the evaluated technology which requires that different methods of coupling at the local level be explored.
4. The legal and institutional policies relative to intellectual property and to patentable inventions which appear to affect both the input and output portions of a transfer program.

Failure to view the transfer process as a function of this set of variables obscures underlying problems in present agency programs. Failure to view the transfer process as a problem that is extremely complex and about which very little is known leads to such ill-fated approaches as that of the early NASA TU Program with its centralized library approach. Since the problems are complex and little

[3] See Edward Roberts, "Facts and Folklore in Research and Development Management," *Industrial Management Review,* VIII, No. 21 (Spring 1967), pp. 5, 11–14, for a discussion of the importance of interpersonal communication for significant transfer.

is known about the horizontal transfer process, what is needed is an experimental program to gather the needed data to determine the feasibility of technology transfer projects both within and outside the government.

Such a program should frankly recognize that certain elements must be built into the framework of the project including the following:

1. It must be experimental in nature and thus results could not be predicted in advance.
2. Little systematic knowledge exists about the transfer process despite numerous federal efforts aimed at transfer. Thus much of the initial work would consist of experimentation and systematic data accumulation.
3. The program would have to work, in the first instance, with technology users capable of providing feedback even if this requires that initial project efforts be devoted to working in regions where there is already a large technology base.
4. To perform useful experiments it may be necessary to work visibly in and to affect the market to some extent, unlike the present TU Program with its orientation toward a passive information service.
5. Initial successful results in terms of measurable end-item use may be accompanied by political pressures to change the geographical areas of experimentation or of the institutional and/or industrial participant.
6. To some extent this political pressure may require that some of the work be done with institutions or industry that will create more favorable comment (such as smaller firms rather than larger ones) ; but each such compromise must be recognized and used as a part of the overall plan to minimize political pressures while maintaining the integrity of a scientific program.

In short, what is needed is an applied social science program aimed at increasing knowledge of the transfer process. The program should concentrate on achieving a few demonstrable successes since such successful transfer would provide useful guides for policy decisions whereas such indirect evidence as document distribution statistics for a larger number of more doubtful successes would provide few guides to policy formulation or to a better understanding of the transfer process. Further, demonstrable success should provide the additional benefit of increased feedback which can be used to structure further experimentation. While many of the items discussed are concerned with the dissemination portion of transfer, a significant portion of the program would also have to focus on means of increasing relevant input from federal science agencies.

These concluding remarks are not meant to present a comprehensive design for an applied social science experimental project in technology transfer; rather, they are intended to note some significant elements needed for the successful implementation of such a project. This study clearly indicates the serious need for truly experimental programs in technology transfer.

Appendix A
Current Federal Programs

U.S. Department of Health, Education, and Welfare—National Library of Medicine (NLM)

Established in 1836 as the Library of the Surgeon General's Office of the U.S. Army, and renamed intermittently, the National Library of Medicine received its present name in 1952. Its statutory authority is as follows:

> In order to assist the advancement of medical and related sciences, and to aid the dissemination and exchange of scientific and other information important to the progress of medicine and the public health, there is established in the Public Health Service a National Library of Medicine.[1]

NLM's mission is to assist the advancement of medical sciences by acquiring publications in all medicine-related sciences, by comprehensively indexing current biomedical literature, and by making its collection accessible to the national medical community.[2]

In 1963, NLM employed an estimated 237 persons and operated on an estimated appropriation of $3.7 million.[3] Its collection in 1964 numbered over a million items, and the library was acquiring 15,000 bound volumes and 13,000 serial publications annually.[4] It is the largest resource of such materials in the world.

In 1964, a computer-based information storage and retrieval sys-

---

[1] National Library of Medicine Act of 1944, 70 Stat. 960, 42 U.S.C.A. 662 (as amended 1956).

[2] National Science Foundation, *Scientific Information Activities of Federal Agencies: National Library of Medicine,* No. 28 (Washington, D.C.: U.S. Government Printing Office, 1964), p. 10.

[3] Department of Health, Education and Welfare, *Handbook on Programs of the U.S. Department of Health, Education and Welfare* (Washington, D.C.: U.S. Government Printing Office, 1963), p. 107.

[4] NSF, No. 28, p. 3.

tem known as MEDLARS (Medical Literature Analysis and Retrieval System) was established in the NLM. MEDLARS stores bibliographic citations prepared by literature analysts and placed on magnetic tape. In 1964, roughly 14,000 articles a month were indexed through the system, with the annual total estimated at 175,000;[5] however, publications are not abstracted. These citations are retrieved for three principal purposes:[6]

1. The preparation of *Index Medicus,* a monthly catalog of articles from over 2,500 biomedical journals.
2. Demand searches in response to individual requests for the literature in particular areas.
3. The preparation of recurring bibliographies in particular branches of the medical sciences.

Since 1964, MEDLARS has undergone a process of decentralization, and search centers have been set up at U.C.L.A., the University of Michigan, the University of Alabama, Harvard University, and the University of Colorado.[7] These search centers accept requests for demand searches, prepare the retrieval punch cards, and forward them to NLM. The requested bibliographies are printed out by the computer's high-speed printer and routed back to the inquirer. The search centers are staffed by up to three searchers, usually undergraduate science majors with degrees in library science. Service may take up to a month. The service is open to the general public, without charge.

In 1966, NLM supplied 3,035 computer-produced demand bibliographies compared with 1,623 in FY 1965.[8]

Department of Commerce—Clearinghouse for Federal Scientific and Technical Information (CFSTI)

The Clearinghouse for Federal Scientific and Technical Information is a part of the Institute for Applied Technology of the Commerce Department's National Bureau of Standards. It offers for

[5] U.S. Department of Health, Education and Welfare, *1964 Annual Report to Congress* (Washington, D.C.: U.S. Government Printing Office, 1965), p. 135.
[6] NSF, No. 28, p. 10.
[7] U.S. Department of Health, Education and Welfare, *1966 Annual Report* (Washington, D.C.: U.S. Government Printing Office, 1967), p. 82.
[8] *Ibid.*

sale, at a low price, unclassified and unlimited reports of scientific and technical R & D generated by federal agencies. With approximately 300 employees, CFSTI operates with an annual budget of $5 million, half of which is transfer funds from other agencies to support the announcement and distribution of their reports.[9]

CFSTI was established in 1964 in response to a recommendation of the Weinberg Report that the Office of Technical Services of the Commerce Department "become a complete Government technical reports sales agency."[10] Its statutory authority is as follows:

> The Secretary of Commerce . . . is directed to establish and maintain . . . a clearinghouse for the collection and dissemination of scientific, technical, and engineering information, and to this end to take such steps as he may deem necessary and desirable—
>
> (a) to search for, collect, classify . . . such information . . .;
>
> (b) to make such information available to industry and business . . . and to the general public . . .; (and)
>
> (c) to effect . . . the removal of restrictions on the dissemination of scientific and technical data where considerations of national security permit.[11]

CFSTI offers the following services:[12]

Sale of Documents. The availability of new documents is announced in accepted announcement journals, including *U.S. Government Research and Development Reports* (USGRDR), and the recent *Government-Wide Index* (both published bimonthly and keyed to the 22 subject categories established by COSATI). Also,

---

[9] Federal Council for Science and Technology, *Recommendations for National Document Handling Systems in Science and Technology,* prepared by the Committee on Scientific and Technical Information (Springfield, Va.: Clearinghouse for Scientific and Technical Information, November 1965), Appendix II, pp. 6–65.

[10] President's Science Advisory Committee, *Science, Government, and Information* (Washington, D.C.: U.S. Government Printing Office, January 1963), p. 47.

[11] Dissemination of Technical, Scientific and Engineering Information Act of 1950, 64 Stat. 823, 15 U.S.C.A. 1152 (1950).

[12] For a more detailed description of CFSTI's services, see Richard Lesher and George Howick, *Background, Guidelines and Recommendations for Use in Assessing Effective Means of Channeling New Technologies in Promising Directions,* prepared for the U.S. National Commission on Technology, Automation and Economic Progress (Washington, D.C.: U.S. Government Printing Office, November 1965), p. 123.

the *Fast Announcement Bulletin* (monthly) identifies those federally sponsored research reports which, after evaluation, appear to be of unusual significance (about 10 percent of all research reports). The subscribers to this service presently number 6,500; 90 percent of them are outside the federal government.[13]

Literature Searching Services. Operated in cooperation with U.S.D.A., the Department of the Interior and the Library of Congress, this service can take either of two approaches: (1) "Current Awareness" bibliographies provided to subscribers on a periodic basis, and listing publications in their field during the period; and (2) Retrospective Searches listing reports in the field at the time of the request.

Referral Services. Operated in cooperation with NRCST, this service refers the inquirer to the source (government or private) most likely to be in possession of the desired information.

Selective Bibliographies. These are compiled in many areas.

Packaging Services. Selected government R & D reports are examined and the technical information therein is distilled into packages for industrial use. The packages are keyed to specific industrial needs and consist of abstracts, indexes, and reviews of technical literature. They are distributed to universities, state and regional economic agencies, professional consultants, and technical assistance organizations.

CFSTI has a file of about 500,000 unclassified documents, including translations. Acquisitions total about 22,000 reports a year from all federal agencies.[14] During FY 1965, in addition to roughly 500,000 requests transferred by DDC, CFSTI serviced about 2,000 direct requests per day.[15]

Science Information Exchange (SIE)

The basic mission of the Science Information Exchange is to "provide information for planning and managing research activity sup-

[13] U.S. Congress, Senate Select Committee on Small Business, Subcommittee on Science and Technology, *Policy Planning for Technology Transfer, Report,* prepared by Richard Carpenter of the Science Policy Research Division of the Legislative Reference Service, Library of Congress, 90th Congress, first session, S. Doc. No. 15 (Washington, D.C.: U.S. Government Printing Office, May 1967).
[14] *Ibid.,* p. 125.
[15] FCST, *loc. cit.*

ported by . . . government and non-government organizations."[16] It therefore does not acquire abstracts, progress reports, or final reports of research results, limiting its acquisition function to summaries of planned or in-progress research. It is designed to avoid duplication and to allow coordination of research.

Begun in 1949 as the Medical Sciences Information Exchange in the National Research Council, its operation was taken over in 1953 by the Smithsonian Institution and it was renamed the Bio-Sciences Information Exchange. Its present name was adopted in 1962 when it underwent reorganization, "with a view to the gradual inclusion of the physical sciences in addition to its original coverage of medicine, biology, and psychology."[17]

Funded principally by NSF, SIE operates at an annual cost of more than $2 million.[18] Of a total staff of about 100 people, 46 are scientists, 8 are data processers, 8 are involved in administration, and the remainder perform clerical functions.[19]

Although input is on a voluntary basis, it is estimated that 90 to 95 percent of all research under way in the life sciences is covered by the Exchange.[20] Coverage of the physical sciences, begun in 1962, is much less adequate. Furthermore, the Exchange records only unclassified and unlimited research.

The information stored concerning each reported research project includes data on the scientists and organizations involved, the annual budget, the projected beginning and completion dates, and a 200-word summary of the work. The 200-word summary is then indexed "with 1 to 45 descriptive words for each project."[21]

SIE provides two types of services, one to individuals and one to organizations.[22] To individuals active in fields covered by the Exchange, it can supply (1) lists of scientists and institutions engaged in similar research, and (2) summaries of active or terminated

---

16 FCST, *op. cit.*, pp. 6–17.

17 National Science Foundation, *Scientific Information Activities of Federal Agencies: Smithsonian Institution*, No. 13 (Washington, D.C.: U.S. Government Printing Office, June 1962), p. 12.

18 FCST, *op. cit.*, Appendix I, pp. 5–17.

19 Lesher and Howick, *op. cit.*

20 *Ibid.*, p. 106.

21 *Ibid.*, p. 105.

22 NSF, No. 13, p. 12.

projects in a particular field. To organizations legitimately interested in planning or managing research, in addition to the services supplied to individuals, SIE can provide (1) reports on geographic distribution of research grants, and (2) information on past and present research performed by applicants for grants.

In 1964, SIE answered 5,000 requests for information concerning who was working in a specific field.[23] A questionnaire mailed to 600 users of this type of service indicated that 97 percent of those responding had learned of work in progress in their field.[24]

Small Business Administration (SBA)

Although the Small Business Administration does not itself generate any scientific or technological information, it does have statutory authority to engage in technology transfer. Its enabling act states, in section 9, that "(b) It shall be the duty of the Administrator, and he is hereby empowered . . . (2) to assist small-business concerns to obtain the benefits of research and development performed under Government contracts or at Government expense; and (3) to provide technical assistance to small business concerns to accomplish the purposes of this section."[25] The purposes of this section of the Small Business Act are to compensate for the inability of small businesses to maintain in-house R & D divisions which can adapt government R & D results to the particular needs of the business.

Until recently, SBA concentrated primarily on assisting small businesses in procuring government R & D contracts under section 9 (b) (1). Despite this effort, contract awards to small businesses for government R & D dropped in FY 1967 to 3.9 percent from 4.4 percent in FY 1966.[26] In 1965, SBA began a pilot program of interagency agreements with NASA and AEC under which three NASA RDC's disseminated technology to certain firms selected by SBA in conjunc-

---

[23] Lesher and Howick, *op. cit.*, p. 108.

[24] *Idem.*

[25] Aid to Small Business—Research and Development Act of 1958, Public Law 85–536, 72 Stat. 391, 15 U.S.C.A. 638 (1958).

[26] Statement of Robert C. Moot, Administrator, Small Business Administration, before U.S. Congress, Senate, Select Committee on Small Business, Subcommittee on Science and Technology, *Technology Transfer, Hearings*, 90th Congress, first session (Washington, D.C.: U.S. Government Printing Office, September 1967), p. 169.

tion with other participating agencies.[27] In 1965, in another pilot program, SBA with Bjorksten Research Laboratories, Inc., collected information on plastics from federal R & D reports and mailed the processed technology information to small businesses.[28]

Present SBA efforts include continued co-sponsorship of conferences in which large audiences of small manufacturers and R & D firms are exposed to technological advances that may have commercial potential for them, issuance of a regular summary of selected innovations generated by government R & D which appear to possess commercial potential, and deployment of eight Technology Utilization Offices at various locations throughout the country.[29]

The services offered by the Technology Utilization Offices are varied and in the Boston area include assistance in specifying the technical problem to be solved, location of government sources of relevant information, limited informational searches in cooperation with NASA, AEC, MIT, and CFSTI, location of managerial and technical consultants, professional organizations and other small businesses knowledgeable in the field, and the seeking out of retired engineers in the SCORE program to assist in technology transfer and utilization.[30]

Atomic Energy Commission (AEC)

In FY 1966, the AEC had estimated R & D expenditures of $1,292 million; only DOD and NASA surpassed it.[31] Section 3 of the Atomic Energy Act of 1954 provides for "a program for the dissemination of unclassified scientific and technical information and for the control, dissemination and declassification of Restricted Data, subject to appropriate safeguards, so as to encourage scientific and industrial progress."[32] The dissemination program, under this mandate, has taken a variety of forms, "some more important, but none pre-

[27] *Ibid.*, pp. 170–71.
[28] *Policy Planning for Technology Transfer*, p. 77.
[29] Moot, *op. cit.*, p. 171.
[30] Small Business Administration, Northeastern Area Office, "Technology Utilization for the Small Manufacturer," policy statement (Boston: SBA Office, 1967).
[31] National Science Foundation, *Federal Funds for Research, Development and Other Scientific Activities: Fiscal Years 1965, 1966 and 1967*, NSF 66–24 (Washington, D.C.: U.S. Government Printing Office, July 1966), p. 3.
[32] Atomic Energy Act of 1946, Public Law 79–585, 60 Stat. 755, 42 U.S.C.A. 1801, 2013 (as amended 1954).

dominating."[33] For convenience, the various programs and mechanisms will be grouped into three major divisions: Publications, Nonpublication Informational Activities, and Programs for Industrial Cooperation.

Publications. The Division of Technical Information manages AEC's publication distribution network and coordinates distribution with the Clearinghouse for Federal Scientific and Technical Information. Among its publications are four Technical Progress Reviews containing state-of-the-art reviews and descriptions of the current status of various R & D programs; "Nuclear Science Abstracts," a comprehensive abstracting and indexing service devoted to nuclear science and technology; and 12 to 15 books and monographs per year. AEC contractors are encouraged to publish Topical Reports on the Status of R & D programs conducted by them. Engineers and scientists working in AEC-sponsored R & D are urged to publish, in trade and technical journals, the unclassified results of their research. In August 1966, AEC and NASA began the "joint issuance of a series of business-oriented summaries of selected non-nuclear devices, processes and techniques developed at Argonne National Laboratory." These AEC-NASA Tech Briefs "are distributed by both AEC and NASA, and are sold by the Clearinghouse for Federal Scientific and Technical Information."[34]

Nonpublication Informational Activities. AEC maintains 78 depository libraries in 55 foreign countries and 97 depository libraries in the United States. A typical library contains over 90,000 titles.[35] In addition, AEC supports, in whole or in part, 25 specialized information centers. These centers are designed to be the most complete repositories of information in their field. Manned by scientists and engineers specializing in the field covered by the center, their primary function is to issue state-of-the-art reviews and to provide "specific information in response to inquiries."[36] Their services are freely available to all.

---

[33] Atomic Energy Commission, *Transference of Non-Nuclear Technology to Industry,* Committee Report to Oak Ridge Operations Office (Oak Ridge, Tennessee: AEC, July 1965).

[34] Atomic Energy Commission, *1966 Annual Report to Congress* (Washington, D.C.: U.S. Government Printing Office, January 1967), p. 319.

[35] *Ibid.,* p. 318.

[36] *Idem.*

In the visual arts, AEC sponsors a battery of exhibits and demonstrations both in the United States and abroad. The 1967 international exhibits were scheduled for Turkey, Panama, Iran, and Ecuador. The United States exhibits were principally held at secondary schools, museums, and state and regional fairs. During 1966, AEC's 10 domestic film libraries loaned prints of films on atomic energy for 91,940 showings.[37] News releases by AEC round out this class of information activities, which, "while they do not contain detailed technology, . . . are useful to highlight the existence of new developments and to provide references for further contact."[38]

In 1966, AEC owned, administered, and made available for nonexclusive licensing 3,912 domestic patents. At present, over 1,100 licenses have been issued on 620 of these patents, with another 623 nonexclusive licenses retained by contractors.[39] The AEC describes its patent policy as ensuring that "atomic energy technology developed with public funds is made available freely to all U.S. citizens."[40]

In support of its other transfer activities, AEC "accredits responsible reviewers at each major contractor site who decide which reports are declassifiable."[41] In 1966, about 14,000 documents were thus found declassifiable and made publicly available.[42] Furthermore, a comprehensive study of AEC's classification policy is underway and is expected to be completed in 1967.

Program for Industrial Cooperation. The most recent and promising direction AEC's technology transfer program has taken is the establishment of a pilot program of two Offices of Industrial Cooperation (OIC) at Argonne National Laboratory and Oak Ridge National Laboratory. Among its functions, each OIC is directed to answer inquiries and to identify and announce innovations. Each is also to become aware of the needs of particular segments of industry.[43]

During 1966, AEC sponsored a limited number of information meetings and conferences for the purpose of acquainting industrial

---

[37] *Ibid.*, p. 330.
[38] AEC, *Transference of Non-Nuclear Technology to Industry,* p. B–4.
[39] AEC, *1966 Annual Report to Congress,* p. 332.
[40] AEC, *Transference of Non-Nuclear Technology to Industry,* p. B–4.
[41] PSAC, *op. cit.*, p. 40.
[42] AEC, *1966 Annual Report to Congress,* p. 334.
[43] Lesher and Howick, *op. cit.*, p. 109.

groups with federal agencies' transfer programs. These meetings were cosponsored by NASA, SBA, the Office of State Technical Services, and the Clearinghouse for Federal Scientific and Technical Information. Also, a limited number of meetings have been held for the "express purpose of transferring AEC-sponsored technology to industry."[44]

The AEC's Access Permit Program, established in 1955, allows industrial organizations to obtain Restricted Data relevant to civilian applications of atomic energy. At the end of November 1966, 427 Access Permits were in effect.[45] The mechanisms of transfer under the Access Permits include plant tours, briefings, and furnishing of reports and drawings."[46]

More indirect transfer techniques include advisory boards and vendor subcontracts.[47] Advisory boards supply advice and suggestions for the AEC, usually in specific areas. In 1965, there were twenty-one such boards, each composed of members who were leaders in their respective fields. Vendor subcontracts not only transfer technology directly to the successful bidder but also alert the different sectors of industry to new levels of requirements in certain fields.

AEC's policy of industrial cooperation permits the agency both to offer consultation services and, on occasion, to work directly for private industry when AEC's unique capabilities are needed. Characteristics of both these services are that they (1) be conducted on a nondiscriminatory basis, (2) be provided on a full cost-recovery basis, and (3) provide "effective" technology transfer.[48]

U.S. Department of Agriculture (USDA)

In 1862, the Department of Agriculture was established and was directed to acquire and diffuse useful information about agriculture. The Hatch Experimental Station Act of 1887 established agricultural experiment stations in connection with each of the Land Grant Colleges of the several states, and the Smith-Lever Act of 1914 established the Cooperative Extension Service to carry to American farmers the results of agricultural research. Some indication of the suc-

---

44 AEC, *Transference of Non Nuclear Technology to Industry,* p. B–3.

45 AEC, *1966 Annual Report to Congress,* p. 334.

46 AEC, *Transference of Non-Nuclear Technology to Industry,* p. B–5.

47 *Ibid.,* pp. B–3, B–4.

48 *Ibid.,* p. B–3.

cess of the program carried out within this statutory framework is given by the statistics, which indicate that during the 1950's, there was an increase of 80 percent in actual production per worker engaged in farming.[49]

The research sponsored by the USDA, both intramurally at over 600 field locations in the United States and extramurally, is largely need-oriented.[50] Funding for USDA research in 1960 exceeded $91.8 million, with an additional $31.8 million available to state agricultural experiment stations as Federal Grant Funds.[51] With state funding of $114 million for agricultural research, total funding for research in 1960 was over $237.6 million. USDA alone employs over 4,800 full-time professional scientists.[52]

The information generated by the agricultural research of both USDA and the State Land Grant Colleges and experiment stations is collected, collated, and made available upon request by the National Agricultural Library. The Office of Information and the Cooperative Extension Service are responsible for its diffusion. The services of the Office of Information fall into three categories: Publications, Mass Media, and Visual Communication.

Publications. USDA publications are directed to three principal groups: scientists, farmers, and the general public. "Thus, the findings of a particular project may be published in technical bulletins written primarily for scientists or specialists; be the basis for a nontechnical article for the general public in one of the Department's periodicals, and presented in a farmer's bulletin written specifically to inform farmers and ranchers how they may put the findings into

---

[49] Department of Agriculture, *1961 Annual Report to Congress* (Washington, D.C.: U.S. Government Printing Office, 1962).

[50] Harvey Brooks, "Organizing Research for Social and Economic Objectives: An Outsider's Appraisal of the Strengths and Weaknesses of Agricultural Research," *Symposium on Research in Agriculture*, sponsored jointly by DOA and the National Academy of Sciences (Washington, D.C.: DOA, August 1966). Brooks suggests that DOA could profit from larger appropriations for opportunity-oriented research.

[51] Department of Agriculture, *Agriculture Information Bulletin No. 224: Questions and Answers on Agricultural Research* (Washington, D.C.: U.S. Government Printing Office, July 1966), p. 4.

[52] The principal DOA agencies engaged in research are the Agricultural Research Service, Agricultural Marketing Service, Forest Service, Farmer Cooperative Service, and the Foreign Agricultural Service.

practical use on the farm."[53] In 1967, an estimated 1,100 scientific and technical reports were issued, with an additional 3,500 articles by USDA researchers appearing in scientific journals. Publications are available to the public, without restriction (except as to supply) from the Superintendent of Documents.[54]

Mass Media. Over 700 radio stations and 100 farm telecasters use current information packages compiled and supplied by the Office of Information. Furthermore, several hundred press releases are issued annually summarizing completed research.

Visual Communication. Exhibits and motion pictures are frequently employed in developing awareness of new techniques and applications which have broad potential for commercial application. Personally conducted tours through USDA field stations and pilot research farms allow farmers to see the results of new agriculture techniques.

The Cooperative Extension Service is a cooperative venture of the Federal Extension Service and State Extension Services which are divisions of their Land Grant Colleges. In 1960, its funding exceeded $142 million and it employed over 14,000 persons.[55] Its statutory mandate in the Smith-Lever Act directs it ". . . to diffuse among the people of the U. S. useful and practical information on subjects relating to agriculture and home economics, and to encourage the application of the same. . . ."[56]

Extension personnel operate on three tiers: federal, state, and county. Federal Extension personnel keep abreast of national research developments and assist State Extension specialists in incorporating these developments into their educational programs. State Extension specialists work with the research staffs of their own college, plan comprehensive educational programs, keep county Extension agents well-informed on research developments and assist them with individual problems. However, because of the Service's recognition that information is not self-motivating, "the Extension Service at the county level is the focal point of the Cooperative Ex-

[53] *Policy Planning for Technology Transfer,* p. 91.

[54] DOA was specifically excluded along with HEW from total and mandatory participation in the Clearinghouse for Scientific and Technical Information.

[55] H C. Sanders, *et al.,* eds., *The Cooperative Extension Service* (Englewood Cliffs, New Jersey: Prentice-Hall, 1966), p. 5.

[56] Smith-Lever Act of 1914, 38 Stat. 372, 7 U.S.C.A. 341 (as amended 1953).

tension organization and program. The national average is about three agents per county, although the number may vary from one to twenty or more."[57]

It is at the county level where the actual transfer takes place. Basically, there are two types of transfer activities in which the county agents engage: (1) creating awareness of the existence and advantages of new agricultural techniques and products, and (2) solving problems in response to individual requests. The mechanisms employed by county agents in the first type of activity include demonstrations, meetings, seminars, workshops, and personally conducted tours through USDA field stations and pilot research farms and through state experiment stations. The new techniques or products are largely the result of research by USDA or the Land Grant Colleges, and are brought to the attention of the county agents by state agricultural agents who are responsible for comprehensive educational programs. The development of hybrid corn presents a classic case of such a transfer activity. The course of diffusion in that case, however, indicates a substantial time lag between the public awareness of an innovation and its public utilization.[58]

In furtherance of the second type of transfer activity, in 1966 over 20.7 million consultations with individuals were held, "most of which required the interpretation and adaptation of research findings."[59] Requests for assistance may be handled in several ways. Since county agents are generally highly qualified,[60] the vast majority of such requests are presumably handled on the county level. When unable to provide assistance himself, however, the county agency can call upon the research staff of the State Land Grant College. Generally, these staffs are broken up into subject-matter specialists and the request will be routed to the appropriate specialist. The requested information will, if available, then be routed back to

---

[57] Sanders, *op. cit.*, p. 38.

[58] Bryce Ryan, "A Study in Technological Diffusion," *Rural Sociology*, XIII (September 1948), p. 273.

[59] *Policy Planning for Technology Transfer*, p. 94.

[60] Gladys Baker, *The County Agent* (Chicago: The University of Chicago Press, 1939), pp. 163–71. The author states that in the late thirties, most states required County Agents to be graduates of 4-yr. agricultural colleges with prior farm training. Presumably, qualifications have, if anything, become more stringent.

the inquirer. If unavailable, the request may become the subject of a new research project. There is, of course, *no direct charge* to the farmer-transferee for these services.

County agents also play an important role in adapting new technologies and products to the level and need of the user. Furthermore, from their personal knowledge of the problems of their clientele, they can inform the State Extension specialists both of the commercial effectiveness of new developments and of production problems uncovered by them which may necessitate new research. To date, however, no formal feedback procedures seem to have been established.

Office of State Technical Services (OSTS)

The State Technical Services Act of September 14, 1965, was designed to provide support and incentives for the states in establishing and maintaining programs to provide technical services to business, commerce, and industry. The Act defines "technical services" as "activities or programs designed to enable business, commerce, and industrial establishments to acquire and use scientific and engineering information more effectively through such means as:

> (1) preparing and disseminating technical reports . . . including the establishment of . . . technical information centers for this purpose;
> (2) providing a reference service to identify services of engineering and other scientific expertise; and
> (3) sponsoring industrial workshops, seminars, training programs, extension courses, demonstrations, and field visits.[61]

The Act provides that the governor of each state wishing to participate should designate an agency or institution to administer and coordinate the program and to submit annual and 5-year plans to the Secretary of Commerce for approval. Some of the criteria for approval include: (1) certification of availability of matching nonfederal funds; (2) certification that the program's services do not duplicate services already available in the state; (3) certification

[61] State Technical Services Act of 1965, Public Law 89–182, 79 Stat. 679, 15 U.S.C.A. 1351 (1965).

that none of the planned services are especially related to any particular business; and (4) a judgment by the Secretary of Commerce that the plans otherwise accomplish the purposes of the Act.

The Act authorizes appropriations of $10 million in fiscal 1966. $20 million in fiscal 1967, and $30 million in fiscal 1968. Twenty percent of the annual appropriation may be reserved by the Secretary of Commerce for programs of special merit. These Special Merit Programs are independent of the state programs and are administered directly by the Office of State Technical Services, Department of Commerce. Although the requirement of matching nonfederal funds still applies, any qualified institution may submit proposals. Special Merit Programs are designed to provide technical services which have a broad regional or national significance or which employ new techniques.

Section 15 of the Act provides for the appointment, by the Secretary of Commerce, of a public committee whose members have not planned, administered, or participated in programs under the Act. The committee is to evaluate the impact of the program and file a recommendatory report with the Secretary of Commerce within 60 days of September 14, 1968. Because of this requirement of public evaluation, OSTS considers "Supporting detail about significant transfers of technology and real or potential economic benefits stemming from State Technical Services projects . . . [to be] essential to the survival and growth of . . . [the] program."[62] Responsibility for feedback rests primarily with project directors, who have been encouraged to identify and document successful transfers.

In fiscal 1966, 24 state and 4 Special Merit Programs were funded with a Congressional appropriation of $3.5 million.[63] The 24 state programs included 427 different activities broken down as follows: information dissemination, 75; referral service centers, 37; educational activities, 282; and demonstrations and field visits, 33. The average state grant was roughly $67,000; the average Special Merit grant about $36,000.

---

62 Department of Commerce, *1966 Annual Report to Congress* (Washington, D.C.: U.S. Government Printing Office, 1967), p. 56.

63 The fiscal and statistical data for 1966 are taken from the *1966 Annual Report to Congress.*

In fiscal 1967, the number of state programs increased to 41 and that of Special Merit programs to 16.[64] The average state grant rose to above $93,000; the average Special Merit grant dropped to roughly $32,000. Of the 678 activities included in the 41 state programs, 85 were information services, 51 were referral services, 424 were educational activities, 71 were demonstrations and field visits, and 47 were administration projects.

National Science Foundation (NSF)

The National Science Foundation was established in 1950 as an independent executive agency. In spite of its heavy involvement in scientific research, NSF is only indirectly involved in the technology transfer process through its concern with increasing the efficiency of information handling processes.[65] Its statutory authority for this concern provides the following:

> The National Science Foundation shall establish a Science Information Service. The Foundation, through such Service, shall (1) provide or arrange for the provision of, indexing, abstracting, translating, and other services leading to a more effective dissemination of scientific information, and (2) undertake programs to develop new or improved methods including mechanized systems, for making scientific information available.[66]

Pursuant to this authority, on November 16, 1958, NSF's Office of Scientific Information was reorganized as the Office of Science

[64] The fiscal and statistical data for 1967 are taken from the *Office of State Technical Services Newsletter,* Vol. III, No. 2, September-October 1967, pp. 1–2. The Newsletter also contains examples of what OSTS considers to be successful transfers by several state programs, including a project to cut management costs in the construction field by use of a large-scale computer on a shared-time basis; a program of field service agents backed up by a Library Information System at Pennsylvania State University; and technical information services in Texas, Utah, and Wisconsin.

[65] "We consider our mission to be completed when the results of research supported by the Foundation have been reported, usually in the appropriate scientific journals. Publication is encouraged. . . , but we do not attempt to identify commercially useful devices, processes or materials for the vast majority of such research activities do not produce new technology having commercial applications." Letter from Charles F. Brown, Head, Legal Office, NSF, to Edward F. Hines, Jr., Nov. 15, 1967.

[66] National Science Foundation Act of 1950, Public Law 81–507, 64 Stat. 149, 42 U.S.C.A. 1861 (as amended 1964).

Information Service (OSIS). Rather than having an operational nature, "the primary role of OSIS . . . is one of coordination, supplementing and research for the improvement of scientific information systems."[67] In fiscal 1966, the requested budget of OSIS was $12.5 million, and it operated with a complement of about 60 employees.[68]

In *Improving the Dissemination of Scientific Information,*[69] OSIS segregates its major activities into 6 categories, three of which are relevant to our purposes and are abstracted here:

Research and Studies Program. (Requested budget for fiscal 1966, $2.5 million.)[70] This program supports research designed to (a) "learn more about the ways in which scientists and engineers communicate information to one another," (b) "evaluate the effectiveness of scientific information sources and services," and (c) "develop improved information-handling techniques that will result in more useful and economical scientific information services."

Information System Program. (Requested budget for fiscal 1966, $1.7 million.) This program's objective is to "continue research and development directed toward systematic, and where possible, mechanized procedures for handling large volumes of scientific information . . . and to extend it [i.e., the R & D] through the application of existing knowledge, techniques, and equipment to the design of improved information systems. . . . Support is provided for research, development, experimental applications, and evaluation of systems in the areas of information retrieval, mechanical translations, libraries and publications."

Federal Science Information Program. (Requested budget for fiscal 1966, $2.5 million.) In addition to supporting SIE and

---

[67] Lesher and Howick, *op. cit.,* p. 131.

[68] U.S. Congress, House of Representatives, Committee on Science and Astronautics, Subcommittee on Science, Research and Development, *The National Science Foundation: A General Review of Its First Fifteen Years, Report,* 89th Congress, second session. H. Report 1219 (Washington, D.C.: U.S. Government Printing Office, 1966), pp. 181, 191–92.

[69] National Science Foundation, *Improving the Dissemination of Scientific Information* (Washington, D.C.: U.S. Government Printing Office, September 1964). The unlisted programs are: 1. Publications Support Program, 2. Domestic and Foreign Science Information Program, and 3. International Scientific Information Exchange.

[70] H. Report 1219, p. 169.

NRCST, this program is conducting a survey of federal scientific and technical information activities and the results are being published in a series of bulletins entitled *Scientific Information Activities of Federal Agencies.* Over 30 individual bulletins in this series are now available at low cost from the Government Printing Office.

Library of Congress—National Referral Center for Science and Technology (NRCST)

Established in 1962 in the Reference Department of the Library of Congress, the primary mission of the National Referral Center for Science and Technology is "to provide access to the Nation's scientific and technical information resources and to assure the fullest possible utilization of these resources."[71] NRCST does not answer specific inquiries; instead, it identifies the sources (information systems or services) capable of supplying the desired information. The Center "acquires all meaningful data relative to the nature, scope, capabilities, key personnel and access procedures of science information systems and services, and identifies and ascertains the nature and characteristics of each."[72]

The Center answers requests through personal consultation, by telephone, and by correspondence and is available without charge to both individuals and organizations. Funded by NSF, the Center operates at an annual cost of about $400,000.[73]

Department of the Interior

Unlike NSF, whose research is discipline oriented, many minor government agencies support R & D programs designed to benefit specific sectors of the economy.[74] Their mission is analogous to that of USDA in the agricultural sector, although on a far smaller scale. Unlike agencies such as NASA and DOD, these agencies have a per-

---

71 National Science Foundation, *Scientific Information Activities of Federal Agencies: Library of Congress,* No. 26 (Washington, D.C.: U.S. Government Printing Office, 1964), p. 5.

72 *Idem.*

73 FCST, *op. cit.,* Appendix I, pp. 5–17.

74 Among these agencies are the Federal Aviation Agency, the Federal Communications Commission, the Bureau of Public Roads, the U.S. Coast Guard, the Maritime Administration, and the Coast and Geodetic Survey.

manently identifiable class of constituents in the industrial sector upon whose needs R & D programs may be based and to whom results may be communicated. The problems, common to the NASA-DOD type agency, of identifying commercially useful applications of R & D results and of locating potential users for them are therefore largely absent, since ordinarily the R & D results were generated with a specific class of applications and a specific class of users in mind. These factors should be considered in evaluating the techniques used by this type of agency in transferring its R & D results to industry. The Department of the Interior is the parent organization of several agencies,[75] two of which are now briefly described.

OFFICE OF COAL RESEARCH (OCR)

The Office of Coal Research was established in July 1960 "to develop through research, new and more efficient methods of mining, preparing and utilizing coal."[76] All information generated by OCR research is, with certain exceptions, required to be available to the general public. OCR contracts out all R & D projects and maintains no facilities for in-house research. Its 19-man staff is concerned with administrative and supervisory tasks.[77] In fiscal 1967, OCR executed 10 new contracts to bring the number of R & D projects under way to a total of 34.[78]

OCR research is concerned with: (1) the mining, preparation, and utilization of coal; (2) increased tonnage output at the mine; (3) efficient, inexpensive methods of transporting coal to the consumer; (4) new products from coal and associated materials; and (5) the design and development of prototype devices and materials. "Emphasis is on projects that can be developed to the point of commercial application in the shortest possible time."[79] In 1966,

[75] In addition to the two described, other Interior agencies with similar missions are the Bureau of Reclamation, Office of Saline Water, Office of Oil and Gas, Office of Geography, Office of Mineral Mobilization, Bureau of Land Management, and the U.S. Geological Survey.

[76] Coal Research and Development Act of 1960, Public Law 86–599, 74 Stat. 336, 30 U.S.C.A. 662 (1958).

[77] Department of Interior, Office of Coal Research, *1967 Annual Report to Congress* (Washington, D.C.: Department of Interior, 1968), p. 55.

[78] *Idem.*

[79] National Science Foundation, *Scientific Information Activities of Federal Agencies: U.S. Department of Interior,* No. 26 (Washington, D.C.: U.S. Government Printing Office, October 1962).

OCR requested a budget for R & D expenditures of $5.7 million; its 1964 actual budget for R & D amounted to $2.6 million.[80]

Reports of R & D results are published upon completion of the project and are made available either through CFSTI, GPO, or OCR itself. OCR also maintains a mailing list of several hundred names to whom new releases are sent upon the completion of research contracts. The mailing list covers news media, trade associations, trade publications, and "relevant congressional committees; members of Congress from coal producing states; interested . . . research organizations; universities having coal technology-related courses; depository libraries; and industry (chiefly coal companies, electric utilities, and railroads).[81] OCR further handles specific requests for reports.

Other methods of dissemination include speeches by OCR officials, and articles by them or by OCR contractors in trade publications.

BUREAU OF MINES (BOM)

The Bureau of Mines was established in 1910 in the Department of the Interior and given the following statutory mandate: "It shall be the province and duty of the Bureau of Mines . . . to conduct inquiries and . . . investigations concerning mining, and the preparation, treatment, and utilization of mineral substances with a view to improving health conditions, and increasing safety, efficiency, economic development, and conserving resources . . . to investigate explosives . . . and to disseminate information concerning these subjects. . . ."[82] Under this statutory authority, the Bureau conducts research in the following areas: mines and mine safety, nonmetallic minerals, fuels and explosives technology, and helium. Its actual 1964 budget appropriation for R & D was $22.6 million; its requested 1966 budget for R & D was $25.4 million.[83]

---

80 U.S. Congress, House of Representatives Committee on Science and Astronautics, Subcommittee on Science, Research and Development, *Science, Technology, and Public Policy During the Eighty-ninth Congress*, 90th Congress, first session (Washington, D.C.: U.S. Government Printing Office, August 1967) (Committee Print), p. 167.

81 Letter from George Fumich, Director, Office of Coal Research, to Edward Hines, Jr., November 17, 1967.

82 Bureau of Mines Act of 1910, 36 Stat. 370, 30 U.S.C.A. 3 (as amended 1934).

83 *Science, Technology, and Public Policy*, p. 167.

The information generated by this R & D is disseminated in a variety of ways which, for convenence, have been divided into two classifications: publications and nonpublication activities. Publications are announced in *New Publications, Bureau of Mines, Monthly List* and in the annual cumulative listing entitled *List of Bureau of Mines Publications and Articles.* They are also announced in U.S. Government R & D Reports (USGRDR) which is distributed through CFSTI, and, in any case, routinely appear in *Monthly Catalog of U.S. Government Publications.* BOM sponsors a large variety of publications, both of a periodic and nonperiodic nature. The following list includes BOM's major recurring offerings:[84]

1. *Bulletins.* These are usually comprehensive restatements of information in a field previously reported in various other BOM publications. Over 600 titles are now available in the series, and usually 10 new titles appear each year.
2. *Reports of Investigations.* These reports have a much more limited scope of inquiry than do the Bulletins; usually they concern a single series of experiments, or a single phase of a large program. Published at the rate of 200 a month, over 6,000 titles are now available.
3. *Information Circulars.* This series contains much economic and marketing data and is aimed specifically at industry. Over 200 a year are issued.
4. *Handbooks.* These are manuals of instruction intended to increase safety and/or efficiency in specific areas. As of 1961, over 30 were in print and those still available are sold through GPO.
5. *Minerals Yearbook.* This is a four-volume summary of significant economic and technical developments in the mineral and fuel industries during the year.
6. *Mineral Industry Surveys.* These are the raw materials for the Yearbook, published periodically and containing an account of trends in national production, distribution, and consumption of about 100 mineral commodities.
7. *Outside Publications.* Articles prepared by BOM authors that

---

[84] This summary of BOM publications was abstracted from NSF, No. 16, pp. 20–23, Lesher and Howick, *op. cit.,* p. A–96; and *Policy Planning for Technology Transfer,* p. 135.

are published in the technical press, in books, and at symposia number about 250 per year.

Bibliographies. Major bibliographies appear as bulletins, others as information circulars.

Mailing lists for each type of publication are maintained by BOM; 300 to 400 names, for example, are on the mailing list for Bulletins, about 300 on the list for Reports of Investigations, and about 200 on that for Information Circulars.[85] "The effectiveness and utility of the information disseminated to the public and private sectors is determined by means of regular or periodic formal and informal inquiries and contacts."[86] Presumably, the mailing lists are the basis of this feedback procedure since GPO keeps no records of the purchasers of individual copies of documents.

Publications may be sold or distributed through CFSTI, GPO, and occasionally the Bureau itself. Furthermore, the publications are collected and made available at over 500 depository libraries in the United States and Puerto Rico.[87] Five Regional Offices also maintain files of BOM publications which may be consulted.

Nonpublication activities consist primarily of motion pictures, patents, and inspection services. In fiscal 1963, there were 4,250 prints of motion pictures in circulation.[88] The films depict mining and manufacturing operations relating to specific commodities, and also are concerned with the mineral resources of various states. Over 200,000 showings of these films are given annually, and the films are distributed free of charge to any responsible organization.

Finally, BOM conducts coal mine inspections under the Federal Coal Mine Safety Act. During fiscal 1963, over 12,000 such inspections were made.[89] These inspections and any violations reported alert the industry to new safety developments required for minimal safety standards.

---

85 Lesher and Howick, *op. cit.,* p. A–96.

86 *Policy Planning for Technology Transfer,* p. 135.

87 NSF, No. 16, p. 24.

88 Department of Interior, *op. cit.,* p. 431.

89 *Ibid.,* p. 440.

Appendix B

Disclosure and Patenting Record of Large NASA Contractors

Table B.1

Disclosure and Patenting Record of the One Hundred Largest NASA Contractors (Business Firms) Listed According to Net Value Direct Awards by NASA* Fiscal Year 1965

Contractor and Place of Contract Performance	Rank as NASA Contractor in FY 1964	NET VALUE OF AWARDS Thousands of Dollars	Percentage of Total Awards to Business	(1) Inventions Disclosed 1958-65	(2) Waivers Requested 1958-65	(3) Waivers Granted (total)	(4) Development or Promotional Effort Reported but No Commercial Application	(5) Inventions Successfully Applied Commercially (through Dec. 31, 1965)
Total Awards to Business		$4,141,434	100.0					
1. North American Aviation, Inc. †Downey, Calif.	1	1,099,448	26.55	811	32	13	2	None
2. Boeing Company †New Orleans, La.	4	305,988	7.39	90	None	None	None	None
3. Grumman Aircraft Eng. Corp. †Bethpage, N.Y.	5	267,226	6.45	26	None	None	None	None
4. Douglas Aircraft Co., Inc. †Santa Monica, Calif.	3	251,668	6.08	96	3	3	1	None
5. General Electric Company †Huntsville, Ala.	7	181,472	4.38	180	3	3	None	None
6. McDonnell Aircraft Corp. †St. Louis, Mo.	2	166,670	4.02	73	8	7	1	None
7. I.B.M. †Huntsville, Ala.	10	128,312	3.10	100	8	7	None	None
8. Aerojet-General Corp. †Sacramento, Calif.	8	123,186	2.97	86	2	1	None	None
9. General Dynamics Corp. †San Diego, Calif.	6	111,148	2.68	109	1	None	None	None
10. Radio Corp. of America †Princeton, N.J.	11	106,552	2.57	182	1	1	None	None

11. Chrysler Corporation †New Orleans, La.	9	85,986	2.08	59	None	None	None	None
12. General Motors Corp. †Milwaukee, Wis.	13	72,531	1.75	22	None	None	None	None
13. Bendix Corporation †Teterboro, N.J.	12	66,100	1.60	24	None	None	None	None
14. TRW Space Tech. Lab. †Redondo Beach, Calif.	16[a]	50,533	1.22	147	11	8	1	None
15. United Aircraft Corp. †West Palm Beach, Fla.	17	43,330	1.05	377	14	1	None	None
16. Sperry Rand Corp. †St. Paul, Minn.	28	39,401	.95	40	4	1	1	None
17. Lockheed Aircraft Corp. †Sunnyvale, Calif.	15	35,796	.86	113	1	None	None	None
18. Collins Radio Company †Richardson, Tex.	51	31,532	.76	25	4	2	None	None
19. Brown Engineering Co., Inc. †Huntsville, Ala.	14	30,850	.74	26	None	None	None	None
20. Philco Corporation †Houston, Tex.	18	30,029	.73	14	None	None	None	None
21. Hayes Internat'l Corp. †Birmingham, Ala.	22	28,496	.69	1	None	None	None	None
22. Honeywell, Inc. †St. Petersburg, Fla.	40	27,068	.65	102	None	None	None	None
23. Hughes Aircraft Company †Culver City, Calif.	25	26,457	.64	158	2	2	None	None
24. Catalytic Construction Co. †Merritt Island, Fla.	44	25,296	.61	0	None	None	None	None
25. Trans World Airlines, Inc. †Various	—	20,862	.50	0	None	None	None	None
26. Union Carbide Corp. †Fontana, Calif.	21	19,954	.48	5	None	None	None	None

Table B.1 (cont'd)

Contractor and Place of Contract Performance	Rank as NASA Contractor in FY 1964	NET VALUE OF AWARDS: Thousands of Dollars	NET VALUE OF AWARDS: Percentage of Total Awards to Business	(1) Inventions Disclosed 1958-65	(2) Waivers Requested 1958-65	(3) Waivers Granted (total)	(4) Development or Promotional Effort Reported but No Commercial Application	(5) Inventions Successfully Applied Commercially (through Dec. 31, 1965)
27. LTV Aerospace Corp. †Dallas, Tex.	20[b]	15,118	.37	8	None	None	None	None
28. Fairchild Hiller Corp. †Hagerstown, Md.	31	14,720	.36	12	None	None	None	None
29. Mason-Rust New Orleans, La.	27	13,097	.32	1	None	None	None	None
30. Westinghouse Electric Corp. †Baltimore, Md.	45	12,647	.31	256	1	1	None	None
31. Radiation, Inc. Melbourne, Fla.	30	12,056	.29	10	None	None	None	None
32. Control Data Corp. †Minneapolis, Minn.	24	11,808	.29	None	None	None	None	None
33. Bellcomm, Inc. Washington, D.C.	37	9,804	.24	17	None	None	None	None
34. Pacific Crane & Rigging Merritt Island, Fla.	—	9,280	.22	None	None	None	None	None
35. Martin Marietta Corp. †Baltimore, Md.	38	8,389	.20	35	None	None	None	None
36. Lear Siegler, Inc. †Anaheim, Calif.	73	8,260	.20	1	None	None	None	None
37. Air Products & Chemicals †Long Beach, Calif.	33	8,135	.20	4	None	None	None	None
38. Republic Aviation Corp. †Farmingdale, N.Y.	35	7,537	.18	5	1	None	None	None

39. Thiokol Chemical Corp. †Brunswick, Ga.	69	7,441	.18	5	None	None	None	None	
40. Northrop Corporation †Hawthorne, Calif.	36	7,297	.18	11	1	None	None	None	
41. Garrett Corporation †Los Angeles, Calif.	57	7,179	.17	34	None	None	None	None	
42. Scientific Data Systems †Santa Monica, Calif.	53	6,800	.16	None	None	None	None	None	
43. Amer. Machine & Found. Co. †York, Pa.	66	6,614	.16	6	None	None	None	None	
44. Dynatronics, Inc. †Orlando, Fla. (s)	—	6,436	.16	5	None	None	None	None	
45. Spaco, Inc. Huntsville, Ala. (s)	46	6,308	.15	9	None	None	None	None	
46. Avco Corporation †Wilmington, Mass.	52	6,299	.15	15	None	None	None	None	
47. Electronic Associates, Inc. †West Long Branch, N.J.	63	6,025	.15	None	None	None	None	None	
48. Motorola, Inc. †Scottsdale, Ariz.	76	5,830	.14	10	None	None	None	None	
49. Sanders Associates, Inc. Nashua, N.H.	—	5,830	.14	None	None	None	None	None	
50. Fed.-Mogul-Bower Bearings, †Los Alamitos, Calif.	32	5,603	.14	None	None	None	None	None	
51. Documentation, Inc. †Bethesda, Md. (s)	39	5,240	.13	7	None	None	None	None	
52. Blount/Chicago Bridge (joint venture) Sandusky, Ohio	—	5,178	.13	None	None	None	None	None	
53. Ball Bros. Research Corp. Boulder, Colo.	43	5,036	.12	15	3	2	None	1	
54. Keltec Industries* †Alexandria, Va. (s)	—	4,749	.11	None	None	None	None	None	

Table B.1 (cont'd)

Contractor and Place of Contract Performance	Rank as NASA Contractor in FY 1964	NET VALUE OF AWARDS Thousands of Dollars	Percentage of Total Awards to Business	(1) Inventions Disclosed 1958-65	(2) Waivers Requested 1958-65	(3) Waivers Granted (total)	(4) Development or Promotional Effort Reported but No Commercial Application	(5) Inventions Successfully Applied Commercially (through Dec. 31, 1965)
55. Ampex Corporation †Redwood City, Calif.	48	4,747	.11	7	5	4	None	None
56. Norair Engineering Corp. Greenbelt, Md.	—	4,736	.11	None	None	None	None	None
57. Electro-Mech. Research, Inc. †Sarasota, Fla.	47	4,615	.11	11	None	None	None	None
58. Vitro Corporation of Amer. †Huntsville, Ala.	72	4,435	.11	6	1	None	None	None
59. Dynamic Corp. of Amer. Garden City, N.Y.	—	4,358	.11	None	None	None	None	None
60. Minnesota Mining & Mfg. Co. †Camarillo, Calif.	—	4,257	.10	None	None	None	None	None
61. Graham Engineering Co. (s) Houston, Tex.	—	4,063	.10	None	None	None	None	None
62. Brown/Northrop (joint venture) Houston, Tex.	—	4,060	.10	None	None	None	None	None
63. Beckman Instr., Inc. †Fullerton, Calif.	77	3,997	.10	22	2	None	None	None
64. Computer Control Co. †Framingham, Mass.	—	3,908	.09	7	1	None	None	None
65. Wolf Res. & Dev., Corp. (s) †Houston, Tex.	—	3,882	.09	None	None	None	None	None
66. Clark David Co., Inc. Worcester, Mass.	—	3,839	.09	20	None	None	None	None

67.	Taag Designs, Inc. College Park, Md.	(s)	—	3,790	.09	None	None	None	None	None
68.	Zia Company Las Cruces, N.M.		91	3,779	.09	None	None	None	None	None
69.	Allis Chalmers Mfg. Co. †Milwaukee, Wis.		—	3,701	.09	5	1	1	None	1
70.	Pennsalt Chemical Corp. Various		—	3,559	.09	None	None	None	None	None
71.	Consolidated Systems Corp. †Monrovia, Calif.		81	3,555	.09	2	None	None	None	None
72.	Calumet & Hecla, Inc. Bartlett, Ill.		—	3,418	.08	None	None	None	None	None
73.	Aero Spacelines, Inc. Van Nuys, Calif.	(s)	—	3,387	.08	None	None	None	None	None
74.	MSI Corporation Greenbelt, Md.		—	3,386	.08	None	None	None	None	None
75.	Bell Aerospace Corp. †Buffalo, N.Y.		49	3,328	.08	3	None	None	None	None
76.	Space-General Corp. El Monte, Calif.		64	3,293	.08	11	None	None	None	None
77.	Hathaway E A & Co. Mountain View, Calif.	(s)	—	3,216	.08	None	None	None	None	None
78.	Systems Engr. Labs., Inc. †Ft. Lauderdale, Fla.	(s)	89	3,019	.07	None	None	None	None	None
79.	Electronic Comm., Inc. †St. Petersburg, Fla.		—	2,952	.07	4	None	None	None	None
80.	Consol. Electrodyn. Corp. †Pasadena, Calif.		58	2,938	.07	7	None	None	None	None
81.	Kiewit/Leavell (joint venture) Sandusky, Ohio		—	2,820	.07	None	None	None	None	None
82.	Electro Optical Sys., Inc. Pasadena, Calif.		84	2,808	.07	29	4	3	None	None

Table B.1 (cont'd)

Contractor and Place of Contract Performance	Rank as NASA Contractor in FY 1964	NET VALUE OF AWARDS: Thousands of Dollars	NET VALUE OF AWARDS: Percentage of Total Awards to Business	(1) Inventions Disclosed 1958-65	(2) Waivers Requested 1958-65	(3) Waivers Granted (total)	(4) Development or Promotional Effort Reported but No Commercial Application	(5) Inventions Successfully Applied Commercially (through Dec. 31, 1965)
83. Sylvania Elec. Prod., Inc. †Waltham, Mass.	—	2,652	.06	21	None	None	None	None
84. Washington Tech. Asso., Inc. Rockville, Md. (s)	—	2,615	.06	3	None	None	None	None
85. Wise Contracting Co. (s) †Hampton, Va.	—	2,561	.06	None	None	None	None	None
86. Sun Shpbldg. & Dry Dock Co. Chester, Pa.	—	2,554	.06	None	None	None	None	None
87. Litton Industries, Inc. †College Park, Md.	—	2,449	.06	3	1	1	1	None
88. Virginia Electric Power Co. Hampton, Va.	—	2,421	.06	None	None	None	None	None
89. Western Union Tele. Co. Various	—	2,397	.06	None	None	None	None	None
90. Universal Marion Corp. Marion, Ohio	—	2,341	.06	None	None	None	None	None
91. Swenson Carl N. Co. Mountain View, Calif.	—	2,324	.06	None	None	None	None	None
92. Whittaker Corporation †Van Nuys, Calif.	83	2,297	.06	9	None	None	None	None
93. Consultants & Designers, Inc. Arlington, Va.	—	2,207	.05	None	None	None	None	None
94. Raytheon Company †Wayland, Mass.	19	2,200	.05	4	None	None	None	None

95. Canoga Electronics Corp. †Van Nuys, Calif.	(s)	95	2,172	.05	None	None	None	None	None
96. Int'l Teleph. & Telegr. †San Fernando, Calif.		71	2,153	.05	6	None	None	None	None
97. Dow Chemical Co. Various		—	2,070	.05	None	None	None	None	None
98. Melpar, Inc. †Falls Church, Va.		—	2,069	.05	22	None	None	None	None
99. Dortech Corporation Various		—	2,064	.05	None	None	None	None	None
100. Management Services, Inc. †Huntsville, Ala.	(s)	74	2,061	.05	None	None	None	None	None
Total				90.55					
All other business				9.45					

* Data for individual companies include awards on R & D contracts of $10,000 and over and on all other contracts of $25,000 and over.

† Awards during period represent awards on several contracts which have different principal places of performance. The place shown is that which has the largest amount of the awards.

(s) Indicates small business concerns.

[a] Rank of Thompson Ramo Wooldridge, Inc., of which TRW Space Technology Labs was then a division.

[b] Rank of Ling Temco Vought, Inc., of which LTV Aerospace Corp. was then a division.

Table B.2

NASA Research and Development Contracts with Educational and Other Nonprofit Institutions
(Exclusive of grants, where single contracts are of $1 million or over)

Institution	Award in 1965	Cumulative Awards under Existing Contracts	Inventions Disclosed 1958-65	Waivers Requested 1958-65	Waivers Granted (total)	Developmental or Promotional Effort Reported but No Commercial Application	Successful Commercial Application
	(In millions of dollars)						
Calif. Inst. of Tech.							
Operation of JPL[1]	247		290 (combined)	15	9	1	1
Other	1.6	2.5					
Mass. Inst. of Tech.	19.2	49.0	44	None	None	None	None
Smithsonian Institution	7.7	27.9	2	None	None	None	None
Univ. of Wisconsin	2.8	6.3	None	None	None	None	None
Univ. of Calif. at L.A.	1.7	3.3	6 (combined)	None	None	None	None
Univ. of Calif. at Berkeley	1.7	2.7		1	1	None	None
New Mexico State Univ.	1.7	—	1	None	None	None	None
Princeton University	1.2	4.9	2	2	2	None	None

1 Contract With California Institute of Technology for Operation of Jet Propulsion Laboratory.

The Jet Propulsion Laboratory (JPL) is a government-owned research and development facility, operated for NASA by the California Institute of Technology. The Laboratory carries out research programs and flight projects and conceives and executes advanced development and experimental engineering investigations to further the technology required for the nation's space program. The primary emphasis of the Laboratory's effort is on the carrying out of unmanned lunar, planetary, and deep-space scientific missions.

Net awards during fiscal 1965 totaled $247 million. Of this amount, $188 million was placed through subcontracts or purchases with business firms; $59 million constituted in-house effort.

Appendix C
Federal Agency Data Policies and Contractor Strategy

Value of Patents in Federal Contracting

Any technology transfer program must face the fact that full disclosure is not likely to be a profitable strategy for a federal contractor since proprietary information that would commonly be accorded some legal protection from competitors in the public sector is not protected in the same ways under government contracts. If a patented item was developed under federal R & D funding, the government usually retains at least an irrevocable, nonexclusive, royalty-free license for any governmental use.[1] Inventions, expertise of "unique" techniques formulated under government-sponsored R & D (not including overhead R & D funding) are, in theory, the property of the government for the purpose of application to any type of government project. The government can and has required that contractors turn over sufficient technical information to a competitor so that the competitor can either take over the project or become a second source.[2]

---

[1] See Robert Solo, *Patent Policy for Government Sponsored Research and Development,* Report prepared for the NASA Administrator's Office (Washington, D.C.: NASA, 1966), part II, p. 34; or Lee Preston, "Patent Rights Under Federal R & D Contracts," *Harvard Business Review,* XLI, No. 5 (September-October 1963), pp. 6–13.

[2] Frederick Scherer, *The Weapons Acquisition Process* (Boston: Division of Research, Graduate School of Business Administration, Harvard University, 1964), pp. 114–18. The example given by Scherer is the Army's breakout of Honest John Rocket production from Douglas's prime contract. Douglas argued that the detailed design drawings required to manufacture the rocket were private property and reflected an accumulated engineering expertise developed over many years of public and private work. But, the Army argued that such data as were needed for the breakdown production were government property in spite of the following ASPR regulations:

> It is the policy of the Department of Defense to encourage inventiveness

Even if a patent was developed under private funding, the patent holder (or his licensee) may find it difficult to charge the government for the patent rights.[3]

A recent law review article noted:

> Although in the commercial realm it has been said that "within his domain the patentee is czar," under present rules a patent owner finds that his patent even if valid, is irrelevant to his bid to furnish the patented item or services to the Government. And a licensee under a valid patent finds that he is actually at a disadvantage compared to his unlicensed competitor.[4]

Even data submitted in proposals have been used by the government, particularly in unsolicited proposals.[5]

For such reasons as these, patent protection plays little part in the market strategy of space/defense contractors. In some instances, the government's appropriation of technical data considered the property of a contractor has also added a strong incentive to bury

---

> and to provide incentive therefor by honoring "proprietary data" resulting from private developments and hence to limit demands for data to that which is essential for Government purposes. ASPR, section 9-202.2 (a) (April 1965, Revision 10).

The ruling that detailed design drawings are government property in this context has been adopted by other agencies, but its effect appears to vary from industry to industry and the government may pay indemnities for violation of trade secrets.

[3] Gerald Mossinghoff and Robert Allnutt, "Patent Infringement in Government Procurement: A Remedy Without a Right?" *Notre Dame Law Review,* XLII (October 1966), pp. 5–28, note that Court of Claims-Patent Cases Act of 1948, 62 Stat. 942, 28 U.S.C.A. 1498 (1948) is interpreted by the Comptroller General in *Herbert Cooper Co.,* B—136916 (August 1958) so that, while patentees must be indemnified for infringement, patent, or license costs should not be considered when an agency has to make a procurement decision. Bidders may, however, be required to post bonds.

[4] Mossinghoff and Allnutt, *op. cit.,* p. 5.

[5] Information was obtained in personal interviews with over 25 Greater Boston R & D contractors and through my own industrial experience. See Allnutt, "Recent Developments in NASA Patent Policy and Data Policies," paper presented before a meeting of NASA contractors (Washington, D.C.: NASA, Office of the General Counsel, February 1966), pp. 2–6, for a discussion of the special care NASA is exercising to protect technical information in proposals, both solicited (if marked) and unsolicited. Allnutt notes that numerous complaints have been made to the Comptroller General about the use of technical information contained in proposals.

other proprietary data and know-how. Any acquisition program must face this reality of the aerospace, weapons-systems industry. DOD and NASA overhead R & D funding policies provide another problem for the Acquisition Branch.

Agency Overhead R & D Funding and Its Effects on Acquisition

Although there is little evidence as to the quantity and quality of weapons-systems innovations developed as a result not of "planned" innovation under direct federal R & D funding, but rather as a result of indirect funding of contractors by way of overhead reimbursement of so-called contractor independent research and development (IR & D or PI or BP), it is at least arguable that a considerable number of innovations result from this class of R & D activity. It can be argued that since innovations discovered under this class of funding belong exclusively to the contractor and need not even be reported, there is considerable motivation to produce and classify innovations under the coverage of overhead R & D funding. As previously observed, a significant portion of federal R & D funding may be spent on this overhead type of R & D funding, perhaps as much as 15 percent of all federally funded R & D.[6]

Both DOD and NASA fund this type of activity not only for R & D contractors but also for those doing more production-oriented work as well.[7] Both DOD and NASA permit contractors to retain exclusive rights to all data, innovations, know-how, and so on, developed under this indirect R & D funding.[8] Not only do contractors retain exclusive rights, they need not reveal the results of this work

[6] See Chapter 2, footnotes 3 to 6, for a discussion of federal R & D funding characteristics.

[7] See Department of Defense, Letter to GAO explaining DOD policy as to Rights in Technical Data Resulting from Independent Research and Development, Defense Procurement Circular #22 (Washington, D.C.: DOD or GAO, January 29, 1965). For a discussion of DOD policy and ASPR, sections 15–205.3 and 15–205.35 (November 1963, Revision 3). See NASA PR, section 15–205.35 (November 1965, Revision 6), for the regulations governing NASA overhead reimbursement for contractor independent R & D. Recently NASA Regulations were brought in line with those of DOD by allowing overhead reimbursement for the preparation of unsolicited proposal work. NASA PRD N. 67–4 (March 1967).

[8] ASPR, section 9–200 (April 1965, Revision 10) and NASA PR, section 9–101–7 (November 1965, Revision 6).

except insofar as they wish to in bidding on new or follow-on contracts. The theory of both agencies is that since a contractor's position in the space/defense industry depends on technological excellence, contractors will, in fact, reveal most of the results of this independent R & D in order to secure new or follow-on contracts.

The GAO, in a somewhat different context, has contended that DOD data policies relating to this overhead R & D funding should be modified so as to provide the results of this public funding to the government free of exclusive contractor rights. The General Accounting Office observed that:

> 1. In instances in which the Government has indirectly borne a substantial portion of the research and development costs of equipment, the Government should negotiate for the acquisition of the technical data needed to obtain competition for the equipment, and
> 2. If a contractor refuses to negotiate for the transfer of its technical data to the Government, consideration should be given to disallowing the contractor's independent research and development costs.[9]

DOD, on the other hand, had contended that this was not public funding, but rather customer financing of private R & D, such as would be done in the commercial market through allocation by the private firm of portions of its higher profit margins in that market.[10] Thus DOD contends that this funding should be considered part of the contractor's risk capital investment needed to maintain his position in the space/defense industry.

This discussion is not intended as a criticism of either the GAO position or that of DOD. Its purpose is to point out that DOD and NASA policies probably have an adverse effect on the input portion of any transfer program. More specifically, it probably adversely af-

[9] Quotation from the DOD Letter, p. 4.

[10] DOD argues in its reply to GAO criticism of overhead R & D funding policies that the difficulty with the GAO position is that it failed to distinguish ". . . between research and development which is directly sponsored and paid for by the Government and research and development which is privately sponsored, with the Government contribution to it only in the sense, that customers generally may be said to contribute to a company's independent research and development—that is, by buying the company's products." DOD Letter, pp. 4–5.

fects the present TU Acquisition Branch substantially in the amount of quality new technology reported for the following reasons:

1. NASA contractors can lawfully refuse to disclose any know-how, inventions, or information attributed to this overhead R & D funding.[11]

2. The possibility exists that a contractor will err on the side of discretion by allocating innovations to overhead R & D charge numbers, thereby preserving his right to withhold information.[12] Scherer notes that defense contractor accounting systems have been notably deficient in accurately allocating cost elements of R & D or production contracts.[13]

3. Both DOD and NASA provide that any patentable items developed under this overhead funding belong solely to the contractor; the contractor need not, generally, grant even license rights to the government.[14]

4. Since most NASA contractors are also DOD contractors, and since DOD overhead R & D funding is several times that of NASA's, even a change in NASA policy requiring disclosure of such innova-

---

[11] NASA PR, section 9.101.7 (November 1965, Revision 6). A significant new technology was developed by a space/defense contractor for whom I had worked. Much of the initial work in this new technology area was funded under various DOD and NASA overhead R & D charge numbers and none had been disclosed under the reporting requirements of the New Technology Clause even though subsequent development was funded directly under NASA R & D contracts. Of course experience with one NASA contractor is not proof of the hypothesis, but it accords well with an optimum reporting strategy in the space/defense market.

[12] There is no other way to prove this assertion than by personal interviews and experience, since there are no data readily available in this area. Contractors are naturally reluctant to discuss their policies with respect to the allocation of charges to overhead R & D charge numbers versus the allocation to directly funded projects.

[13] Scherer, *op. cit.,* pp. 65–67.

[14] NASA PR, section 9.101.7 (November 1965, Revision 6) contains the following provision: "Any invention made in the performance of any work by the Contractor under the Contractor's own product improvement program, or the Contractor's independent research and development program, even though supported by an allowance of costs for such program as a part of the overhead costs hereof, will not be subject to the 'New Technology' clause or the 'Property Rights in Inventions' clause (whichever is included in this contract) unless said work is identified in writing as being required in the performance of this contract."
See also ASPR section 9.101.7 (October 1966, Revision 11).

tions would probably still allow contractors to avoid disclosure for long periods by charging innovation development costs to DOD overhead R & D charge numbers.

5. Since there is no incentive to disclose these overhead-funded innovations under the policy of either agency, many significant innovations may be disclosed, if at all, only as needed in bid proposals. There is little business advantage to disclosure even for a diversified space/defense contractor. Thus, this overhead funding policy on disclosure further reinforces and provides a legal basis for a business strategy of selective disclosure in space/defense contracting.

Some of the TU Program's problems with low reporting rates of "quality" disclosures may be explained by this policy.[15] Moreover, so long as DOD continues to follow a contractor-keep-all policy, the NASA Acquisition Branch is likely to continue to report a low disclosure rate of quality innovations. The issue is really whether contractors need to retain *exclusive* rights to insure a continuing high rate of innovation in the space/defense industry or whether some means (higher profit margins, for example) could be found for rewarding innovative contractors other than by allowing them to retain exclusive and enduring nondisclosure rights to this overhead R & D work product.

It may be simpler administratively for DOD not to attempt to reward contractors for inventions developed under this overhead R & D funding other than by awards of contracts in the usual bid-proposal cycle. But, unless some form of disclosure is required, any transfer program is likely to be severely handicapped in the amount of quality inventions and significant new technical information available for dissemination.

---

[15] The only measure of "quality" presently available for NASA contractor disclosures is whether either the contractor or NASA has been willing to expend the effort and money to file a patent. (Admittedly this is a crude measure of "quality.") Donald Watson and Mary Holman, *Evaluation of NASA's Patent Policy* (Washington, D.C.: George Washington University, 1966), pp. 49–53.

Appendix D
Table of Commonly Used Acronyms and Abbreviations

ACDA	Arms Control and Disarmament Commission
AEC	Atomic Energy Commission
ARPA	Advanced Research Project Administration (DOD)
ASPR	Armed Services Procurement Regulations
ASTIA	Armed Services Technical Information Agency (DOD)
BP	Bid proposal (overhead costs)
CFSTI	Clearinghouse for Federal Scientific and Technical Information
DDC	Defense Documentation Center (DOD)
DOD	Department of Defense
DOA	Department of Agriculture
FCST	Federal Council for Science and Technology
FY	fiscal year
GAO	General Accounting Office
GNP	Gross National Product
HEW	Department of Health, Education and Welfare
IITRI	Illinois Institute of Technology Research Institute
IR & D	independent research and development (overhead costs)
MRI	Midwest Research Institute (Kansas City, Mo.)
NAA	North American Aviation (Corporation)
NASA	National Aeronautics and Space Administration
NASA PR	NASA Procurement Regulations
NERAC	New England Research Application Center (RDC at the University of Connecticut)
NIH	National Institutes of Health
NPA	National Planning Association
NSF	National Science Foundation
OTU	Office of Technology Utilization (NASA)
PI	product improvement (overhead costs)
PSAC	President's Science Advisory Committee
RDC	Regional Dissemination Center
R & D	research and development
RDT & E	research, develoment, test, and evaluation (DOD category)
SBA	Small Business Administration
Stat.	U.S. Statutes at Large
STID	Scientific and Technical Information Division
STS	State Technical Services (Department of Commerce Program)
TUD	Technology Utilization Division
TUO	Technology Utilization Officer (NASA)
TUP	Technology Utilization Program (NASA)
U.S.C.A.	United States Code Annotated
USDA	U.S. Department of Agriculture

Bibliography

Books

Baker, Gladys. *The County Agent.* Chicago: University of Chicago Press, 1939.

Barber, Bernard. *Science and the Social Order.* 2nd ed. New York: Collier Books, 1962.

Barber, Bernard, and Walter Hirsch, eds. *The Sociology of Science.* New York: The Free Press of Glencoe, 1962.

Bolton, Roger. *Defense Purchases and Regional Growth.* Washington, D.C.: The Brookings Institution, 1966.

Blood, Jerome, ed. *Utilizing R & D Pay-Products.* New York: American Management Association, 1967.

Bright, James. *Research, Development, and Technological Innovation.* Homewood, Illinois: Richard B. Irwin, 1964.

Bright, James, ed. *Technological Forecasting for Industry and Government.* Englewood Cliffs, New Jersey: Prentice-Hall, 1968.

Brooks, Harvey. *The Government of Science.* Cambridge: The M.I.T. Press, 1968.

Cleaveland, Frederick. *Science and State Government: A Study of State Government Activities in Six States.* Chapel Hill: University of North Carolina Press, 1959.

Colm, Gerhard, and Peter Wagner. *Federal Budget Projections.* Washington, D.C.: The Brookings Institution, 1966.

Corbin, Arthur. *Corbin on Contracts.* (One-volume edition.) St. Paul, Minnesota: West Publishing Company, 1952.

Denison, Edward. *The Sources of Economic Growth in the United States and the Alternatives before Us.* New York: Committee for Economic Development, 1962.

Dorfman, Robert, ed. *Measuring Benefits of Government Investments.* Washington, D.C.: The Brookings Institution, 1963.

Dupré, Stefan, and Sanford Lakoff. *Science and the Nation.* Englewood Cliffs, New Jersey: Prentice-Hall, 1962.

Dupree, A. Hunter. *Science in the Federal Government: A History of Policies and Activities to 1940.* New York: Harper & Row, 1964.

Etzioni, Amitai.*The Moon Doggle, Domestic and International Implications of the Space Race.* Garden City, New York: Doubleday, 1964.

Farrand, Max. *Record of the Federal Convention of 1787.* Vol. 2 of 3. New Haven: Yale University Press, 1911.

Forman, Howard. *Patents: Their Ownership and Administration by the United States Government.* New York: The Central Book Company, 1957.

Green, Harold, and Alan Rosenthal. *Government of the Atom: The Integration of Powers.* New York: Atherton Press, 1963.

Gilpin, Robert, and Christopher Wright, eds. *Scientists and National Policy Making.* New York: Columbia University Press, 1964.

Sherwin, Chalmers, and Raymond Isenson, "Project Hindsight, A Defense Department Study of the Utility of Research," *Science,* CLVI, No. 3782 (1967), pp. 1571–77.

Silk, Leonard, "The Impact on the American Economy," in *Outer Space: Prospects for Man and Society,* Lincoln Bloomfield, ed., Englewood Cliffs, New Jersey: Prentice-Hall, 1962, pp. 64–83.

Solo, Robert, "Gearing Military R & D to Economic Growth," *Harvard Business Review,* XL, No. 6 (November-December 1962), pp. 49–60.

Solow, Robert, "Technical Change and the Aggregate Production Function," *Review of Economics and Statistics,* XXXIX, No. 3 (August 1957), pp. 312–20.

Toulmin, Stephen, "The Complexity of Scientific Choice: A Stock-taking," *Minerva* (Spring 1964), pp. 343–59.

Watson, Donald, and Mary Holman, "Patents from Government Financed Research and Development," *Patent, Trademark and Copyright Journal of Research and Education,* V, No. 2 (Summer 1964), pp. 199–222.

Watson, Donald, Harold Bright, and Arthur Burns, "Federal Patent Policy in Contracts for Research and Development," *Patent, Trademark, and Copyright Journal of Research and Education,* IV, No. 4 (Winter 1960), pp. 299–434.

Webb, James, "The Economic Impact of the Space Program," *Business Horizons,* VI, No. 3 (Fall 1963), pp. 4–26.

Weinberg, Alvin, "Can Technology Replace Social Engineering?" *Bulletin of the Atomic Scientists* (December 1966), pp. 4–8.

Welles, John, and Robert Waterman, "Space Technology: Pay-Off from Spin-Off," *Harvard Business Review,* XLII (July-August 1964), pp. 106–18.

"Will Space Research Pay Off on Earth?" *New York Times,* May 26, 1963.

Wille, Frank, "Government Ownership of Patents," *Fordham Law Review,* XII, No. 2 (May 1943), pp. 105–29.

Wright, Robert, "Wright on Patents," *Bulletin of the Atomic Scientists* (October 1964), p. 34.

———, "U.S. Patent Policy and Government Research," *Bulletin of the Atomic Scientists,* (December 1963), pp. 9–13.

Public Documents

Allen, Thomas. *Managing the Flow of Scientific and Technological Information.* Final Report to Office of Science Information Service, NSF. Springfield, Va.: Clearinghouse for Scientific and Technical Information, September 1966.

Brooks, Harvey, "Organizing Research for Social and Economic Objectives: An Outsider's Appraisal of the Strengths and Weaknesses of Agricultural Research," *Symposium on Research in Agriculture.* Conference sponsored jointly by the DOA and the National Academy of Sciences. Washington, D.C.: DOA, August 1966.

Crawford, J. H., *et al. Scientific and Technical Communications in the Government.* Task Force Report to the President's Special Assistant for Science and Technology. Springfield, Va.: Clearinghouse for Scientific and Technical Information, April 1962.

Denver Research Institute. *The Commercial Applications of Missile/Space Technology*. NASA Sponsored Report. Springfield, Va.: Clearinghouse for Scientific and Technical Information, 1963.

———. *Channels of Technology Acquisition in Commercial Firms and the NASA Dissemination Program*. NASA Sponsored Report. Springfield, Va.: Clearinghouse for Scientific and Technical Information, June 1967.

Gough, William. *The Relation of Controlled Fusion Research to American Science and Industry*. Washington, D.C.: AEC, 1965.

Harbridge House, Inc. *Government Patent Policy Study: Final Report*. Vol. I. Prepared for the FCST Committee on Government Patent Policy. Washington, D.C.: U.S. Government Printing Office, May 1968.

Howell, Richard, *et al. The Structure and Dynamics of Research and Exploratory Development in Defense R & D Industry*. Stanford Research Institute Report, prepared for the Director of Defense Research and Engineering, Office of Secretary of Defense. Springfield, Va.: Clearinghouse for Scientific and Technical Information, August 1966.

Lesher, Richard, and George Howick. *Background, Guidelines, and Recommendations for Use in Assessing Effective Means of Channeling New Technologies in Promising Directions*. Prepared for U.S. National Commission on Technology, Automation, and Economic Progress. Washington, D.C.: U.S. Government Printing Office, November 1965.

———. *Assessing Technology Transfer*. NASA. SP–5067. Washington, D.C.: U.S. Government Printing Office, 1966.

Little, Arthur D., Inc. *Centralization and Documentation*. Springfield, Va.: Clearinghouse for Scientific and Technical Information, July 1963.

———. *Patterns and Problems of Technical Innovation In America*. Report to the NSF. Washington, D.C.: U.S. Department of Commerce, 1963.

———. *Projective Economic Studies of New England*. Report to U.S. Army Engineer Division, New England Corps of Engineers. Cambridge: A. D. Little, Inc., October 1964.

———. *Technology Transfer and the Technology Utilization Program*. Report to the NASA OTU. Washington, D.C.: NASA Headquarters, January 1965.

———. *Technology Transfer and the Technology Utilization Program*. Report to the NASA OTU. Washington, D.C.: NASA Headquarters, April 1966.

———. *Transfer of Aerospace Technology in the United States—A Critical Review*. Report to the Subcommittee of Enquiry into the Aircraft Industry, United Kingdom (known as the Plowden Committee). Cambridge: A. D. Little, Inc., July 1966.

Lynn, Frank. *An Investigation of the Rate of Development and Diffusion of Technology in Our Modern Industrial Society*. Report to the U.S. National Commission on Technology, Automation and Economic Progress. Washington, D.C.: U.S. Government Printing Office, 1966.

National Academy of Sciences, Committee on Science and Public Policy. *Basic Research and National Goals*. A Report to the Committee on Science and Astronautics, U.S. House of Representatives. Washington, D.C.: U.S. Government Printing Office, 1965.

———. *Applied Science and Technological Progress*. A Report to the Committee on Science and Astronautics, U.S. House of Representatives. Washington, D.C.: U.S. Government Printing Office, 1967.

National Planning Association. *Technology Transfer and Industrial Innova-*

tion. Unpublished Report prepared for the National Science Foundation by Sumner Myers, *et al.* Washington, D.C.: NSF, February 1967.

New England Research Application Center. *NASA Technology Utilization Project—Feasibility Study for Establishment of Regional Dissemination Center for New England.* Springfield, Va.: Clearinghouse for Scientific and Technical Information, April 1967.

North American Aviation, Inc. *Technology Utilization Program Management and Operation Plan.* Washington, D.C.: NASA OTU, September 1965.

A National Program of Research for Agriculture. Sponsored jointly by the Association of State Universities and Land Grant Colleges and the U.S. DOA. Washington, D.C.: U.S. DOA, October 1966.

Office of Industrial Application, University of Maryland. *Final Report of 1964 Activities.* Greenbelt, Md.: NASA, Goddard Space Flight Center, 1965.

———. *Final Report of 1965 Activities.* Greenbelt, Md.: NASA, Goddard Space Flight Center, 1966.

Rosholt, Robert. *An Administrative History of NASA, 1958–1963.* NASA SP–4101. Washington, D.C.: U.S. Government Printing Office, 1966.

Sherwin, Chalmers, and Raymond Isenson. "First Interim Report on Project Hindsight." Report to the Director of Defense Research and Engineering. Washington, D.C.: DOD, June 1966, revised October 1966.

Technology Transfer and Innovation. Conference under the Auspices of the National Planning Association and the National Science Foundation. Washington, D.C.: U.S. Government Printing Office, May 1966.

U.S. Arms Control and Disarmament Agency. *The Implications of Reduced Defense Demand for the Electronics Industry.* Prepared by Battelle Memorial Institute. Washington, D.C.: U.S. Government Printing Office, September 1965.

———. *Defense Industry Diversification: An Analysis with 12 Case Studies.* Prepared by John Gilmore and Dean Coddington of the Denver Research Institute. Washington, D.C.: U.S. Government Printing Office, January 1966.

———. *Technological Innovation in Civilian Public Areas.* Prepared by Ronald Black and Charles Forman. Washington, D.C.: U.S. Government Printing Office, September 1967.

U.S. Atomic Energy Commission. *Tranference of Non-Nuclear Technology to Industry.* Committee Report to Oak Ridge Operations Office. Oak Ridge, Tennessee: U.S. AEC, July 1965.

———. *1966 Annual Report to Congress.* Washington, D.C.: U.S. Government Printing Office, January 1967.

U.S. Attorney General. *Report on Investigation of Government Patent Practices and Policies.* Washington, D.C.: U.S. Government Printing Office, 1947.

U.S. Bureau of the Budget. *Report to the President on Government Contracting for Research and Development.* Prepared by the Bureau of the Budget and referred to the Senate Committee on Government Operations. Washington, D.C.: U.S. Government Printing Office, 1962. (87th Congress, second session, 1962 Senate Document, No. 94.)

U.S. Department of Agriculture. *1961 Annual Report to Congress.* Washington, D.C.: U.S. Government Printing Office, 1962.

———. *Agriculture Information Bulletin No. 224: Questions and Answers on Agricultural Research.* Washington, D.C.: U.S. Government Printing Office, July 1966.

U.S. Department of Commerce. *Technological Innovation: Its Environment and Management*. Prepared for the Secretary of Commerce. Washington, D.C.: U.S. Government Printing Office, January 1967.

———. Office of State Technical Services Newsletter, Vol. II, No. 5, November 1966.

———. Vol. III, No. 2, September-October 1967.

———. *1966 Annual Report to Congress*. Washington, D.C.: U.S. Government Printing Office, 1967.

CONGRESSIONAL HEARINGS*—HOUSE

U.S. Congress. House of Representatives. Subcommittee of the Committee on Appropriations. *1967 Department of Defense Appropriations. Hearings*. 89th Congress, second session. Washington, D.C.: U.S. Government Printing Office, 1966. Part 2.

———. *1968 Department of Defense Appropriations. Hearings*. 90th Congress, first session. Washington, D.C.: U.S. Government Printing Office, 1967. Part 3.

———. Committee on Government Operations. *Conflict Between Federal Research Programs and the Nation's Goals for Higher Education. Hearings*. 89th Congress, first session. June 1965. Washington, D.C.: U.S. Government Printing Office, June 1966.

———. *Federal Research and Development Programs: The Decision Making Process*. Thirty-fourth report. 89th Congress, second session. House Report No. 1664. Washington, D.C.: U.S. Government Printing Office, June 1966.

———. Research and Technical Programs Subcommittee. *The Use of Social Research in Federal Domestic Programs. Report*. 90th Congress, first session, 4 parts. Washington, D.C.: U.S. Government Printing Office, April 1967 (Committee Print).

———. Select Committee on Government Research. *Documentation and Dissemination of Research and Development Results*. Study No. 4. 88th Congress, second session. H. Report 504. Washington, D.C.: U.S. Government Printing Office, 1964.

———. Committee on Science and Astronautics. *An Evaluation of the Patent Policies of the National Space and Aeronautics Administration. Report*. 89th Congress, second session. Washington, D.C.: U.S. Government Printing Office, 1966 (Committee Print).

———. *Proposed Studies on the Implications of Peaceful Space Activities for Human Affairs. Report*. Prepared for NASA by The Brookings Institution. 87th Congress, first session. H. Report 242. Washington, D.C.: U.S. Government Printing Office, April 1961.

———. Subcommittee on Advanced Research and Technology. *The Practical Values of Space Exploration. Report*. 86th Congress, second session. H.R. 2091. Washington, D.C.: U.S. Government Printing Office, 1960 (Committee Print).

———. *1963 NASA Authorization. Hearings*. 87th Congress, second session. H.R. 10100. Washington, D.C.: U.S. Government Printing Office, 1962.

* Arranged alphabetically by committee and by subcommittees (if any) within that committee, and chronologically within each committee or subcommittee.

Hamberg, Daniel. *R & D Essays on the Economics of Research and Development.* New York: Random House, 1963.

Harris, Seymour. *The Economics of New England.* Cambridge: Harvard University Press, 1962.

Hitch, Charles, and Roland McKean. *The Economics of Defense in the Nuclear Age.* Cambridge: Harvard University Press, 1960.

Horowitz, Irving, ed. *The Rise and Fall of Project Camelot: Studies in the Relationship Between Social Science and Practical Politics.* Cambridge: The M.I.T. Press, 1967.

Jewkes, John, David Sawers, and Richard Stillerman. *The Sources of Invention.* New York: St. Martin's Press, 1961.

Keenan, Boyd, ed. *Science and the University.* New York: Columbia University Press, 1966.

Kidd, Charles. *American Universities and Federal Research.* Cambridge: Harvard University Press, 1959.

Lakoff, Sanford, ed. *Knowledge and Power: Essays on Science and Government.* New York: Free Press, 1966.

Lapp, Ralph. *The New Priesthood: The Scientific Elite and the Uses of Power.* New York: Harper & Row, 1965.

Lave, Lester. *Technological Change: Its Conception and Measurement.* Englewood Cliffs, New Jersey: Prentice-Hall, 1966.

McLaurin, William. *Inventors and Innovation in the Radio Industry.* New York: Macmillan, 1949.

National Bureau of Economic Research. *The Rate and Direction of Inventive Activity: Economic and Social Factors.* Princeton: Princeton University Press, 1962.

Nelson, Richard, Merton Peck, and Edward Kalachek. *Technology, Economic Growth, and Public Policy.* Washington, D.C.: The Brookings Institution, 1967.

Patents and Technical Data. Washington, D.C.: The George Washington University Government Contracts Program, 1967.

Peck, Merton, and Frederick Scherer. *The Weapons Acquisition Process: An Economic Analysis.* Boston: Division of Research, Graduate School of Business Administration, Harvard University, 1962.

Price, Don K. *Government and Science: Their Dynamic Relation in American Democracy.* New York: Oxford University Press, 1962.

———. *The Scientific Estate.* Cambridge: Harvard University Press, 1965.

Rodgers, Everett. *Diffusion of Innovation.* New York: The Free Press of Glencoe, 1962.

Sanders, H. C., *et al.*, eds. *The Cooperative Extension Service.* Englewood Cliffs, New Jersey: Prentice-Hall, 1966.

Scherer, Frederick. *The Weapons Acquisition Process: Economic Incentives.* Boston: Division of Research, Graduate School of Business Administration, Harvard University, 1964.

Schmookler, Jacob. *Invention and Economic Growth.* Cambridge: Harvard University Press, 1966.

Schon, Donald. *Technology and Change.* New York: Delacorte Press, 1967.

Silk, Leonard. *The Research Revolution.* New York: McGraw-Hill Book Company, Inc., 1960.

Truman, David. *The Governmental Process: Political Interests and Public Opinion.* New York: Alfred A. Knopf, 1965.

Published Articles and Reports

Abramovitz, Moses, "Resource and Output Trends in the United States Since 1870," *American Economic Review,* XLVI (May 1956), pp. 5–23.

Allison, David, "The Civilian Technology Lag," *International Science and Technology,* No. 24 (December 1963), pp. 24–34.

Berger, Peter, "Utilization or Dispensation—Suggestions for the Government's Patent Procurement Program," *Journal of the Patent Office Society,* XLVIII, No. 7 (July 1966), pp. 449–69.

Cooper, Arnold, "R & D Is More Efficient in Small Companies," *Harvard Business Review,* XLII, No. 3 (May-June 1964), pp. 75–83.

Comanor, William, "Market Structure, Product Differentiation and Industrial Research," *The Quarterly Journal of Economics,* LXXXI (November 1967), pp. 639–57.

Deuterman, Elizabeth, "Seeding Science-Based Industry," *Federal Reserve Bank of Philadelphia Business Review* (May 1966), pp. 3–10.

Doctors, Samuel, "Technology Utilization: NERAC Service," *Industry,* XXXII, No. 11 (November 1966), pp. 33, 89.

———. "Transfer of Space Technology to the American Consumer: The Effect of NASA's Patent Policy," *Minnesota Law Review,* LII, No. 4 (March 1968), pp. 789–818.

Ewing, Thomas, "Government Owned Patents," *Journal of the Patent Office Society,* X, No. 4 (January 1928), pp. 149–56.

Fenning, Carl, "The Origin of the Patent and Copyright Clause of the Constitution," *Georgetown Law Journal,* XVII, No. 2 (February 1929), pp. 109–17.

Freeman, Christopher, "Research and Development in Electronic Capital Goods," *National Institute Economics Review* (November 1965), pp. 40–91.

Furash, Edward, "Businessmen Review the Space Effort," *Harvard Business Review,* XLI (September-October 1963), pp. 14–48.

Glocker, George, "The Contract Versus the Grant Approach to Basic Research Activities," *Federal Bar Journal,* XVII (July-September 1957), pp. 265–80.

"The Great American Purchase," *Newsweek* (Feb. 27, 1967; de Borchgrave, Paris Editor).

Green, J. C., "The Information Explosion—Real or Imaginary?" *Science,* CXLIV, No. 3619 (May 8, 1964), pp. 646–48.

Hartwig, Quentin, and David Bendersky, "Guidelines to the Application of Space Technology to Medicine," *Research/Development,* XVII, No. 9 (September 1966), pp. 44–46.

Hinrichs, Robert, "Proprietary Data and Trade Secrets under Department of Defense Contracts," *Military Law Review,* XXXVI (1967), pp. 61–90.

Holman, Mary, "Government Research and Development Inventions—A New Resource?" *Land Economics,* XLI (August 1965), pp. 231–38.

Holst, Helge, "Government Patent Policy—Its Impact on Contractor Cooperation with the Government and Widespread Use of Government Sponsored Technology," *Patent, Trademark and Copyright Journal of Research and Education,* IX, No. 2 (Summer 1965), pp. 273–96.

Howick, George, and James Mahoney, "Technology–A Resource," *Research/Development,* XVII, No. 9 (September 1966), pp. 18–22.

Howick, George, *et al.*, "R & D Inputs from Space Technology," *Research/Development,* XVII, No. 9 (September 1966), pp. 18–46.

International Economic Policy Association, *U.S. Government-Financed Research and Development: Policies and Practices in Protection and Use of Results.* Washington, D.C.: IEPA, June 1967.

"Is the Moon Race Hurting Science?" *New York Times Magazine,* May 26, 1963.

"Is the Moon Project a Waste of Brainpower?" *U.S. News and World Report,* July 29, 1964.

Little, Arthur D., Inc. *Strategies for Survival in the Aerospace Industry.* Prepared by Thomas Miller. Cambridge: Arthur D. Little, Inc., 1964.

Lorsch, Jay, and Paul Lawrence, "Organizing for Product Innovation," *Harvard Business Review,* XLIII (January-February 1965), pp. 109–22.

Marquis, Donald, and Thomas Allen, "Communication Patterns in Applied Technology," *American Psychologist,* XXI (November 1966), pp. 1052–60.

Michaelis, Michael, "A Strategy for Innovation," *Bulletin of the Atomic Scientists* (April 1964), pp. 19–23.

Machlup, Fritz, "Patents and Inventive Effort," *Science,* CXXXIII, (May 12, 1961), pp. 1463–66.

MacLaurin, Rupert, "The Process of Technological Innovation," *The American Economic Review,* LX (March 1950), pp. 90–112.

McKie, James, *Proprietary Rights and Competition in Procurement.* Report prepared for United States Air Force Project Rand, Rand Corporation, Santa Monica, California: The Rand Corporation, June 1966.

Mainzer, Louis, "Scientific Freedom in Government Sponsored Research," *Journal of Politics,* XXIII (1961), pp. 212–30.

Mansfield, Edwin, "Diffusion of Technological Change," *Reviews of Data on Research and Development,* No. 31. NSF 61–52. Washington, D.C.: U.S. Government Printing Office, October 1961.

———, "Technical Change and the Rate of Imitation," *Econometrics,* XXIX (October 1961), pp. 741–66.

———, "Size of Firm, Market Structure and Innovation," *Journal of Political Economy,* LXXI, No. 6 (December 1963), pp. 556–76.

———, "Industrial Research and Development Expenditures: Determinants, Prospects and Relation to Size of Firm and Inventive Output," *Journal of Political Economy,* LXXII, No. 4 (August 1964), pp. 319–40.

———, "Technical Change and the Management of Research and Development," in Michigan University Graduate School of Business Administration, *Technological Change and Economic Growth, Michigan Business Papers,* Floyd Bond, ed., No. 41 (1965), pp. 19–51.

Michigan University Graduate School of Business Administration, *Technological Change and Economic Growth,* Floyd Bond, ed. *Michigan Business Papers,* No. 41 (1965).

Morton, Jack, "From Research to Technology," *International Science and Technology,* No. 29 (May 1964), pp. 82–92.

Mossinghoff, Gerald, and Robert Allnutt, "Patent Infringement in Government Procurement: A Remedy Without a Right," *Notre Dame Law Review,* XLII (October 1966), pp. 5–28.

Myers, Sumner, "The Space Program: A Model for Technological Innovation," *Space Digest* (August 1966), pp. 81–85.

"NASA Cuts Back Spin-off Program," *Electronics* (September 30, 1968), p. 63.

O'Meara, Robert, *Employee Patent and Secrecy Agreements,* A Research Report for the National Industrial Conference Board, Studies in Personnel Policy, No. 199 (April 1966).

Orlans, Harold, "Ethical Problems in the Relations of Research Sponsors and Investigators," in Gideon Sjoberg, ed., *Ethics, Politics, and Social Research.* Cambridge: Schenkman Publishing Company, 1967, pp. 3–24.

Parker, Gayle, "Comparison of the Patent Procedures of the National Aeronautics and Space Act and the Atomic Energy Act," *Patent, Trademark, and Copyright Journal of Research and Education,* III, No. 3 (Fall 1959), pp. 303–16.

Preston, Lee, "Patent Rights Under Federal R & D Contracts," *Harvard Business Review,* XLI, No. 5 (September-October 1963), pp. 6–13.

Quinn, Brian, "Technological Forecasting," *Harvard Business Review,* XLV, No. 2 (March-April 1967), pp. 89–106.

Roberts, Edward, "Facts and Folklore in Research and Development Management," *Industrial Management Review,* VIII, No. 2 (Spring 1967), pp. 5–18.

Rosenbloom, Richard, *Technology Transfer—Process and Policy: An Analysis of the Utilization of Technological By-products of Military and Space R & D.* Washington, D.C.: Special Report No. 62, NPA, July 1965.

———, "The Transfer of Military Technology to Civilian Use," in *Technology in Western Civilization,* V. II, Melvin Kranzberg and Carroll Pursell, eds. New York: Oxford University Press, 1967, pp. 601–12.

Rosebloom, Richard, and Francis Wolek. *Technology, Information and Organization: Information Transfer in Industrial R & D.* Report prepared for NSF. Boston: Graduate School of Business Administration, Harvard University, June 1967.

Ryan, Bryce, "A Study in Technological Diffusion," *Rural Sociology,* XIII (September 1948), pp. 273–85.

Ryan, Bryce, and Neal Gross, "The Diffusion of Hybrid Seed Corn in Two Iowa Communities," *Rural Sociology,* VIII, No. 1 (March 1943), pp. 15–24.

Sanders, Berkev, "Patterns of Commercial Exploitation of Patented Inventions by Large and Small Companies," *Patent, Trademark, and Copyright Journal of Research and Education,* VIII, No. 1 (Spring 1964), pp. 51–93.

———, "What Should the Federal Government's Patent Policy Be?" *Patent, Trademark, and Copyright Journal of Research and Education,* VIII, No. 2 (Summer 1964), pp. 168–98.

———, "Comparative Patent Yield from Government versus Industry Financed R & D," *Patent, Trademark, and Copyright Journal of Research and Education,* IX, No. 1 (Spring 1965), pp. 1–24.

Scherer, Frederick, "Government Research and Development Programs," in *Measuring Benefits of Government Investment,* Robert Dorfman, ed. Washington, D.C.: The Brookings Institution, 1965, pp. 12–57.

———, "Firm Size, Market Structure and the Output of Patented Inventions," *The American Economic Review,* LV (December 1965), pp. 1097–1125.

Schon, Donald, "Champions for Radical New Inventions," *Harvard Business Review,* XLI, No. 2 (March-April 1963), pp. 77–86.

———, "Innovation by Invasion," *International Science and Technology,* No. 27 (March 1964), pp. 52–60.

National Science Foundation. *Scientific Information Activities of Federal Agencies: Smithsonian Institution.* No. 13. June 1962. *U.S. Department of the Interior.* No. 26, October 1962. *Library of Congress.* No. 26, 1964. *National Library of Medicine.* No. 28, 1964. Washington, D.C.: U.S. Government Printing Office.

———. *Improving the Dissemination of Scientific Information.* Washington, D.C.: U.S. Government Printing Office, September 1964.

———. *Basic Research, Applied Research, and Development in Industry, 1964.* NSF 66–28. Washington, D.C.: U.S. Government Printing Office, June 1966.

———. *Federal Funds for Research, Development and Other Scientific Activities: Fiscal Years 1965, 1966 and 1967.* NSF 66–24. Washington, D.C.: U.S. Government Printing Office, July 1966.

———. *Geographic Distribution of Federal Funds for Research and Development: Fiscal Year 1965.* NSF 67–8. Washington, D.C.: U.S. Government Printing Office, April 1967.

———. *Basic Research, Applied Research, and Development in Industry, 1965.* NSF 67–12. Washington, D.C.: U.S. Government Printing Office, June 1967.

———. *Federal Support to Universities and Colleges: Fiscal Years 1963–1966.* Prepared for the Office of Science and Technology. NSF 67–14. Washington, D.C.: U.S. Government Printing Office, July 1967.

———. *Federal Funds for Research, Development, and Other Scientific Activities: Fiscal Years 1966, 1967 and 1968.* XVI, NSF 67–19. Washington, D.C.: U.S. Government Printing Office, August 1967.

———. *Scientific Activities of Nonprofit Institutions, 1964.* NSF 67–17. Washington, D.C.: U.S. Government Printing Office, September 1967.

———. *R & D Activities in State Government Agencies: Fiscal Years 1964 and 1965,* NSF 67–16. Washington, D.C.: U.S. Government Printing Office, September 1967.

———. *American Science Manpower 1966.* A Report of the National Register of Scientific and Technical Personnel. NSF 68–7. Washington, D.C.: U.S. Government Printing Office, December 1967.

U.S. Office of Scientific Research and Development. *Science, The Endless Frontier: A Report to the President on a Program for Postwar Scientific Research.* By Vannevar Bush, Director. July 1945. Washington D.C.: NSF, reprinted 1960.

U.S. President's Science Advisory Committee. *Science, Government, and Information: The Responsibilities of the Technical Community and the Government in the Transfer of Information.* Washington, D.C.: U.S. Government Printing Office, January 1963.

U.S. Small Business Administration, Northeastern Area Office. "Technology Utilization for the Small Manufacturer." Policy Statement. Boston: SBA Office, 1967.

Court and Administrative Decisions and Presidential Memoranda

Bouford v. *Houtz,* 133 U.S. 320 (1889).

Herbert Cooper Co., unpublished division of the Comptroller General, B–136916 (August 25, 1958).

Opinion of the Hon. Harlan Fiske Stone, 34 Op. Att'y Gen. 320 (1924). 38 Op. Att'y Gen. 164 (1936). 39 Op. Att'y Gen. 425 (1938).

Tennessee Electric Power v. *TVA,* 306 U.S. 118, 59 S.Ct. 336 (1937).

Tektronix, Inc. v. *U.S.,* 351 Fed. Rep. 2d 630 (Ct. of Claims 1965).

United States v. *Midwest Oil Co.,* 236 U.S. 459 (1915).

President Kennedy's Memorandum and Statement of Government Patent Policy, 28 Fed. Rep. 200 (October 12, 1963).

White House Memorandum, "Strengthening Academic Capability for Science Throughout the Country," September 13, 1965.

Unpublished Papers and Reports

Aaronson, David. "Legislative History of the Property Rights in Inventions Provisions of the National Aeronautics and Space Act of 1958." A paper that appears as Appendix A in the report, Donald Watson and Mary Holman. *Evaluation of NASA's Patent Policies.* Washington, D.C.: George Washington University, Department of Economics, 1966.

Allen, Thomas. "The Differential Performance of Information Channels in the Transfer of Technology." Working paper, Alfred P. Sloan School of Management. Cambridge: MIT Sloan School, June 1966.

Blaschke, Charles. "Federal Procurement: An Instrument to Increase the Rate of Innovation." Paper prepared for Science and Public Policy Seminar, Kennedy School of Government, Harvard University (available at the Science and Public Policy Library), May 1966.

Dinnell, Thomas. "The Encounter of State Government with Research and Development." Paper prepared for Science and Public Policy Seminar, Kennedy School of Government, Harvard University (available at the Science and Public Policy Library), May 1965.

Lambright, William. "NASA and the Politics of Patents: A Study of Administrative Pluralism." Unpublished Doctoral Dissertation, Faculty of Political Science, Columbia University, 1966.

Moore, Michael, and Samuel Doctors. "NERAC and Potential Legal Interfaces." A report prepared for the New England Research Application Center (NERAC). Storrs, Connecticut: NERAC, August 1967.

National Planning Association. *The Impact of the U.S. Civilian Space Program on the U.S. Domestic Economy.* Report prepared for the Lockheed Aircraft Corp., Washington, D.C.: NPA, July 1965.

Shimshoni, Daniel. "Aspects of Scientific Entrepreneurship." Unpublished Doctoral Dissertation, Kennedy School of Government, Harvard University, 1966.

Solo, Robert. *Studies in the Anatomy of Economic Progress.* Report prepared for the National Planning Association. Washington, D.C.: NPA, 1965.

———. *Patent Policy for Government Sponsored Research and Development.* Report in three parts prepared for the NASA Administrator's Office. Washington, D.C.: NASA, 1966.

Wainer, Herbert, and Irwin Rubin. "Motivation of R & D Entrepreneurs: Determinants of Company Success." Working paper, Alfred P. Sloan School of Management. Cambridge: MIT, January 1967.

Watson, Donald, and Mary Holman. *Evaluation of NASA's Patent Policies.* Washington, D.C.: George Washington University Department of Economics, 1966.

Miscellaneous

ADDRESSES

Allnutt, Robert. "Recent Developments in NASA Patent Policy and Data Policies." Paper presented before a meeting of NASA contractors, February 1966.

Eisenhower, Dwight. Farewell Message from the White House, January 19, 1961.

Gavin, James. Speech to the International Bankers Association, Bal Harbor, Florida, December 1958.

Kerr, Breene. "Maximizing the Return on the Nation's Investment in Research and Development." Paper presented to R & D symposium of the National Security Industry Association, October 10, 1965.

Myers, Sumner. "The Role and Impact of Government R & D Information." Paper presented to a meeting of the National Association of Business Economists, December 2, 1966.

Roberts, Edward. "Marketing and Engineering Strategies for Winning R & D Contracts." Paper presented at the 4th annual Conference on Marketing in the Defense Industries, Boston, May 27, 1965.

Roberts, Edward, and Herbert Wainer. "Technology Transfer and Entrepreneurial Success." Paper presented to the Twentieth National Conference on the Administration of Research, Miami Beach, Florida, October 26, 1966.

Rosenbloom, Richard. "Product Innovation in a Scientific Age." Paper presented to the 49th Annual American Marketing Association Meeting, June 14, 1966.

Rubel, John. "The Impact of Government Research and Development on Industrial Growth: Trends and Challenges in Research and Development." Paper presented to R & D Symposium of the National Security Association, March 13, 1963.

INTERVIEWS

Series of interviews with Arthur D. Little, Inc., personnel, Cambridge, Massachusetts, August 1966 to April 1967.

Series of interviews with NASA Electronic Research Center, Technology Utilization Officers, Cambridge, Massachusetts, August 1966 to March 1967.

Series of interviews with NASA OTU personnel, Branch Chiefs, RDC administrators, and RDC operations personnel, August 1966 to March 1967.

Series of interviews with NASA Patent Counsel, August 1966 to September 1968.

MEETING MINUTES

Minutes of the Meetings of the NASA Industrial Applications Advisory Committee, January 1963, September 1963, and January 1964.

Federal Statutes and Regulations

ARMED SERVICES PROCUREMENT REGULATIONS (ASPR'S)

ASPR, section 9.100 (April 1965).

ASPR, section 9.101–7 (October 1966, Revision 11).

ASPR, section 9.200 (April 1965, Revision 10).
ASPR, section 9.202 (April 1965, Revision 10).
ASPR, section 15–205 (November 1963, Revision 3).

NASA PROCUREMENT REGULATIONS (NASA PR'S)

NASA PR, section 9.101–4 (June 1966).
NASA PR, section 9.101–7 (November 1965, Revision 6).
NASA PR, section 15.205–35 (November 1965, Revision 6).
NASA Procurement Regulation Directive (PRD) No. 67–4, paragraph II, pp. 2–3 (March 1967).

ENTRIES IN U.S. CODE OF FEDERAL REGULATIONS (C.F.R.)

(NASA Patent/License Regulations)
14 C.F.R., section 1245 (1966).
———, section 1245.100 (May 1966).
———, section 1245.103 (May 1966).
———, section 1245.104 (May 1966).
———. section 1245.105 (May 1966).
———, section 1245.106 (May 1966).
———, section 1245.107 (May 1966).
———, section 1245.108 (May 1966).
———, section 1245.112 (May 1966).
———, section 1245.113 (May 1966).
———, section 1245.200 (October 1962).
———, section 1245.200 (c) (October 1962).
———, section 1245.205 (October 1962).
———, section 1245.206 (October 1962).

ENTRIES IN U.S. FEDERAL REGISTER (FED. REG.)

32 Fed. Reg. section 11,262 (August 1967).
27 Fed. Reg. section 3289 (1961).
28 Fed. Reg. section 10,943 (October 1963).

PUBLIC LAWS (LISTED BY U.S. CODE ANNOTATED)

Public Law 89–554, 80 Stat., 5 U.S.C.A. 301 (1966).
Cooperative Extension Work by Colleges Act of 1914 (Smith-Lever Act) 38 Stat., 7 U.S.C.A. 341 (as amended 1953).
Aid to Small Business—Research and Development Act of 1958, Public Law 85–536, 72 Stat., 15 U.S.C.A. 638 (1958).
Dissemination of Technical, Scientific and Engineering Information Act of 1950, 64 Stat., 15 U.S.C.A. 1152 (1950).
State Technical Services Act of 1965, Public Law 89–182, 79 Stat., 15 U.S.C.A. 1351 (1965).
Tennessee Valley Authority Act of 1933, Public Law 73–17, 48 Stat., 16 U.S.C.A. 831 (as amended 1964).
Court of Claims—Patent Cases Act of 1948, 62 Stat., 28 U.S.C.A. 1498 (as amended 1960).
Bureau of Mines Act of 1910, 36 Stat., 30 U.S.C.A. 3 (as amended 1934).

———. *1965 NASA Authorization. Hearings.* 88th Congress, second session, part 4. H.R. 9641. Washington, D.C.: U.S. Government Printing Office, 1964.

———. *1966 NASA Authorization. Hearings.* 89th Congress, first session, part 4. Washington, D.C.: U.S. Government Printing Office, 1965.

———. *1967 NASA Authorization. Hearings.* 89th Congress, second session, parts 1 and 4. H.R. 12718. Washington, D.C.: U.S. Government Printing Office, 1966.

———. *Inquiries, Legislation, Policy Studies re: Science and Technology; Review and Forecast. Report.* 89th Congress, second session. Washington, D.C.: U.S. Government Printing Office, 1966 (Committee Print).

———. *1968 NASA Authorization. Hearings.* 90th Congress, first session, parts 1 and 4. H.R. 4450 and H.R. 6470. Washington, D.C.: U.S. Government Printing Office, 1967.

———. Subcommittees Nos. 1, 3, and 4. *1962 NASA Authorization. Hearings.* 87th Congress, first session. H.R. 3238 and H.R. 6029. Washington, D.C.: U.S. Government Printing Office, 1961.

———. Subcommittee on Patents and Scientific Inventions. *Ownership of Inventions Developed in the Course of Federal Space Research Contracts. Report.* 87th Congress, second session. Washington, D.C.: U.S. Government Printing Office, April 1962 (Committee Print).

———. *Patent Policies Relating to Aeronautical and Space Research. Hearings.* 87th Congress, second session, H.R. 1934 and H.R. 6030. Washington, D.C.: U.S. Government Printing Office, 1962.

———. Subcommittee on Science, Research, and Development. *The National Science Foundation: A General Review of Its First Fifteen Years. Report.* 89th Congress, second session. H. Report 1219. Washington, D.C.: U.S. Government Printing Office, 1966.

———. *Science, Technology, and Public Policy During the Eighty-ninth Congress.* 90th Congress, first session. Washington, D.C.: U.S. Government Printing Office, August 1967 (Committee Print).

———. Subcommittee on Space Sciences and Applications. *1964 NASA Authorization. Hearings.* 88th Congress, first session, part 4. H.R. 5466. Washington, D.C.: U.S. Government Printing Office, 1963.

CONGRESSIONAL HEARINGS—SENATE

U.S. Congress. Senate. Committee on Aeronautics and Space Science. *NASA Authorization for Fiscal Year 1962. Hearings.* 87th Congress, first session. S.1300. Washington, D.C.: U.S. Government Printing Office, 1961.

———. *NASA Authorization for Fiscal Year 1963. Hearings.* 87th Congress, second session. S. 1633. Washington, D.C.: U.S. Government Printing Office, 1962.

———. *NASA Authorization for Fiscal Year 1965. Hearings.* 88th Congress, second session. S. 1245. Washington, D.C.: U.S. Government Printing Office, 1963.

———. *NASA Authorization for Fiscal Year 1966. Hearings.* 89th Congress, second session, parts 2 and 3. S. 927. Washington, D.C.: U.S. Government Printing Office, 1965.

———. *NASA Authorization for Fiscal Year 1967. Hearings.* 89th Congress, second session. Washington, D.C.: U.S. Government Printing Office, 1966.

———. *NASA Authorization for Fiscal Year 1968. Hearings.* 90th Congress, first session, part 2. S. 1296. Washington, D.C.: U.S. Government Printing Office, 1967.

———. Committee on Government Operations. Subcommittee on Reorganization and Internal Organizations. *Coordination of Information on Current Federal Research and Development Supported by the United States Government.* 87th Congress, first session. S. Rep. 263. Washington, D.C.: U.S. Government Printing Office, May 1961.

———. *Coordination of Information on Current Federal Research and Development Projects in the Field of Electronics. Report.* 87th Congress, first session. Washington, D.C.: U.S. Government Printing Office, September 1961 (Committee Print).

———. Committee on the Judiciary. Subcommittee on Patents, Trademarks and Copyrights. *Patent Practices of the Tennessee Valley Authority.* 86th Congress, first session. Washington, D.C.: U.S. Government Printing Office, 1959 (Committee Print).

———. *Government Patent Practices. Hearings.* 86th Congress, second session. S. 3156 and S. 3550. Washington, D.C.: U.S. Government Printing Office, May 1960.

———. *Patent Practices of the Department of Defense. Report.* 87th Congress, first session. Washington, D.C.: U.S. Government Printing Office, September 1961 (Committee Print).

———. *Patent Practices of the Department of Agriculture. Report.* 87th Congress, first session. Washington, D.C.: U.S. Government Printing Office, September 1961 (Committee Print).

———. *Government Patent Policy. Hearings.* 87th Congress, first session, parts 1 and 2. S. 1084 and S. 1176. Washington, D.C.: U.S. Government Printing Office, 1961.

———. *Patent Practices of the Federal Communications Commission. Report.* 87th Congress, second session. Washington, D.C.: U.S. Government Printing Office, August, 1962 (Committee Print).

———. *Government Patent Policy. Hearings.* 89th Congress, first session, parts 1 and 2. S. 789, S. 1809, and S. 1899. Washington, D.C.: U.S. Government Printing Office, June 1965.

———. *Patents, Trademarks and Copyrights. Report.* 89th Congress, second session. Washington, D.C.: U.S. Government Printing Office, June 1966.

———. Committee on Labor and Public Welfare. Subcommittee on Employment and Manpower. *Convertibility of Space and Defense Resources to Civilian Needs: A Search for New Employment Potentials.* 88th Congress, second session, vol. 2. Washington, D.C.: U.S. Government Printing Office, 1964 (Committee Print).

———. Select Committee on Small Business. *Fourteenth Annual Report.* 88th Congress, second session. S. Report No. 1180. Washington, D.C.: U.S. Government Printing Office, July 1964.

———. Subcommittee on Monopoly. *Patent Policies of Government Departments and Agencies. Conference on Federal Patent Policies.* 86th Congress, second session. Washington, D.C.: U.S. Government Printing Office, June 1960 (Committee Print).

———. *Economic Aspects of Government Patent Policies. Hearings.* 88th Congress, first session. Washington, D.C.: U.S. Government Printing Office, March 1963.

———. *Economic and Legal Problems of Government Patent Policies. Report.* 88th Congress, first session. Washington, D.C.: U.S. Government Printing Office, June 1963 (Committee Print).

———. Subcommittee on Retailing, Distribution and Marketing Practices. *The Role and Effect of Technology on the Nation's Economy.* 88th Congress, first session. Washington, D.C.: U.S. Government Printing Office, May 1963.

———. Subcommittee on Science and Technology. *Policy Planning for Technology Transfer. Report.* Prepared by Richard Carpenter of the Science Policy Research Division of the Legislative Reference Service, Library of Congress. 90th Congress, first session. S. Doc. No. 15. Washington, D.C.: U.S. Government Printing Office, May 1967.

———. *The Prospects for Technology Transfer. Report.* 90th Congress, second session. Washington, D.C.: U.S. Government Printing Office, May 1967 (Committee Print).

———. *Technology Transfer. Hearings.* 90th Congress, first session. Washington, D.C.: U.S. Government Printing Office, 1967.

U.S. Congress, Joint Economic Committee. *Background on Economic Impact of Federal Procurement.* 89th Congress, second session. Washington, D.C.: U.S. Government Printing Office, 1966 (Committee Print).

U.S. Department of Defense. Letter to General Accounting Office Explaining DOD Policy as to Rights in Technical Data Resulting from Independent Research and Development. Defense Procurement Circular #22. Washington, D.C.: DOD or GAO, January 29, 1965.

U.S. Department of Health, Education and Welfare. *Handbook on Programs of the U.S. Department of Health, Education and Welfare.* Washington, D.C.: U.S. Government Printing Office, 1963.

———. *1964 Annual Report to Congress.* Washington, D.C.: U.S. Government Printing Office, 1965.

———. *1966 Annual Report to Congress.* Washington, D.C.: U.S. Government Printing Office, 1967.

U.S. Department of Interior. *1963 Annual Report.* Washington, D.C.: U.S. Department of Interior, 1964.

———. Office of Coal Research. *1967 Annual Report.* Washington, D.C.: Office of Coal Research, 1968.

U.S. Federal Council for Science and Technology. *Annual Report on Government Patent Policy.* Washington, D.C.: U.S. Government Printing Office, June 1965.

———. *Recommendations for National Document-Handling Systems in Science and Technology.* Prepared by the Committee on Scientific and Technical Information. Springfield, Va.: Clearinghouse for Federal Scientific and Technical Information, November 1965 (Report in 3 parts).

———. *The Role of the Federal Council for Science and Technology: Report for 1963 and 1964.* Washington, D.C.: U.S. Government Printing Office, 1965.

———. *Annual Report on Government Patent Policy.* Washington, D.C.: U.S. Government Printing Office, June 1966.

———. Patent Advisory Council. "Request for an Opinion of the Attorney

General on the Authority of Agencies to Grant Limited Exclusive and Irrevocable Non-Exclusive Licenses Under Government-Owned Patents." Washington, D.C.: FCST, July 7, 1966 (Draft).

———. *Annual Report on Government Patent Policy.* Washington, D.C.: U.S. Government Printing Office, June 1967.

U.S. Library of Congress, Legislative Reference Service. *Government Assistance to Invention and Research: A Legislative History.* Study of the Subcommittee on Patents, Trademarks and Copyrights of the Committee on the Judiciary. U.S. Senate. 86th Congress, second session, Study No. 22. Washington, D.C.: U.S. Government Printing Office, 1960.

U.S. National Aeronautics and Space Administration. *Proceedings of the Second National Conference on the Peaceful Uses of Space.* Washington, D.C.: U.S. Government Printing Office, November 1962.

———. *Proceedings of the University Program Review Conference.* Washington, D.C.: U.S. Government Printing Office, March 1965.

———. *Symposium on Technology Status and Trends.* Washington, D.C.: U.S. Government Printing Office, April 1965.

———. *Proceedings of the Fifth National Conference on the Peaceful Uses of Space.* Washington, D.C.: U.S. Government Printing Office, May 1965.

———. *Technology Utilization Program.* NASA No. N65–3650. Washington, D.C.: U.S. Government Printing Office, 1965.

———. *Patent Program—A Review Document.* Washington, D.C.: NASA, Office of the General Counsel, April 1966.

———. Management Instruction No. 1134.8, June 1966.

———. *Management Guidelines for New Technology Reporting,* NASA Handbook No. 2170.1. Washington, D.C.: NASA, OTU, October 1966.

———. *Reportable Items under the New Technology Clause. Report.* NASA Handbook No. 2170.2. Washington, D.C.: U.S. Government Printing Office, October 1966.

———. *Petitions for Patent Waiver: Findings of Fact and Recommendations of the NASA Inventions and Contributions Board.* NASA Handbook No. 5500.1 and 5500.1A. Washington, D.C.: U.S. Government Printing Office, 1966.

———. *Technology Utilization Program Review.* Washington, D.C.: NASA, OTU, February 1967.

———. News Release No. 67–50. Washington, D.C.: NASA, March 1967.

———. *A Review of NASA's Patent Program.* Washington, D.C.: NASA, Office of the General Counsel, March 1967.

———. Memorandum Concerning Selected Provisions for Inclusion in Technology Utilization Division Contracts as Appropriate. Washington, D.C.: NASA, OTU, October 15, 1967.

———. *The Technology Utilization Program.* Washington, D.C.: NASA, OTU, 1967.

———. *Documentation Requirements Handbook: Technology Utilization Division.* Washington, D.C.: NASA, OTU, 1968 (Draft—not official).

U.S. National Commission on Technology, Automation and Economic Progress. *Technology and the American Economy.* Appendix I. *Outlook for Technological Change and Employment.* Appendix V. *Applying Technology to Unmet Needs.* Washington, D.C.: U.S. Government Printing Office, February 1966.

Coal Research and Development Act of 1960, Public Law 86–599, 74 Stat., 30 U.S.C.A. (1960).

Public Law 85–857, 72 Stat., 38 U.S.C.A. 101 (1958).

Management and Disposal of Government Property Act of 1949, 63 Stat., 40 U.S.C.A. 472 (as amended 1964).

National Library of Medicine Act of 1944, 70 Stat., 42 U.S.C.A. 662 (as amended 1956).

Atomic Energy Act of 1946, Public Law 79–585, 60 Stat., 42 U.S.C.A. 1801 (as amended 1954).

National Science Foundation Act of 1950, Public Law 81–507, 64 Stat. 149, 42 U.S.C.A. 1861 (as amended 1964).

National Aeronautics and Space Act of 1958, Public Law 85–568, 72 Stat., 42 U.S.C.A. 2451 (as amended 1964).

U.S. Congress. House of Representatives. *H.R. 9847*. 85th Congress, second session, sections 2 and 4. Washington, D.C.: U.S. Government Printing Office, 1958. Early House version of NASA Act, introduced by Congressman Lane.

U.S. *Constitution,* Article I, section 8.

———, Article IV, section 3.

Index